MOTORSPORTS
MEDICINE

RACE FASTER! LONGER! SAFER!

11-93

Dr. Harlen C. Hunter
&
Rick Stoff

Lake Hill Press
St. Louis, Missouri

Passages from Stock Car Racing and Open Wheel magazines reprinted by permission of Dick Berggren, Stock Car Racing Publishing Ltd. and Open Wheel Publishing Ltd., New York, N.Y.

Acknowledgements
The authors gratefully acknowledge the cooperation and assistance of the many people who made this book possible. We sincerely thank Dick Berggren, Stock Car Racing and Open Wheel magazines; Keith Clark, Corinne Economaki, National Speed Sport News; George England, North American Racing Insurance; Jack Gilmore, Indianapolis Motor Speedway; Dr. Michael Henderson; Patc Henry, Sports Car Club of America; Dick Jordan, United States Auto Club; John Kilroy, Performance Racing Industry; Arnold S. Kuhns, SFI Foundation Inc.; Bob McKee, McKee Engineering Corporation; G. Terry Smith; and Suzanne A. Snively, M.D., Snell Memorial Foundation, Inc.

Photographs by the authors and Todd Hunter.

Manuscript assistance provided by Janet Stone, Catherine Sorrell, Kathleen Billington, Michelle Crouch, JoAnn Hunter, Juliann Hunter and Ron Nelson.

Library of Congress Cataloging-in-Publication Data

Hunter, Harlen C., 1940-
    Motorsports medicine : race faster! longer! safer! / Harlen C. Hunter & Rick Stoff
      p. cm.
    Includes index.
    ISBN 0-9634819-0-8 (pbk.) : $19.95
    1. Motorsports--Physiological aspects. 2. Motorsports--Accidents and injuries. I. Stoff, Rick, 1954- . II. Title
RC1220.M57H86 1992
617.1 027--dc20
                                   92-39754
                                   CIP

THE AUTHORS

DR. HARLEN C. HUNTER is an orthopedic surgeon certified by the American Osteopathic Board of Surgery, a member of the International Council of Motorsport Sciences and president of Mid-States Orthopedic Sports Medicine Clinics of America, Ltd.

Dr. Hunter graduated from Drake University and the College of Osteopathic Medicine and Surgery of Des Moines, Iowa. He has served as medical director to the Sports Car Club of America (SCCA) and Automobile Racing Club of America (ARCA). His Hunter Trauma Team has provided medical coverage at hundreds of SCCA Pro Racing, United States Auto Club (USAC) and local races.

He has served as an advisor to the Motor Sport Research Group at McGill University in Montreal, Canada; medical director to the U.S. Biathlon Association; chairman of the committee on athletic injuries of the American Osteopathic Academy of Orthopedics; and founding member of the American Osteopathic College of Sports Medicine and American Sports Health Association. His research has been published in Osteopathic Annuals, Osteopathic Physician and the Journal of the American Osteopathic Association.

A serious collector of motorsports memorabilia, Dr. Hunter has served as an official photographer at the Indianapolis 500 and NASCAR and ARCA events.

RICK STOFF is a graduate of the prestigious University of Missouri School of Journalism and a former reporter and assistant city editor of the St. Louis Globe-Democrat. He has covered motorsports events including the Indianapolis and Daytona 500s and profiled Mario Andretti, Bobby Rahal, Benny Parsons, Terry Labonte, Ken Schrader, Rusty Wallace, Willy T. Ribbs, Janet Guthrie, Sleepy Tripp, New Zealand midget champion Barry Butterworth and others. Recent works have appeared in Stock Car Racing, Open Wheel and American Motorcyclist magazines.

He was publications editor of one of the nation's largest pediatric institutions, St. Louis Children's Hospital, before forming his marketing and public relations firm, Stoff Communications. The company's clients have included racing teams, a national racing series, a race track, a motorsports equipment manufacturer and an international pharmaceutical and medical supply producer.

Stoff grew up on the grounds of the now-closed Lake Hill Speedway in Valley Park, Mo. While a college student he handled public relations duties for the track as it was launching the careers of Schrader and Wallace. He also has experience as an Indy-car crew member and dirt-track announcer.

TABLE OF CONTENTS

FOREWORD   1

Chapter 1   THE SURPRISING DEMANDS OF   9
MOTORSPORTS
Racers really <u>are</u> athletes!

Chapter 2   MEDICAL SCREENING FOR RACERS   17
Who should race?

Chapter 3   ENDURANCE (AND) RACING   21
Racing truly is an endurance sport

Chapter 4   MUSCLING PAST THE COMPETITION: 33
STRENGTH IN RACING
Power for enhanced performance

Chapter 5   BE A FLEXIBLE FLYER   53
Staying loose for performance
& injury prevention

Chapter 6   BEATING THE HEAT: 61
YOU CAN'T WIN IF YOU CAN'T FINISH
Withstanding heat & dehydration

Chapter 7   EAT FOR SPEED:
NUTRITION AND THE RACER   75
A common-sense guide to eating right

Chapter 8   VISION FOR RACING   89
Optimizing sight & reaction times

Chapter 9   AGING & RACING   99
Older racers don't have to stop
. . . or slow down

Chapter 10   PSYCHOLOGY OF WINNERS   119
Successful attitudes & teamwork

Chapter 11   HEARING: 131
             YOUR LOSS IS NOBODY'S GAIN
             Preventing injury from racing noise

Chapter 12   SUNBURN: 135
             AN OCCUPATIONAL HAZARD
             The importance of skin protection

Chapter 13   DRUGS & RACING   137
             Warnings on medications, legal or not

Chapter 14   SLEEP: 143
             SLOWING DOWN TO STAY FAST
             Sometimes you must leave the fast lane

Chapter 15   THE OBLIGATORY SEX SCENE   145
             The latest word on an age-old question

Chapter 16   UNDERSTANDING RACING INJURIES   147
             What's likely to get hurt & how

Chapter 17   UNDERSTANDING TRAUMA   173
             Crashes & the human body

Chapter 18   UNDERSTANDING BURNS   189
             The skin is more tender than you think

Chapter 19   UNDERSTANDING SAFETY EQUIPMENT   195
             Why you need and deserve the best

Chapter 20   UNDERSTANDING TRACK SAFETY   207
             Tips for accident prevention & response

Chapter 21   RESPONDING TO INJURIES   221
             First aid at the track,
             in the shop, on the road

             INDEX   244

FOREWORD

Motor racing is among the most physically demanding sports, yet much of the public does not consider racers to be athletes. From the looks of many racers, they don't think they're athletes, either.

Motorsports, while not as suicidal as many people would like to believe, are, of course, hazardous. Yet many participants, in apparent ignorance of the risks they face, compete without taking readily-available safety precautions .

While sports medicine books are available for activities as demanding as tennis and golf, to our knowledge only one volume devoted to racing has preceded <u>Motorsports Medicine</u>. It was <u>Motor Racing in Safety: The Human Factors</u>, published in 1968 by Dr. Michael Henderson of New Zealand.

While the U.S. government can provide estimates on the annual injury toll resulting from the use of golf clubs, water skis, bowling balls, croquet mallets, billiard cues, table tennis paddles, toasters and toothpicks, it can provide no data on motor racing injuries or fatalities. Surprisingly, apparently no one in the sport can provide comprehensive statistics, either.

While researching and writing this book, the authors consulted hundreds of articles and chapters in medical journals, motorsports publications and medical books. Hundreds of hours were devoted to analyzing, by computer, several thousand injury reports filed with one of the country's largest racing insurers. This database afforded, we believe, one of the larger studies of racing injuries ever undertaken. The second part of the book describes the nature and causes of racing injuries and offers thought-provoking discussion of preventive measures. These chapters also relate, in understandable terms, the biomechanics of crash injuries -- the nature of "G" forces and the body's ability to withstand them; the body's uncomfortably limited tolerance of heat and fire; and first-aid tips. The importance of adequate protective equipment, particularly helmets, driving suits and restraint systems, is stressed in a chapter that describes Snell Foundation and SFI Foundation ratings and testing procedures.

Often the findings of this research were more fascinating than anticipated. Much of the information never before has been published in a form applicable to motorsports.

FOREWORD

We believe this material -- presented in a non-technical, easy-to-understand style -- will prove vitally useful to participants and provide fans a deeper understanding of the sport. (Many chapters also may help fans better understand their own health needs.)

As for the physical demands of motorsports, research suggests that driving a race car can be as strenuous as endurance sports such as distance running and bicycling and can require more upper-body muscular stamina than football. Furthermore, the traditional fancy that driving a race car itself keeps a driver in shape is just that -- a fancy. Four chapters detail reasons that race drivers, crew members and fans need to do more to stay in shape and provide an outline for a complete endurance, strength and flexibility program.

Racing excels like no other activity at imposing life-threatening perils of heat and dehydration upon participants, so a chapter is devoted to explanations of the body's heat tolerances and fluid needs. Society as a whole holds many misconceptions about nutrition, so another chapter is devoted to eating right, especially on the road. Because a racing environment demands the highest levels of physical and mental ability, potential side effects of prescription, non-prescription and "recreational" drugs are summarized.

Other chapters explore the importance of vision and sleep; the psychology of handling stress, promoting team work and maintaining productive self-confidence; and the avoidance of "occupational" hazards such as sunburn and hearing loss. For example, the typical large-displacement, V-8 racing engine running unmuffled can create noise as severe as repeated gunshots -- so much noise, in fact, that the ears can be injured in as little as 30 minutes of exposure unless hearing protection is worn.

The research showed that racing, while extremely demanding, is far from a young person's sport. Experience can offset youth and costs prevent many from starting careers until later in life, so racing tends to harbor an older population than other popular sports.

But that's great, because there is no reason a healthy, fit individual should not be able to race into his or her 50s and sometimes 60s. But many physical abilities do begin to decline after the 20s so racers need to understand them and compensate for them. Of course we devote a chapter to the processes of aging and their implications in racing.

We believe the availability of better information on fitness and safety precautions, as well as frank discussion of risks, will make racing safer. To date several obstacles seem to have blocked the starting line to such enlightenment.

Racing is a fragmented sport. Little of its activity is overseen by national or even regional organizations, so compiling comprehensive data looms as a monumental undertaking. Some data that are compiled, however, are kept out of view because the owners of it do not want competitors or the general public to know how much business they handle or how many injuries competitors incur. Many potential sources of data were contacted by the authors. Few could or would provide information. Appallingly, a handful of people in the industry did not even bother to acknowledge correspondence.

Sometimes it seems too many people associated with our sport are more concerned with image than the well-being of our friends. On the other hand, there have been many efforts to fill this broad health-and-safety-information gap. People like Dick Berggren and Doug Gore of Stock Car Racing and Open Wheel magazines, for example, have addressed tough issues such as the extraordinary incidence of fatalities in northeastern pavement modified racing. These reports, in which Berggren wrote, "Everyone wants to see an end to these awful accidents, but almost everyone expects someone else to come up with the fix," are a model of the type of investigative journalism of which motorsports could use more.

We believe the available statistics suggest that racing truly is much safer than many people think -- but could be considerably safer than it is as present. We hope this book and the efforts of others will spur greater cooperation in disseminating safety knowledge by the sport's leaders. Open discussion of health and injury prevention in motorsports can only make the sport still safer and more popular than it is today.

Most major sanctioning bodies conduct exemplary safety programs. But it takes only a quick look around some race tracks to see that many racers, smoking cigarettes while their bellies protrude under their driving suits, do not realize how strenuous competitive driving can be. Statistics listed in coming chapters show that a significant percentage of racing fatalities result not from accidents but from heart attacks suffered during the stress of competition.

And speaking of driving suits, too many racing organizations, mostly operating at the smaller tracks that are racing's backbone, do not require adequate use of driver suits and other equipment that can offer a reasonable amount of protection. Car safety also is lacking in many cases, as is the safe construction of race tracks and conduct of race meets. A leading goal of this book is convincing racers that they need to do more to keep themselves fit and safe.

The authors were given access to the files of North American Racing Insurance of Independence, Mo., one of the largest racing insurers in the U.S. Too many of the company's accident reports suggest that unnecessary injuries result from unsafe and easily-eliminated practices. Beyond the sadness we experience when a racing friend is injured or killed, there are other reasons to advance the cause of fitness and safety in racing.

One is expense. Even so-called "budget" racing classes cost a ton of money these days. Escalating medical and legal expenses force insurers and equipment manufacturers to raise prices. That in turn forces track operators, sanctioning bodies and equipment dealers to raise fees and prices. That finally forces participants, potential participants and fans to pay more to go racing -- or do something else with their money.

Another factor to be considered is the image of the sport. If the sport shall continue to grow, prosper and attract new fans, participants and sponsors, it will need a wholesome image. Frankly, many opinion-leaders outside the sport do not view racing as such.

We recall a Sunday morning a couple of years ago when, flipping through the television channels, we found a cable talk show populated by sports writers. The subject of stock car racing came up and a New York "expert," who obviously had visited few, if any, auto races, smugly offered his learned assessment of the sport: "red necks, beer bellies and bib overalls." We, of course, agree the gentleman knew not of what he spoke. But we cannot overlook that such opinions continue to linger from days when motor racing was far less safe and its competitors were commonly viewed as self-destructive playboys, punks or criminals. Here are some reminders:

> Despite safety precautions and safety records, auto racing's tragedies are spectacular and are viewed, repeatedly, in slow motion, by hundreds of thousands. Races without incident get little attention.
>> -- Hal Quinn, "Death and Safety
>> in the Fast Lane," Maclean's, June 28, 1982

"Marred" is the handy word regularly inserted in the second sentence of news reports after the race driver wins his race or loses it or qualifies for it in record time. "The day was marred . . . " Not ruined completely, just slightly marred, as our small pleasures are forever being slightly marred. Gordon Smiley was slightly marred at Indianapolis two weekends ago, just as Gilles Villeneuve had been in Belgium the week before that. They are dead, of course.

Some 450,000 people will perch or picnic at the Speedway on Sunday. Nobody knows how many of them are ghouls spreading their blankets beside a bad intersection.

> -- Tom Callahan, "A 'Marred' Day: More Death at Indianapolis," TIME, May 31, 1982

These accidents demonstrate two sides to motor racing's approach to safety: Officials usually make effective changes when there is a bad accident, but it can take a bad accident to show where change is needed. And no matter how many safety improvements are made, the fact remains that auto racing, by its very nature, is a dangerous sport for drivers, spectators and crew members.

> -- Joseph Siano, "Indy Cars Safest Ever, in Theory That Is," New York Times, May 22, 1991

The Los Angeles Times tabulated damage from the 1992 Indianapolis 500: the crashes leading to and during the race involved 27 cars that sustained $6 million in damage. The human toll included one fatality and 14 other drivers hospitalized with broken limbs. Comment: This is easily the dumbest, sorriest excuse for a "sport" that we have in this country.

> -- Bernie Miklasz, "Commentary,"
> St. Louis Post-Dispatch, June 6, 1992

FOREWORD

We in motorsports obviously must put in a few more laps on best behavior before securing universal acceptance as an equal of those in the "ball" sports. Those of us within the sport already realize that racing largely is safe, that race after race is contested without so much as a moderate injury. We know racing does not need to be "the dumbest, sorriest excuse for a sport," so we must do our best to prevent incidents that hurt friends and the sport's image. We must frankly acknowledge that people can get hurt so we can openly discuss risks and convince others to take the steps that can prevent needless tragedy.

The tools for the mission already are available. Thousands of people have devoted careers to nurturing racing and advancing its safety. We have the knowledge and equipment, available at competitive, reasonable prices from many quality sources, to make racing even safer than it already has become.

As this book is being written the International Council of Motorsport Sciences, an organization of respected leaders in health and safety, is undertaking a significant effort to advance the knowledge base of racing. Wrote Dr. M. Rick Timms, chairman of ICMS, in the organization's December 1991/January 1992 newsletter:

It is clear that analysis of accident data can identify those accident factors that predispose to injury. Hopefully the system for data collection and accident analysis currently under development by the ICMS can help identify specific elements of the race car and race course, as well as the elements of driver behavior and race organization, which could be modified to improve safety.

To be successful this effort will obviously require the active support and participation of the major race sanctioning organizations and the insurance industry. Some may choose to do accident/injury analysis independently and internally, because of concerns about liability, adverse publicity, or simply through an unwillingness to share accident information with other sanctioning bodies.

A single large accident database, representing a wide variety of cars, race courses, barrier types, and other race factors, could be of tremendous value if collected and analyzed scientifically and used in a cooperative manner to help develop recommendations for race car and course construction based on the hard data of accident/injury analysis.

These efforts would undoubtedly serve to improve upon the already impressive safety record of automobile racing and, by emphasizing that record to the motoring public, contribute to improvements in highway safety as well.

We dedicate this book to the efforts of the ICMS and all others who strive to make racing a safe, healthy and enjoyable hobby and career.

Men and women who drive racing machines in competition face astonishing physical demands which even they may not recognize.

Chapter 1

THE SURPRISING DEMANDS
OF MOTORSPORTS

" . . . what gifted physical creatures -- indeed, what
truly phenomenal <u>athletes</u> -- auto racers really are."
-- Ted West, "Fit to Win,"
<u>Road & Track</u>, June 1987

Are race drivers athletes? For most of the history of motorized
competition, the safe answer probably would have been "No."

In 1979 Dr. Glenn A. Dawson, a cardiac rehabilitation specialist,
published the results of his research into this long-debated
question. He prepared fitness profiles of 10 volunteers from the
ranks of the NASCAR Grand National (now Winston Cup) stock car
division. The drivers were compared to six non-racers described as
"sedentary" -- the polite medical term for "couch potato."

While Dawson found that racing drivers faced unique and
severe heart, muscle and heat stresses in their work, they were no
better prepared for racing than men who drank beer while watching
races on the tube. The racers were found to have twice the body fat
and nearly half the cardiopulmonary capacity of soccer, football
and track athletes -- who in many ways face lesser demands in their
sports.

"The data . . . support the conclusion that the NASCAR drivers
are not highly conditioned athletes," Dawson reported. "However,
better physical condition would surely help them cope with the
physical and mental stress of this hazardous sport."

That observation has proven prophetic. In the decades since
his study sports medicine knowledge has mushroomed. Records in
professional and amateur athletics have been broken repeatedly
and continue to be broken.

THE SURPRISING DEMANDS OF MOTORSPORTS

Why? Because better understanding of the human body permits intelligent sportsmen and sportswomen to prepare themselves ever better for the demands of competition. Even non-competitive adults, by the millions, are following sensible dietary guidelines, frequenting health clubs and taking to jogging, walking and biking paths in pursuit of healthier lives.

While increasing numbers of racers follow serious fitness regimens, too many remain in the dark ages. In the minds of many, the slogan "Win on Sunday, Sell on Monday" begins with "Party on Saturday."

Many drivers, even at the highest levels of the sport, contend that they do not need conditioning regimens because racing keeps them in shape. That view, to put it bluntly, belongs with the other stuff that stops when the green flag drops. Ever notice that the last set of tires put on a race car during a long race tends to be the worst set of the day? Ever wonder how many of the disappointing finishes blamed on used-up tires really result from used-up drivers?

Racing once -- even two or three times -- a week is not enough to enable a driver to attain and maintain peak athletic performance. Drivers who say they can stay in shape just by racing are merely using a psychological ploy to convince themselves they don't have to work during the week. It is obvious that many do not themselves realize that motorsports is one of the most physically demanding and strenuous competitive pursuits.

Medical research devoted to motorsports has found that racing requires levels of stamina and strength equalling or surpassing other endurance sports. Cranking a steering wheel in a hot cockpit for a couple of hours combines, to an astounding degree, the physiologic demands of distance running and football.

Racing, however, is a curious sport. Poor health habits do not prevent gifted drivers from shining in qualifying, heat races or occasional main events. When few racers exercised, none were penalized for being out of shape. Let's face it, if the Triple Crown was contested by cattle, a cow could win the Kentucky Derby.

The image of motorsports has been confused further by the fact that a high percentage of racers, including successful ones, are middle-aged. Experience and mechanical knowledge contribute greatly to success in racing, giving older drivers a means of overcoming physical decline. In addition, many men and women can afford to start racing only in their 30s or 40s, skewing participant demographics toward middle-age.

It is easy to understand the evolution of the perception that racers truly are not athletes. But nature increasingly is going to separate the athletes from the amateurs when it's time to bang wheels on dirt all night, guide a 200-mile-per-hour tank 500 miles under a blazing sun or survive a weekend of long and winding road courses.

And let us not forget our crew members, track officials, safety workers and fans who have unique fitness needs, too. It should be common knowledge that eating right and getting even a little bit of regular exercise enables anyone to live a longer, higher-quality life.

Why Racers Really Are Athletes

Motor races, like all sports activities, that last longer than a few minutes require aerobic fitness for endurance and performance; muscle conditioning and flexibility for car control; and good nutrition and personal habits for stamina and resistance to dehydration.

The Cardiovascular System

Racing severely tests the cardiovascular system -- the body's heart, lungs and blood distribution network. Each link in this chain must be strong enough to provide sufficient amounts of oxygen to every stressed muscle and organ of the body. Oxygen is crucial to the conversion of energy needed for every function from muscle movement to thinking.

The human heart beats 40 to 80 times per minute while its owner is at rest. That is less than half the heart's potential BPM -- beats per minute. Athletes in many sports typically cruise at 110 to 130 beats per minute, roughly 60 to 70 percent of cardiac redline, and peak at 180 beats during their most strenuous moments.

In most sports such peaks are short-lasting. While basketball, football, hockey and soccer players work hard for an hour or more, they enjoy the benefits of substitutions, timeouts and half-times.

Racing, however, puts as much strain on the heart as distance running or bicycling. Repeated studies have found that race drivers work at around 80 percent of maximum heart rate, 140 to 180 beats per minute, and remain at that level as long as the green flag waves.

Doctors Dan Marisi and Jacques Dallaire of the McGill University Motor Sport Research Group in Montreal have reported sustained heart rates of 170 to 180 beats per minute in Formula 1,

Indy car and endurance racing drivers. Glenn A. Dawson's 1979 study of NASCAR stock car drivers found average heart rates of 181 beats per minute.

The excitement and stresses of racing -- particularly at the drop of the green flag and during crashes -- send the heart beating even faster. A Formula 1 driver fitted with a heart monitor achieved his highest rate -- 190 BPM -- at the start of a race. Two stock car drivers involved in a 1979 wreck reached 184 and 214 BPM while another uninvolved driver, who previously had suffered a heart attack, got excited enough to send his heart 186 beats.

The work load placed on the upper body by racing is responsible for much of the demand placed on the heart, but the high rates result primarily from psychological stresses. Ever been walking through a dark room or alley and had someone sneak up right behind you? Remember the sensations of the hair-rising, heart-pounding rush you felt as you turned to face the danger?

In a way, that is what happens to racing drivers. Racing provides enormous sensory inputs to the brain and demands a like number of decisions and commands. The brain copes with this rush of activity by kicking the body into top gear and summoning the primitive "fight or flight" response which puts the body on alert when faced with danger. This response includes a discharge of the hormone adrenaline which boosts the heart rate.

Coping efficiently with the cardiovascular demands of racing requires a high degree of aerobic fitness and conditioning which can be provided only by intense and regular exercise.

Strength and Flexibility

Racing creates muscle demands similar to those required of football linemen, a combination of strength and endurance. Yes, linemen require more total strength but race drivers require greater endurance because they do not get to take turns driving offensive and defensive laps or pull over and park for 15 minutes at halftime.

Racing poses the additional strain of sustained gravitational forces, in particular on the arms and neck. To appreciate fully the effects of g-forces, think of your head as a bowling ball -- that's the weight of a head wearing a helmet. In high-speed corners, g-forces can push the head sideways at pressures equalling one to several times its weight. Drivers competing in races longer than sprints must have sufficient strength in the neck and shoulders to be finishers.

Flexibility in the muscles and joints also is needed to assist racing participants in withstanding extended seat time, doing their best during pit stops and tolerating the impact forces created by collisions.

Heat and Hydration

Racing excels most of all at placing participants under severe heat stress and dehydration. In many sports, athletes are discouraged -- even barred -- from competing during the hottest months or hours of day, allowed to dress lightly and encouraged to swallow cold drinks constantly.

By its nature racing breaks all the rules of handling heat and fluid needs. Motorsports activity centers on the hottest seasons and times of day and further requires drivers and support crews to toil in steaming-hot, enclosed cockpits or under blazing sunshine. In addition, many participants wear heavy protective clothing that prevents the sweat evaporation that is vital to maintaining a safe body temperature.

Football linemen are known to lose typically four to eight pounds during a game -- and they get to catch their breath and get a drink on the sideline every few minutes. Race drivers can lose 10 to 12 pounds during a two-hour race. Pit crews, track officials, corner workers, and rescue squads face heat and dehydration hazards that may be slower to develop but are just as dangerous. Everyone needs to understand the body's fluid needs and mechanisms for coping with heat. Dehydration can do more than slow you -- it can kill.

Reaction Times

Good racing drivers have much faster reflexes than the average man on the street. A study conducted a decade ago for U.S. Tobacco Co. found that NASCAR racing drivers were able to respond to a stimulus in an average time of 162.4 milliseconds. The typical driver on the highway needed 180 milliseconds to react. In a test requiring drivers to discriminate stimuli and make a choice of reactions, NASCAR drivers averaged 485 milliseconds; the general population averaged 600 milliseconds. When foot-brake reaction time was measured the NASCAR drivers scored 197.1-millisecond elapsed times while road drivers turned in 250-millisecond scores.

Formula 1 drivers have shown better reaction times than athletes from other sports in driver evaluations conducted by Drs.

THE SURPRISING DEMANDS OF MOTORSPORTS

Marisi and Dallaire at McGill University and published in Road & Track magazine (June 1987). In a test requiring one decision, Formula 1 drivers averaged 258 milliseconds while other athletes averaged 275 milliseconds. On a multiple-choice reaction test, the Grand Prix pilots turned in 296-millisecond times to beat the 316-millisecond scores of other athletes. In both cases, the F1 times were just a tick off the results achieved by members of Mensa, the organization for people whose intelligence scores fall in the top two percent of the population.

Psychology

The right frame of mind is essential to success in a sport as demanding as racing. A fit body is healthier mentally, too. Exercise makes the body feel better all over and better able to maintain rational concentration under stress. Research has proven that exercise actually alters chemical processes in the brain in ways that promote athletic performance as well as a positive outlook on life and its challenges.

Injury Prevention

While many prefer not to discuss it, the risk of injury does pervade our sport. Many injuries that occur in racing could be prevented or minimized. Again, fitness is one of the keys.

A healthy heart is better able to withstand and recover from the stresses of competition and injury. Bone density, muscle strength and flexibility also are enhanced by a good fitness regimen and can reduce the risks of fractures, sprains and strains.

And let's not forget the importance of taking all the safety precautions possible when building racing machines, equipping our workshops and pit areas and clothing our drivers, pit crews and track workers. Too many people are killed or maimed simply because they drove or worked in unsafe conditions.

Yes, We Are Athletes

So why does the myth persist that race drivers are not athletes? Why do so many race drivers, who place themselves at the greatest risks in all of sports, continue to insist that they have no need for exercise programs or athletic nutritional regimens?

The human body is a wonderful machine. If trained hard and often and adequately prepared, it actually performs better and lasts longer. The heart, lungs, blood stream and muscles adapt to handle heavier work loads at higher levels of performance while utilizing energy more efficiently.

The coming chapters will describe the workings of the human body and the ways in which fitness enables it to function better in a racing environment. We'll also take detailed looks at the forces and conditions that cause injuries and present suggestions for avoiding those that are avoidable.

This information applies not only to those who compete in long-distance races and rallies. A lifestyle designed around fitness can assist all of us -- drivers, mechanics, flagmen, scorers and fans -- in enjoying healthier, longer and more productive lives.

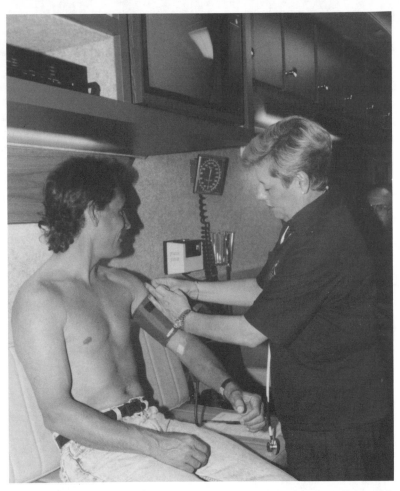

There is no reason an aspiring racer of any age shouldn't be able to hit the track, but an annual physical examination is needed to make sure there are no hidden health problems that can put a driver or his competitors in danger. Trans Am champion Dorsey Schroeder gets a blood-pressure check from Cathy Sorrell of the Hunter Trauma Team during his examination.

Chapter 2

MEDICAL SCREENING FOR RACERS

Who should race? A better question is, "Who shouldn't race?"
Men and women of a broad range of ages safely enjoy participation in racing. As long as one's skills and health are sufficient for the type of racing being pursued, go for it!

Nonetheless, all people who drive racing vehicles should undergo a physical examination every year to assure the safety of themselves and fellow competitors.

The medical requirements of the U.S. Federal Aviation Administration for a second-class medical certificate physical provide a good basis for determining who should race and who should not. These physical requirements are used by several racing organizations and are reproduced below in language taken directly from Federal Aviation Regulations Part 67. (Parenthetical clarifications added by the authors). The standards of this physical examination which are pertinent to motorsports are:

Eye:

(1) Distant visual acuity of 20/20 or better in each eye separately, without correction; or of at least 20/100 in each eye separately corrected to 20/20 or better with corrective lenses (glasses or contact lenses), in which case the applicant may be qualified only on the condition that he wears those corrective lenses while exercising the privileges of his airman certificate (motorsports participation).

(2) Enough accommodation (ability to change focus among objects at varying distances) to pass a test prescribed by the Administrator based primarily on ability to read official aeronautical maps.

(3) Normal fields of vision.

(4) No pathology of the eye.

(5) Ability (color vision) to distinguish aviation signal red, aviation signal green, and white.

(6) Bifoveal fixation and vergencephoria relationship (coordinated focusing and tracking by the eyes) sufficient to prevent a break in fusion under conditions that may reasonably occur in performing airman (motorsports) duties.

MEDICAL SCREENING FOR RACERS

Equilibrium:
   No disturbance in equilibrium.

Mental:
   (1) No established medical history or clinical diagnosis of any of the following:
>   (a) A personality disorder that is severe enough to have repeatedly manifested itself by overt acts.
>   (b) A psychosis (mental disturbance involving loss of contact with reality).
>   (c) Alcoholism, unless there is established clinical evidence . . . of recovery, including sustained total abstinence from alcohol for not less than the preceding two years. As used in this section, "alcoholism" means a condition in which a person's intake of alcohol is great enough to damage physical health or personal or social functioning, or when alcohol has become a prerequisite to normal functioning.
>   (d) Drug dependence. As used in this section, "drug dependence" means a condition in which a person is addicted to or dependent on drugs other than alcohol, tobacco, or ordinary caffeine-containing beverages, as evidenced by habitual use or a clear sense of need for the drug.

   (2) No other personality disorder, neurosis, nor mental condition that . . . :
>   (a) Makes the applicant unable to safely perform the duties or exercise the privileges of the airman certificate (motorsports participation); or
>   (b) May reasonably be expected, within two years after the finding, to make him unable to perform those duties or exercise those privileges . . .

Neurologic:
   (1) No established medical history or clinical diagnosis of either of the following:
>   (a) Epilepsy.
>   (b) A disturbance of consciousness without satisfactory medical explanation of the cause.

(2) No other convulsive disorder, disturbance of consciousness, nor neurologic condition that . . . :

(a) makes the applicant unable to safely perform the duties or exercise the privileges of the airman certificate (motorsports participation) . . . ; or

(b) May reasonably be expected, within two years from the finding, to make him unable to perform those duties or exercise those privileges.

Cardiovascular:

(1) No established medical history or clinical diagnosis of:

(i) Myocardial infarction (heart attack);

(ii) Angina pectoris (severe pain and constriction about the heart); or

(iii) Coronary heart disease that has required treatment or, if untreated, that has been symptomatic or clinically significant.

General medical condition:

(1) No established medical history or clinical diagnosis of diabetes mellitus that requires insulin or any other hypoglycemic drug for control.

(2) No other organic, functional or structural disease, defect or limitation that . . . :

(i) Makes the applicant unable to safely perform the duties or exercise the privileges of the airman certificate (motorsports participation); or

(ii) May reasonably be expected, within two years after the finding, to make him unable to perform those duties or exercise those privileges.

(For motorsports this includes uncontrolled hypertension or hypertension controlled by potassium-depleting diuretics.)

Exceptions:

(The FAA regulations permit an applicant not meeting these provisions to apply for the discretionary issuance of a medical certificate if he can show "to the satisfaction of the Federal Air Surgeon that the duties authorized by the class of medical certificate applied for can be performed without endangering air commerce . . . The Federal Air Surgeon may consider the applicant's operational experience . . . ")

Drivers and crew members who don't prepare for the extraordinary physical demands of motor competition are sacrificing performance and safety. Racing truly is an endurance sport.

Chapter 3

ENDURANCE (AND) RACING

"One thing all endurance athletes have in common is that they are operating very close to the limit of steady state respiratory and circulatory performance. All breathe very hard and all find that their ability to perform as an oxygen-conversion organism defines the limit of their excellence at their sport."

> -- Peter S. Riegel, "Athletic Records and Human Endurance," <u>American Scientist</u>, May-June 1981

In motorsports we think endurance races last 12 to 24 hours -- or 500 miles at least. In terms of the human body's physiological capacities, however, any athletic activity exceeding THREE MINUTES is an endurance sport. Few motor races, therefore, are shorter than the threshold of human endurance.

It's a fact that racers who are not in good physical condition shape can not drive hard for as long as drivers who are fit. Out-of-shape drivers also are prone to "brain fade" and crashes.

But there is good news: The human body is astonishingly capable of expanding its energy reserves to handle extraordinary athletic demands. People of almost any age can achieve competitive physical conditioning and become capable of racing harder while using less energy -- and delaying aging processes while doing it!

The Endurance Threshold

The body quickly reaches the threshold of endurance because most athletic activities demand 10 to 20 times as much energy as the body uses while resting.

Muscles store energy in two enzymes, adenosine triphosphate and creatine phosphate. These can fuel only about 20 consecutive muscle contractions, enough for sports such as weightlifting, sprint running, baseball, gymnastics and golf. These activities are "anaerobic," meaning they require little oxygen.

ENDURANCE (AND) RACING

Racing, on the other hand, is an "aerobic" sport (one that consumes great quantities of oxygen). Racing's physical and mental demands quickly devour muscle energy stores. The body then must use energy from glycogen, which is stored in fat and food. The chemical reactions that convert glycogen into work require oxygen, which must be supplied by the cardiovascular system.

At rest the muscles consume 20 percent of blood flow. Exercise forces the body to increase blood flow to up to 25 times the resting rate and divert flow from the internal organs to the muscles. Under strain the muscles may command 85 percent of blood flow.

No driver or athlete can repeatedly run his or her fastest laps without slowing. Analyses of world-class performances by runners, swimmers, skiers, skaters, rowers and bicyclists show a predictable rate of decline in average speed -- five to eight percent -- as events extend past 3.5 minutes. In endurance events the odds of success belong to those who come closest to attaining this optimal "fatigue factor."

Put another way, a driver who trains to turn in 100 laps at peak human form still begins to slow slightly after 3.5 minutes of action. By the end of a theoretical 100-lap race this driver may be driving at 92 percent of peak physical capacity -- at best. A driver whose conditioning leaves him capable of only 50 peak laps will fall to 92 percent of work capacity by lap 50 and continue slowing over the final 50 laps. If these drivers have equal skills and cars and start the last 10 laps side by side, there will be no contest.

When the lap charts show slowing times toward the end of a race, it isn't always the tires that are wearing out.

The Respiratory Express: How the Human Machine Works

The oxygen delivery process starts with the lungs. When oxygen demand builds the lungs compensate first by increasing their tidal volume, the amount of air inhaled and exhaled with each breath. As the lungs reach 50 to 60 percent of maximum volume, however, the effort required to make the lungs expand also increases so breathing frequency must increase. A normal, fit man breathes 12 times a minute at rest and 40 times a minute at maximum effort.

Within the lungs oxygen is absorbed by gas-exchange tissues and sent to the heart. The heart compensates during exercise by increasing in stroke volume and heart rate. In engine builders' terms, that's cubic inches and revolutions per minute. The typical well-conditioned man averages 70 beats per minute at rest and 190 beats per minute at maximum effort.

Exercise also expands blood vessels that deliver oxygen to the heart. The process is similar to increasing the oil passages in a hard-working engine.

Training also boosts the body's oxygen-carrying capacity and oxygen-handling efficiency. A body that is used to working hard learns to do a better job of using its oxygen. A 10- to 20-fold increase in oxygen consumption is possible in fit individuals.

Racers as Athletes

Motorsports are as physiologically demanding as any games on earth. Since football, hockey, basketball, soccer and even BASEBALL players follow intense, year-round fitness regimens, why don't most racers? Probably because even they don't realize how demanding racing is.

The mental excitement of racing prompts a hormone and adrenaline surge that sends the body into a frenzied buzz. Remember the heart-pounding, hair-raising sensations that followed a scary experience in a dark room or alley? Racing creates physiological reactions comparable to this "fight or flight" response, named because it gives scared creatures a better shot at survival by enabling them to better defend themselves or run like the dickens.

The fact that racing heavily involves the upper-body muscles also places an inordinate demand on the cardiovascular system. Racing stimulates the heart to work harder but does not utilize the large muscle masses in the legs. That leaves limited outlet for all the increased blood flow, greatly elevating blood pressure.

(That is why upper-body activities such as shoveling snow cause heart attacks -- just another reason for racers, especially those getting older, to stay in shape.)

These continuous physiologic phenomena make racing more strenuous than sports in which players get to rest between plays and periods.

Unfortunately, racing also requires a lot of time for equipment preparation and travel, so racing people may get to exercise less than the U.S. population as a whole. Only 20 percent of Americans exercise enough to maintain cardiovascular fitness. Another 40 percent exercise too little and the last 40 percent do none at all.

ENDURANCE (AND) RACING

Racers should be as fit as marathon runners because their hearts face the same strenuous demands. Machinery is not the only thing strained to the limit during motorsports competition.

Racing into Shape?

Drivers who claim racing is enough to keep them in shape are just kidding their car owners, themselves or both. The only way to derive any degree of physical fitness from racing would be to run feature-length races four times a week.

Even baseball players (who spend much of their competitive time scratching and spitting) do conditioning year-round. Golfers find that aerobic exercise enables them to maintain their energy and concentration under stress. Other athletes do not risk their lives when they pull on their uniforms, yet they know that you don't play the game to get in shape -- you get in shape to play the game.

Medical research has conclusively proven that athletes cannot play themselves into shape because the benefits of conditioning are lost more quickly than gained. One study examined college football players, whose competition schedules are similar to those of racers. Football players who stopped lifting weights after their season commenced lost conditioning while those who kept working out between weekend games became fitter still.

The off-season is not a time to stop exercising, either. Aerobic capacity diminishes significantly in three to four weeks of inactivity. Long-distance runners can lose entirely in two to three months the fitness they spent a decade building.

How Exercise Works

Each of us has an endurance threshold defined by our maximum oxygen volume, or VO2 max, consumption. Think of it as the body's air flow -- and remember that engines flowing more air go faster.

The body can be conditioned to increase its VO2 max through aerobic exercise, an activity characterized by heavy breathing and an advanced heart rate. Many forms of exercise provide aerobic stimulation -- running, bicycling, swimming, brisk walking, rowing, aerobic dancing, rope-jumping, cross-country skiing and vigorous calisthenics are just a few. The effectiveness of aerobic training is dependent upon its intensity, duration, frequency and type.

INTENSITY is the most important factor: Lasting aerobic benefit is derived when the body attains 60 to 90 percent of its potential maximum heart rate. As a rule of thumb, one's maximum heart rate is 220 beats per minute minus one beat for each birthday. Maximum heart rate declines with age, so the aerobic range translates to 114 to 143 b.p.m. for a 30-year-old and 108 to 135 b.p.m. for a 40-year-old.

As for DURATION, any intense workout of 30 minutes will provide substantial fitness benefits. Extremely longer workouts do not produce substantially increased benefits. Overtraining can produce fever, muscle wasting and disease-like changes in the blood and immune system.

FREQUENCY? Many athletes try to schedule endurance workouts four or five days a week. Three days weekly is sufficient during the racing season when racers work up a good sweat on the track each weekend.

What TYPE of exercise works? Any that meets the above criteria and is enjoyable. In fact, pleasant exercises are the best because they are the most likely to be continued.

The Benefits of Exercise

When routinely subjected to aerobic loads, the body responds in a number of helpful ways. It becomes capable of doing more work with less effort for longer periods. It also grows more tolerant of heat, dehydration and psychological stress.

Exercise causes the normal person's oxygen uptake to increase from about 0.3 liter per minute to 4 liters per minute. Cardiac blood flow increases five to six times, from about 5 liters per minute to 25 liters per minute. The potential is even greater for the world-class athlete, who may achieve 40 liters per minute of blood flow. This person can absorb six liters of oxygen per minute and attain lung volume of 3.5 liters per minute. This is possible while breathing only 50 times a minute, fewer times than a poorly-conditioned person must breathe at a heavy work load.

More important are exercise's benefits to health in general: medical study after study has shown that people who exercise are less prone to heart disease, high blood pressure, osteoporosis (loss of bone density), diabetes, fatigue, and dozens of other ailments. Active people feel better and enjoy life more, too.

AEROBIC CAPACITY: The human body, like an engine, is limited in speed and endurance by its ability to absorb and burn oxygen. The first benefit of endurance training is an increase in aerobic capacity. A 15- to 20-percent increase in aerobic capacity is possible with just six months of serious training.

ENDURANCE (AND) RACING

HEART RATE: A gain in work capacity is not permitted by a higher maximum heart rate since heredity and age serve as built-in rev limiters. In fact, the fit heart beats at a slower pace while producing more oxygen flow. An athlete's heart can pump the same amount of blood at 45 to 50 beats per minute as an unconditioned person's heart can pump at 75 to 80 beats. The American Heart Association reports that the heart rate can begin to decline after only three to six weeks of training. By exercising regularly, one conceivably can save millions of heartbeats over a lifetime and maybe prolong life.

HEART VOLUME: Cardiologists measure the displacement of hearts by stroke volume -- the amount of blood pumped with each beat. Exercising conditions the heart to grow larger. Stroke volume can increase from roughly 70 milliliters to 140 milliliters per beat during exercise, enough to take the body to 40 to 50 percent of its maximum potential oxygen consumption. Physical fitness can bring still greater benefits. Highly conditioned athletes can achieve heart stroke volumes of about 180 milliliters.

HEART STRENGTH: Exercise makes heart muscles stronger, too, enabling the heart to work harder longer into a race.

BLOOD PRESSURE: After 16 weeks of exercise blood pressure should begin to decline.

Blood pressure is measured by the millimeters of mercury in a manometer that are displaced when the heart beats (systolic pressure) over the millimeters displaced between beats (diastolic pressure). Normal, relaxed systolic pressure ranges from 100 to 140 mm; average normal diastolic pressure is 80 mm.

Just a slight decrease in blood pressure, from 130/80 to 120/75, reduces the risk of mortality 40 percent in men who are 40 years old -- an age at which many folks are still racing or just starting.

BLOOD STREAM: Exercise spurs the body to increase its blood volume, increasing resistance to dehydration and heat. There also is a higher concentration of hemoglobin, the red cells that deliver oxygen throughout the body. This increases the body's ability to carry oxygen to working muscles.

RESPIRATORY RATE: The intercostal muscles between the ribs become stronger and better able to fully expand the lungs for long periods of time.

MUSCLE EFFICIENCY: Endurance training facilitates the efficiency of energy conversion by increasing blood flow and the oxidation capacity in muscle cells. The blood vessels dilate to handle greater blood volume and the number of functioning capillaries within muscles may rise from 200-400 per square milliliter at rest to 600-5,000 when oxygen needs are greater.

CALORIE CONSUMPTION: Exercise, of course, increases calorie consumption. This in turn brings a more desirable body weight. People who exercise can lose weight while eating more food. During strenuous exercise or competition, the body has to supply blood and oxygen to its fat as well as its muscles and organs. Each pound of fat contains ten miles of capillaries, so it takes blood longer to circulate through a fat body and return to the heart.

MENTAL PERFORMANCE: Because more oxygen flow in the body means more energy for the brain, drivers who are in better shape stay alert longer and out-think gasping competitors at the end of a race. They also will be better able to make quick judgments that might help them avoid incidents on the track.

FEEL GOOD: People who are in good physical condition simply feel better. This may be due in part to the brain's release of norepinephrine, a natural, morphine-like hormone generated during exercise. Happy people have been found to have higher levels of norepinephrine in the blood than depressed people. Some doctors claim a 15-minute walk can be more relaxing than a tranquilizer.

Exercise helps people sleep better, too.

What about the REAL Short Races?

Yes, as many of you may be thinking, not all motor races are aerobic undertakings. When looking at the event times for drag races, most closed-course qualifying sessions and some heat races on short tracks, it is obvious that some drivers do compete intensely within the 3.5-minute anaerobic barrier.

These racers must include short-burst, anaerobic exercises in their fitness programs. Maximum-effort wind sprints of 20 to 40 yards, with brief pauses between, can get the body accustomed to the all-out surge needed to succeed in these races.

Fitness for Pit Crews, Track Workers, Officials and Fans

People who don't race can benefit from a fitness programs, too. Their goals, however, may differ.

PIT CREWS: People who perform pit stops need anaerobic (short-burst) conditioning in addition to the aerobic exercises that improve general health. To condition their bodies for quick action, pit crew-men and -women should include such activities as wind sprints in their endurance workouts. Group drills, such as passing a medicine ball or kicking a soccer ball, can provide team activities that build agility and coordination.

SAFETY WORKERS: Folks involved in rescue and extrication operations need a combination of aerobic and anaerobic endurance. Short-burst fitness usually is required to put out fires and help drivers to safety. In extreme instances, however, lengthy extrications or cardiopulmonary resuscitation may be needed.

The sudden, intense exertion experienced by rescue personnel can increase the risks of muscle injury and heart attacks. Obesity, smoking and lack of physical conditioning push the risks higher. Heart attacks account for about half of all job-related firefighter deaths.

OFFICIALS AND FANS: Those who supervise or watch races need exercise programs, too. Why? To live longer and healthier. Taking a break from daily life for a 30-minute workout makes it easier to handle stress, keep off pounds, avoid illness, stall aging processes and enjoy more healthy years at the track.

Carbon Monoxide

There is another reason for racers to stay physically fit and give up smoking -- the occupational hazard of carbon monoxide poisoning.

When we breathe air containing petroleum exhaust gases, carbon monoxide accompanies oxygen into the lungs and blood stream. Unfortunately, carbon monoxide bonds to hemoglobin in the blood 400 times more strongly than oxygen bonds to the blood cells. Hemoglobin cells that are bound to carbon monoxide molecules cannot carry oxygen. Increasing one's cardiovascular capacity forestalls the fatigue and illness that carbon monoxide exposure can cause.

Carbon monoxide also is one of the many harmful compounds in tobacco smoke. Racers who smoke are giving themselves carbon monoxide poisoning before the green flag flies.

Getting Started

Always consult a sports medicine doctor before beginning a fitness program, especially if you are middle-aged or badly out of shape. The doctor can help you plan a program that gets you into winning form as soon as possible without injuries or setbacks.

When starting any exercise session spend a few minutes warming up. This prevents injury to the muscles and the heart, which is a muscle, too.

Gentle aerobic activity that uses large muscles (legs and arms) will raise the body temperature to its operating range, increase circulation, respiration and oxygen flow through the blood and loosen tight muscles. Light jogging, calisthenics or bicycling are good warm-up activities.

A cool-down period also is important to keep blood from pooling in the lower half of the body and to prevent thrombophlebitis (blood clots) and muscle soreness. The cool-down period also diminishes the risk of a heart attack. Keep moving slowly for 5 to 15 minutes, without a hot shower or bowel movement, to avoid straining the heart. A gradual cool-down removes lactic acid (a by-product of exercise) from the muscles and helps avoid lingering soreness.

A Caution Flag: Exercise Warning Signs

The body has signs that warn when you are going too fast.

Extreme shortness of breath, a rapid pulse lasting more than five minutes after a workout or prolonged fatigue suggest that you are doing too much, too soon. Your heart rate should return to normal within two to three minutes after ceasing exercise. Nausea or vomiting may indicate the need to slow down or to avoid eating within two hours of workouts.

You should stop exercising immediately and consult your physician if the above problems persist or if:

-- You experience abnormal heart activity such as irregular pulse, fluttering, palpitations in the chest or throat, sudden burst of rapid heart beats or sudden slowing of a rapid pulse rate.

-- Pain or pressure is felt in the center of the chest, in the arm or in the throat during or immediately following exercise.

-- You feel dizzy, light-headed, uncoordinated or confused or experience a cold sweat, glassy stare, pallor, blueness of the skin or fainting.

Running Tips

Running is one of the most time-efficient means of achieving aerobic fitness. It also can lead to injuries. To avoid them, warm up gradually and, after running a short distance (up to 1/4 mile), stop and stretch your legs. Some good leg stretches are described in the chapter on flexibility.

Also take steps to avoid BEING injured. When on streets and sidewalks, runners are responsible for staying out of the way of cars. If a runner is struck it doesn't matter who had the right of way -- the runner always is the loser.

Avoid running during rush hours when auto pollution is at its worst. Wear bright, reflective clothing and carry identification, emergency medical information and telephone numbers to speed medical treatment in case of an accident.

Avoid busy roads without sidewalks or safe shoulders. When possible, tell someone your planned route and expected time of return. That may avoid a wait if you are injured or become sick along the way. Carry an extra house key, too. In cold weather a runner wearing wet clothes can quickly suffer from exposure if locked outside. If you do twist an ankle or break down while running, don't hesitate to find a phone and ask police for a ride home.

Do NOT run while wearing radio or cassette headphones. You can't trust drivers to avoid you -- YOU must hear what is happening around you.

Summing Up

A commitment to fitness will benefit racers in competition and in the long years after their racing careers are over. People who exercise into old age are leaner, healthier and more likely to live longer. Beginning an exercise program at any age produces real benefits.

Unfortunately, 40 to 50 percent of the people who start a fitness program drop out within one year. The most common excuses are inconvenience, lack of time, conflicts with work or lack of support from spouses.

However, surveys have found that inactive people have just as much leisure time as exercisers. So -- no excuses! Make better use of your time, take up activities that are convenient, time-efficient and enjoyable, and get your spouse and friends to support you and join you -- they need the exercise, too!

Comparison of Exercise Activities

Calorie expenditures are one way of comparing the intensity of various types of exercise. The following list indicates the number of calories burned per each minute of activity in many popular sports.

Climbing	10.7-13.2
Cycling	
5.5 m.p.h.	4.5
9.4 m.p.h.	7.0
13.1 m.p.h.	11.1
Football	8.9
Golf	5.0
Gymnastics	
Balancing	2.5
Abdominal exercises	3.0
Trunk bending	3.5
Arm swinging, hopping	6.5
Rowing	
51 strokes/minute	4.1
87 strokes/minute	7.0
97 strokes/minute	11.2
Running	
Short-distance	13.3-16.6
Cross-country	10.6
Skating (fast)	11.5
Tennis	7.1
Skiing	
Moderate speed	10.8-15.9
Uphill, maximum speed	18.6
Squash	10.2
Swimming	
Breaststroke	11.0
Backstroke	11.5
Crawl	14.0
Wrestling	14.2

Few sports require more total upper-body strength and over-all muscular endurance than auto racing.

Chapter 4

MUSCLING PAST THE COMPETITION: STRENGTH IN RACING

"Until I started, I didn't know how much a difference it was going to make in my performance. I hope not many drivers read this."
> -- Emerson Fittipaldi, "Auto Racer's Latest Tools: Diet and Exercise," New York Times, May 18, 1991

Emerson Fittipaldi was well into his 40s when he won his first Indianapolis 500. Working regularly with free weights (up to 130 pounds for his upper body and up to 300 pounds for his legs) had given Fittipaldi's neck, arms and hands the endurance to compete 500 miles in a high-g race car. He said his dedication to exercise and nutrition had revitalized his career at an age when most athletic careers are simply winding down.

Few sports require more total upper-body strength than racing. Weightlifting, wrestling and some positions at football, maybe, and that's about it.

But those sports do not require the muscular endurance of motorsports. Nor do they pose the high risks of muscular and skeletal injury that can be reduced by making the musculoskeletal system stronger.

Weightlifters might do a minute or two of actual work during a competition. Wrestling matches last three minutes. Football linemen actually work five to ten minutes a game; they spend more time catching their breath than playing.

Racers, as we know, don't get much rest between the green and checkered flags. The shortest feature race requires a longer upper-body exertion than ever demanded of a football player or weightlifter.

Racers face the added strain of gravitational forces, which can exert several times the force of gravity on muscles normally accustomed only to downward gravitational pull. To your neck muscles, your head is like a bowling ball trying to roll off your shoulders in every turn.

Stronger muscles and more flexible joints are better equipped to withstand crashes, too. Many racing injuries result not from impact but from whiplash-like strains that tear at muscles, ligaments and tendons. Such injuries can occur even during spins without wall or car-to-car contact.

Muscle Tech

In its capacity for muscular development the human body again is a wonderful machine. Unlike mechanical devices that wear with usage, muscles grow bigger, stronger and more durable when faced with repeated work.

Strength is the maximum force generated during muscle contractions. Strength can be exerted without joint movement (isometrically) or with joint movement (isotonically). Activities that require more than a few seconds of muscle work require a combination of strength and endurance.

Racers don't need as much total strength as some other athletes, but they definitely need far more muscle endurance. It's like the difference between building an engine for drag-racing or for the 24 Hours of LeMans.

The skeleton provides the framework for more than 600 muscles, each consisting of bundles of tiny fibers. Each part of the body moves through the contraction of some combination of muscles.

It is not believed that the body can create additional muscle fibers. However, the repeated contraction of muscles against resistance -- an outside force such as a weight or gravity -- clearly causes physiologic changes in muscle fibers. As the muscles recover from microscopic injuries caused by training, they adapt by growing in size and tone. If allowed to remain inactive the fibers shrink back toward their unconditioned size.

Men and women have identical muscle fibers but men generally have more of them due to larger body size and their testosterone, a hormone that builds muscles.

Muscles can perform four roles. This is why it can take time to develop good conditioning and the coordination needed for a sport. The muscle roles are:

-- Agonist: Muscle contraction that creates body movement.

-- Antagonist: Relaxation of an opposing muscle that permits agonist movement.

-- Stabilizer: Multi-use muscles, such as the biceps, can move more than one joint. Stabilizer muscles tighten isometrically to hold one joint (such as the shoulder) in place while another (such as the elbow) moves.

-- Synergist: Muscles that work together. For example, muscles on the sides of the abdomen can turn the trunk to the left or right when contracting independently. By contracting simultaneously, or synergistically, rotation is neutralized and the trunk bends forward at the waist.

Unused muscles, despite popular belief, do not turn to fat. Muscle and fat are completely different tissues. Generally, however, people who stop exercising lose muscle tone and grow more fat.

Year-round, three-times-per-week effort is required to achieve and maintain peak muscular conditioning because the benefits of training are lost with inactivity. Remember those football players mentioned in the previous chapter? Those who stopped weight training between games lost strength while those who continued lifting during the season kept getting stronger.

Muscular strength does not fade as quickly as aerobic fitness, however. After regular exercise is halted it may take six to 12 months for strength to diminish completely to an unconditioned state. But a muscle put completely at rest, as when it is placed in a cast, will lose 10 percent of its strength in only one week.

Developing Muscle Endurance

The only way to make a muscle stronger and more durable is to put it under stress. The last chapter described an aerobic conditioning program covering three to four alternating days a week. This chapter provides activities for those left-over, in-between days.

Exercise enhances muscle endurance in several ways:

* Stronger muscles handle sustained work with less effort. By increasing maximum strength, training reduces the percentage of maximum muscle exertion needed to complete a task. Imagine trying to draw a continuous 100-horsepower load during a long race from a 100-horsepower engine or from a 300-horsepower engine -- which is more likely to last until the finish?

* By increasing muscle stores of the energy sources adenosine

triphosphate (ATP) and creatine phosphate (CP), exercise expands the cruising range of muscle fibers. Five months of weight training have been found to produce an 18-percent increase in ATP storage and a 22-percent increase in CP reserves.

* By increasing blood circulation through the muscles, repeated exercise provides more oxygen needed to convert that stored energy to work. Test subjects have experienced a 43 percent boost in forearm blood flow simply by working a handgrip for 30 minutes, four days a week, for one month. A flow bench isn't needed to prove that a lot more blood is going to race through an entire body submitted to regular workouts!

Increased blood flow makes the removal of waste products from muscles more efficient, too. Fit muscles, therefore, are less prone to soreness after racing and exercise. A lot of racers consider tight shoulders and a sore neck a routine part of Monday mornings during the racing season. Proper conditioning should make the muscles practically invisible after all but the longest events.

Getting Started

Before starting any conditioning program, seek advice from your doctor. If you are in poor shape or have suffered injuries in the past, special planning may be needed to work your body up to optimum speed and strength. Do not attempt to build the perfect body in a day. Forget the "no pain, no gain" theory -- that approach does more harm than good. It makes muscles unnecessarily sore and thwarts succeeding workouts.

Aerobic endurance workouts should be sufficient to provide all the lower-body strength most racers need. Three weekly weight sessions of 30 minutes each should be sufficient to develop the arm, shoulder, hand and neck endurance that will delay fatigue and facilitate vehicle control all the way to the victory lap.

Weight sessions should be performed on alternating days because muscles need 48 hours to recover from strenuous workouts. Daily weight workouts are unnecessary and even counter-productive.

Because motorcycle racing does place significant demands on the feet, legs, hips and back, some lower body exercises should be included. The needs of pit and safety crew members will be addressed, too.

The Program

Athletes in all sports utilize some weightlifting work in their fitness programs. Achieving strength endurance does not require grunting and straining under massive loads. That is fine if your goal is grossly oversized muscles. Racers instead need a much more pleasant regimen of high repetitions at low weights to build endurance and efficiency without unneeded bulk.

The results of weight training depend on the intensity, volume and frequency of work, the length of rest periods between sets of exercises and, finally, the range of motion utilized in weight movements.

INTENSITY: The intensity of weight training is expressed by an individual's maximum resistance (MR). One MR is the amount of weight that can be lifted, pushed or pulled only one time without rest; 5 MRs is the weight that can be moved in sets with five repetitions but not six. Weight selection generally is discussed as the percentage of an individual's personal 1 MR capacity.

VOLUME: The total amount of work performed during a training session -- the weight moved multiplied by the number of repetitions executed in each set and the number of sets. The intensity and volume of a training session determine whether it will produce endurance or total strength and bulk.

To produce strength and bulk, training at loads of extremely high intensity, 85 to 90 percent of 1 MR, and corresponding low repetitions, 4 to 6, is most effective.

For racing, however, moderate-intensity lifts, 50 to 60 percent of 1 MR, at 20 to 25 repetitions per set have been found to produce the greatest gains in muscle endurance.

FREQUENCY: This is beginning to sound like a broken record, but three weight training sessions a week are necessary to provide the maximum muscular endurance possible. Taking days off in between weight sessions gives the upper-body muscles time to recover. Even serious weight lifters and body builders who train up to six days a week do "split routines," meaning they do not use the same muscle groups on consecutive days.

Low-speed, high-weight exercises produce an increase in muscular force only for slow movements, like weightlifting or rescue work. What racers need is muscular force at all speeds of fiber contraction, which is what is provided by high-speed, low-load repetitions. A weight training program that is optimum for these needs will promote increases in strength and endurance indefinitely.

REST PERIODS: The amount of time spent catching one's breath between sets determines the benefits that will be derived. At weight-lifter work loads, two to three minutes of recovery are needed between sets. To accustom muscles to racing-style endurance demands, however, only 30 to 60 seconds of rest should be taken between sets.

Weight training conducted at this pace also can produce a modest aerobic benefit that will be far out-stripped by the aerobic training a racer should be doing on alternating days. High-speed weight training has produced VO2 max gains of five percent in men and eight percent in women, about one-third of the potential benefits of aerobic endurance training. Weight training aimed at only strength and bulk development delivers no increase in VO2 max.

RANGE OF MOTION: It is important to move each part of the body through its full range of possible motion. This insures that the newly-developed strength is available throughout the body's range of movement and that flexibility is not limited. For the latter reason, it also is desirable to equally work both agonist and antagonist muscles.

Either free weights or weight machines can get the job done. If weights aren't available, a problem faced by traveling racers, surgical rubber tubing or other devices can provide resistance against which to work the muscles. When working with free weights or resistance devices, one must concentrate on proper technique in order to derive the best benefit.

Fittipaldi's weight program includes 18 different exercises designed for the chest, back, shoulders, biceps, triceps, forearms, legs, neck and abdomen. He does two to six sets of each movement. Each set consists of 10 to 20 repetitions.

Weightlifting sessions should mimic as much as possible the motions involved in racing. This insures effective training and can benefit coordination. The term "muscle memory" refers to the body's ability to learn a sequence of muscle contractions, making a movement go more smoothly and quickly. It takes about 12 weeks of training for muscle size and strength to begin increasing. It is believed that the first gains experienced from exercise actually result from better nervous system coordination of the muscles.

Before hitting the weights, warm up by doing five or ten minutes of light jogging, bicycling or calisthenics. The muscles work better and are less likely to be strained after being warmed.

The strain of weight work can boost the blood pressure, but breathing steadily while working minimizes this adverse effect. Exhale whenever raising a weight and inhale while lowering it.

Types of Muscle Training

There are three types of muscle training:

-- Static or isometric, in which muscles contract against fixed resistance without movement.

-- Isotonic, in which muscles contract against resistance.

-- Isokinetic, in which constant resistance is provided against the muscle's full range of motion.

A product called the "Ortho-Rehab Bar," manufactured by Ortho Technology Inc., consists of a steel rod and latex tubing and provides an excellent, portable strength exercise tool. A similar device can be fabricated from a short length of round wood or metal and surgical latex tubing, which can be found in larger pharmacies or medical supply stores. Some exercises can be recreated by using latex tubing without the bar. To increase the resistance of any exercise, simply shorten the length of latex.

The following diagrams identify the major muscle groups used in racing and describe Ortho-Rehab Bar exercises that racers can follow to build the strength needed to successfully drive, crew or rescue in racing.

Muscle Identification

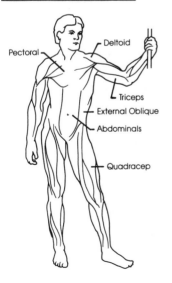
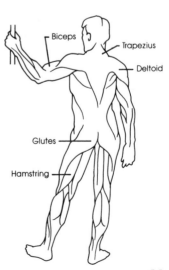

STRENGTH IN RACING

Deltoids

Stand upright and place tubing under feet. Grip handles or tubing so that tubing crosses in front of body. Raise each arm out to the side and overhead. Hold up for one count and return to starting position before repeating in three sets of 10 repetitions.

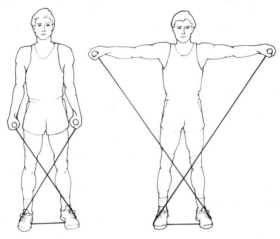

Deltoids

Stand upright and placing tubing under feet. Grip handle in front of body, keep arms fairly straight and raise bar overhead in an arching motion. Slowly lower bar to starting position. Do three sets of 10.

Deltoids and Back

Loop tubing around foot, bend at waist and perform rowing motions along body, flexing elbow to maximum. Do three sets of 10.

Deltoids

Standing upright with tubing under feet, grab bar in center. Keep back straight and raise bar to chest, keeping elbows high and out to sides of body. Do three sets of 10.

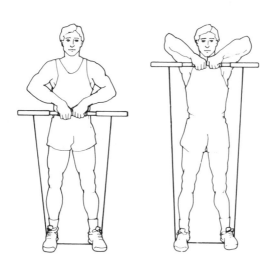

STRENGTH IN RACING

Upper Back

Sit on floor and extend legs. Wrap tubing around feet, keep back erect and repeat rowing motions that pull bar to chest. Entire movement should be executed by the upper back and arms. Do three sets of 10.

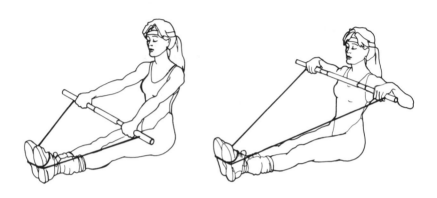

Deltoids and Triceps

Stand upright and place tubing under feet and behind the body. Rest the bar on the shoulders then press upward to fully extend the arms. Do three sets of 10.

Biceps

Stand upright and place tubing under feet. Lower and raise bar using only the arms while holding the body still. Do three sets of 10.

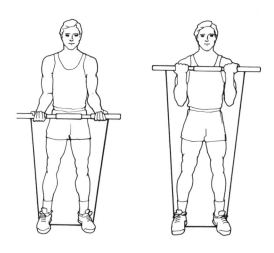

Biceps

Sit and support elbow on inner thigh with tubing under one foot. Lower arm to full extension and slowly raise to full curled position. Do three sets of 10.

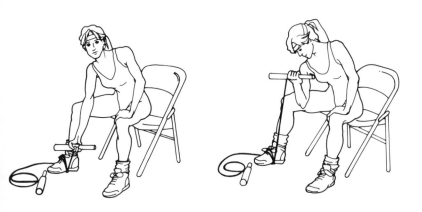

Wrists

Stand upright with the back straight and the arms fully extended. Place tubing under feet. Alternately using the right and left hands, curl latex tubing around the bar. Do sets with palms facing down and palms facing up. Do three sets of 10 repetitions.

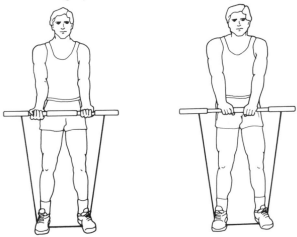

Triceps

Stand upright and place tubing under feet. Keeping back straight with bar behind body, extend arms outward as far as possible. Hold extension for a count of one and return to starting position. Repeat for three sets of 10 repetitions.

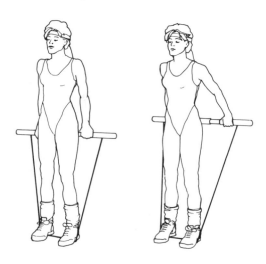

Pectoralis and Triceps

Lying flat on back and place tubing around lower portion of shoulder blades. If needed, wrap towel around latex tubing for padding. Extend arms above body to stretch tubing, return to starting position and repeat in three sets of 10.

Pectoralis

Sit on floor and secure latex tubing around feet. Spread feet and grip tubing. Cross arms in front of chest, hold for a count of one and return to starting position. Do three sets of 10 repetitions.

Triceps

Stand upright and place tubing under feet. Grip bar in center. Starting with bar behind head and elbows close to the ears, raise bar over head, lower and repeat in three sets of 10.

Abdominal/Lower Back Obliques

Stand upright, place tubing under feet, with feet at shoulder width, and rotate bar so loop crosses front leg and bar is behind back. Rotate hips horizontally in slow, smooth repetitions. Switch tubing across both legs so resistance is felt to both right and left sides of body. Do three sets of 10 repetitions.

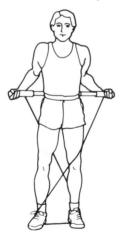

Lower Back, Abdominal, Biceps, Triceps,
Deltoids, Quadriceps, Hips

Sit and loop tubing around feet. Step 1: Pull arms to chest. Step 2:
Lie back. Step 3: Bring arms overhead to fully extended position.
Step 4: Bring knees to chest. Step 5: Straighten legs, spread legs
apart. Step 6: Let legs come back together, bring bar back to chest,
sit up and repeat. Do three sets of 10.

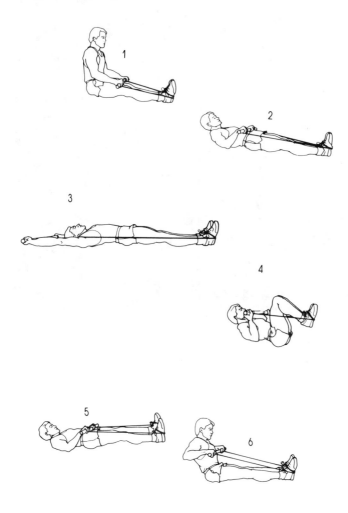

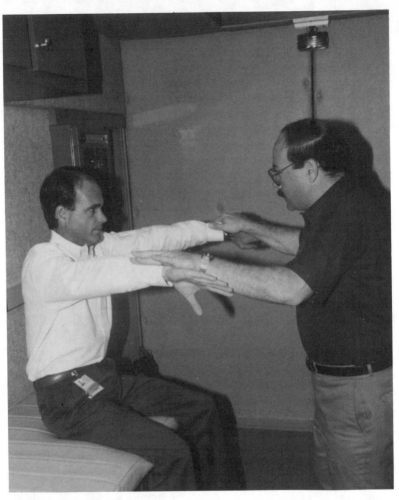

Flexibility keeps the body loose and comfortable farther into long races and reduces the risks of injury. Randy Biggerstaff, right, of the Hunter Trauma Team instructs Trans Am driver Max Jones in exercises for upper-body flexibility.

Chapter 5

BE A FLEXIBLE FLYER

Often overlooked in the pursuit of physical fitness is simple flexibility, which enhances speed, agility and performance and reduces the risks of injuries. A few minutes of each day should be devoted to stretching the muscles and joints of the arms, legs, neck and back.

Racers who are following a proper strength program must work on flexibility to counteract the effects of muscle conditioning. Strength exercise can cause muscle tightness by shortening the resting length of muscle fibers. In addition, racers need to work on flexibility because, in a contradictory way, they actually don't move most of their muscles very much during races.

Drivers sitting in cars can quickly feel tightness in the hamstring and calf muscles because the legs remain stationary while exerting considerable pressure through the toes to the pedals. Back muscles, particularly in the lower back, become stiff from being kept strapped into a seat. Wrists, fingers and thumbs seemingly become locked to the steering wheel. The arms become tired, too, from staying in a raised position.

The muscles and joints can survive the rigors of racing more comfortably if effort is devoted to keeping them limber and loose. The stiffness and limited range of motion that develop as we get older also can be prevented by paying attention to flexibility. As with most of the physical deficits that accompany aging, stiffness results more from inactivity than birthdays. The tissues that support joints are elastic, so exercise can increase their flexibility.

Flexibility contributes to improved performance and reduces the likelihood of injury. Muscles, ligaments and tendons that are accustomed to a full range of movement are more likely to accommodate centrifugal forces than joints that haven't been flexed fully in years. For example, the introduction of flexibility training has decreased injuries in football and other sports.

Pit and safety workers benefit from flexibility as much or more than drivers. Their jobs can demand considerable muscle movement, so flexibility enables them to do their jobs better and with less risk of muscle pulls and ligament sprains.

BE A FLEXIBLE FLYER

Stretching might even help relieve some stress -- at least the stress that develops into muscle tension. Some athletes use their daily flexibility sessions as a time to shut the world out for a few minutes. Many add deep breathing and meditation techniques to relax their minds as well as their bodies.

All it takes to keep the body flexible is a trio of five-minute stretching sessions (in the morning, at noon and after dinner) every day. The following simple stretches can be done anywhere -- at home, in the aisle of an airplane, in hotel rooms or in the pit area at a race track.

Stretching each part of the body and holding it for only 20 seconds will keep it loose and comfortable for four hours. The order in which stretches are done does not make much difference. Doing the easier ones first, however, may help the body get loose and warm for those that are more demanding.

Do stretches slowly and gently -- bouncing (sometimes referred to as ballistics) during stretching can cause muscle tears and other tissue injuries.

When muscles are stretched slowly, they relax to prevent tearing. Done repeatedly, this tendency permits muscles to stretch further and further. Never stretch muscles to the point of pain.

Slow, controlled breathing, even closing the eyes to focus concentration on the muscles, can make the flexibility session more refreshing. So breathe deep, relax, and stretch!

Wrist Stretch
With palms facing up and down, pull hand downward and hold 20 seconds. Do four repetitions on each hand three times daily.

 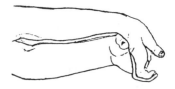

Standing Quadricep Stretch
Steadying self against wall, hold foot, pull toward buttock and hold for 20 seconds. Do four repetitions on each leg three times daily.

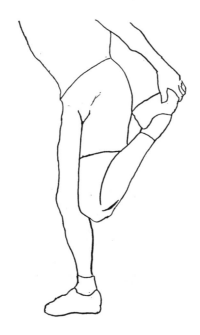

Prone Quadricep Stretch
Lying on stomach, arch back, hold ankle and attempt to pull leg toward head. Hold 20 seconds; do four repetitions three times daily.

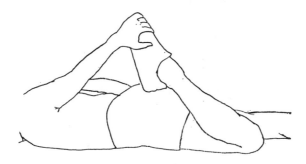

BE A FLEXIBLE FLYER

Neck Stretch

Place arm over head and pull head to side and forward. Hold for 20 seconds and do four repetitions for each side of neck, three times daily.

Hip Twist

Lying on back with arms stretched to sides at shoulder height, bring feet together with knees straight. Lift left leg from floor and roll over right leg while keeping shoulders on floor. Repeat for right leg. Hold up to 3 minutes on each side, one time daily.

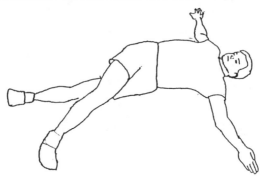

Isometric Leg Stretch

In seated position, press foot against table leg or other solid object. Hold leg in tension for 20 seconds. Do four repetitions with each leg, three times daily.

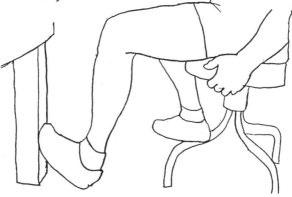

Back Stretch

Sit in chair with thighs parallel to floor and calves upright. Bend over, place elbows between knees and place fingers under arches of feet. Stretch spine fully; hold 1 minute and repeat three times daily.

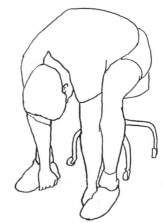

Leg Stretch (Front)

Kneel on floor with legs parallel. Bend backward to stretch muscles on fronts of legs. Hold 20 seconds. Do four repetitions, three times daily.

Ankle/Calf Stretch

Stand approximately two feet from wall, place hands on wall at shoulder level and lean forward. Do a half knee bend, without arching the back, and hold for 1 minute. Do one time daily.

Arm Raise

Stand upright with feet apart at shoulder width. Slowly raise arms parallel to shoulder with left palm turned up and right palm turned down. Hold as long as possible or up to five minutes. Then, while taking a deep breath, raise arms over head and lower them on exhaling. Do one time daily.

Iliotibial Band (Muscles on Outsides of Legs) Stretch

Sitting on floor with one knee crossed over other leg, bent on floor, and foot flat on floor, place elbow on outside of knee. Push knee toward opposite leg. Hold 20 seconds. Do four repetitions on each leg three times daily.

Adductor (Muscles on Insides of Legs) Stretch

Stand with legs spread apart. Lean to one side with hand on leg and feel stretch along inside of other leg and hold for 20 seconds. Repeat for both legs, doing four repetitions three times daily.

Hamstring Stretches

Lie along corner and lift foot onto end of wall. Keeping leg straight, press foot against wall and feel stretch along inside of lifted leg. Hold for 20 seconds and do four repetitions, three times daily.

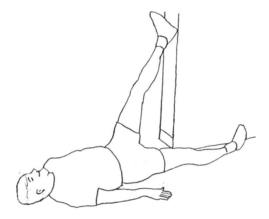

In sitting position. Flex one knee and rotate hip to form a figure four with legs. Extend other leg slowly, bend upper body and touch foot with both hands, then hold 20 seconds. Do four repetitions for each leg, three times daily.

Gastrocnemius (Upper Calf) Stretch

Lean against wall, place one heel flat on ground with toes pointed straight ahead. Keep the back of the leg in a straight line with the back and head. Feel the stretch and hold for 20 seconds.

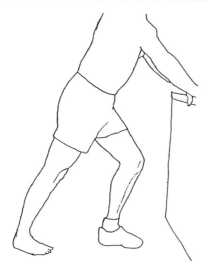

Soleus (Lower Calf) Stretch

Face the wall and stretch again, this time with the knee bent.

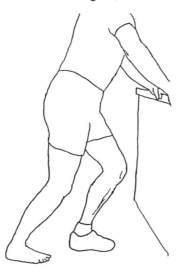

Chest Wall Stretch

Stand facing corner approximately 18 inches from walls. Place hands on walls at shoulder height, 12 inches from corner, with fingers horizontal. Slowly lean forward into corner as far as possible and hold for 20 seconds, then return to starting position. Do four repetitions, three times daily.

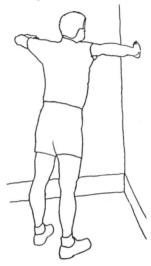

Lower Calf Muscle

To stretch lower calf muscle, again face wall and place one foot behind the other and stretch straightened leg. Hold 20 seconds and do four repetitions for each leg, three times each day.

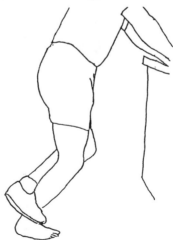

Heat and dehydration rank among the greatest hazards facing racers. Understanding and addressing the body's needs can keep you from having to throw in the towel early.

Chapter 6

BEATING THE HEAT:
YOU CAN'T WIN IF YOU CAN'T FINISH

"In July, the heat can be miserable. It can get so hot, sweat is just dripping off your arms when you try to turn the steering wheel. If you don't take precautions, you could dehydrate in a matter of minutes. I've seen it be almost bad enough that a driver starts wanting a caution period so he can duck into the pits."
-- Bobby Allison,
Stock Car Racing, 1988

Temperatures inside race cars easily can surpass 150 degrees. In one of the few medical studies of heat's effects in motorsports, doctors found that drivers sweated off 5 to 11 pounds of fluid weight while competing in a 500-mile stock car race in 1974.

Two of the six drivers studied drank only a pint or two of water through the whole miserable afternoon. Not coincidentally, those two were unable to complete the race. Two other drivers who swallowed more than 200 ounces of fluid during the race both finished -- and one of them, who drank nearly seven quarts, won!

We now know that fluid loss will severely impair the skills of even the best-prepared driver. The human body is 70 percent water, the blood 90 percent water. Water powers the body's cooling system and the chemical reactions which enable the muscles and organs to function. On the other side of the equation, about 75 percent of the oxygen burned to produce energy is converted into heat -- making our cooling systems crucial to life and performance.

When fluid losses are not replaced, the volume, pressure and flow of blood are decreased. This impairs the delivery of oxygen to muscles and organs which depend on it for energy conversion. Yes, "brain fade" does occur!

In racing environments extreme dehydration and heat stroke --

accompanied by life-threatening organ damage -- are real hazards. Nonetheless, many race drivers and other athletes still follow the out-dated belief that drinking during competition causes nausea. To the contrary, NOT replacing lost fluids is hazardous because dehydration can diminish muscle strength, coordination and mental alertness and, in severe cases, cause heat stroke.

The body's own perception of thirst does not completely reflect its water needs. By the time the first thirst warning is flashed by the brain, the body already has lost one percent of its weight and is halfway to physical impairment. We stop feeling thirsty after replacing only 60 to 70 percent of the water we have lost. Conscious, intelligent effort is needed to maintain a functional fluid level.

One of the six drivers studied in 1974 foolishly endeavored to drive the 500-mile, hot-weather, high-humidity race while drinking only 18 ounces of water. Heat exhaustion put him out of the race. A driver who drank 32 ounces needed relief to last until the checkered flag.

Another Risk of Racing

Heat and dehydration rank right alongside crashes as racing dangers. The peculiarities of motorsports force drivers, crews and fans to break many common-sense rules for coping with heat. To make matters worse, many people continue to follow dangerous and now out-dated misconceptions learned during less enlightened times.

Not long ago coaches and other "experts" wrongly advised athletes not to drink while playing or practicing -- and thousands suffered heat-related illnesses, occasionally fatal. During the 1960s there were 46 heat-stroke football deaths in America.

As recently as 1988 a prominent NASCAR Winston Cup driver told Stock Car Racing magazine that he refused to carry water in his car. "I don't keep a water jug in the car because once I drink any water, I can't quit," he said. He wrongly believed, as did many athletes of the era, that he should not have been drinking water. We now know that misconception is dangerously foolish.

The Heat of Competition

Organizers of most intense outdoor sports, such as running, football and soccer, schedule events in the spring and fall. Warm-weather activities often are planned for mornings and evenings.

Athletes in these sports are directed to wear light clothing, drink fluids at every opportunity and seek shade during time-outs.

Motorsports, due to economics and logistics, are centered on the warmest months and daylight hours. It would make little sense to attempt to schedule races during the winter when few fans would attend and weather could prevent completion of races. It also would be unrealistic to light the larger racing circuits for night competition.

Heavy clothing stifles sweat evaporation, elevating body temperature and prompting higher body fluid losses. An early sports medicine study found that football uniforms caused athletes to sweat 70 percent more than hospital scrub clothing. Imagine how sweating must accelerate when one is swaddled in a three-layer fire suit, Nomex underwear, gloves, a head sock and full-face helmet!

Racing is an intense physical activity. It places heavy demands on the large muscles of the arms and upper torso which are second in mass only to the legs. The chemical reactions that create muscle movement also create heat. During exercise the body accumulates heat faster than it can be dispelled. Even on cool days drivers encounter high body temperatures due to rapid heart and respiration rates and the use of the large muscles.

In addition, the body absorbs heat from exterior sources -- the exhaust pipes running beside the driver and the sun beating down on people in the pits and bleachers.

Sports medicine experts recommend that runners should not start races when air temperatures exceed 82 degrees Fahrenheit. Some advise that distance running can be hazardous when air temperatures are as low as 65 to 70 degrees. Temperatures within enclosed race cars, on the other hand, routinely reach 120-130 degrees and occasionally approach 200 degrees in tight vehicles such as Trans Am cars. In open-cockpit cars high heat retention may occur due to sunlight energy absorbed by safety clothing.

Crew members, track workers and fans spend hours soaking in heat, humidity and sunshine, too. These conditions place them at risk of heat illnesses that may be slower to develop but just as severe as those threatening drivers. Pit firesuits and fire-fighting gear can simulate the conditions facing drivers. Fans drinking beer on hot days can be in greater danger of serious injury than the drivers they are watching.

The Human Cooling System

The human body uses several mechanisms, together known as

thermoregulation, to maintain a temperature near 98.6 degrees Fahrenheit. During heavy exercise core body temperatures typically reach 100 to 104 degrees. The ability to regulate core temperature in the face of heat diminishes slightly with age.

The body attempts to rid itself of excess heat through the breath, through radiation to surrounding air and through convection to colder objects -- such as swallowed fluids, cool suits or the blocks of ice that crew members sit on in the pits. When surrounding air is 85 degrees or cooler, the body expels excess heat primarily through these processes.

Above 86 degrees Fahrenheit the body has to start sweating to maintain a safe temperature. Radiation and convection cease to be useful at all when air temperature exceeds 92 degrees.

Our sweat glands can produce about one ounce of sweat per minute. That is a couple of quarts or three or four pounds of fluid per hour. While women sweat less than men, it does not seem to reduce their ability to regulate body temperature.

Under ideal conditions (exposed skin, low humidity and constant air movement) sweating can dissipate 1,080 calories of heat each hour. That's enough energy to raise the temperature of 1,080 cubic centimeters of water (66 cubic inches or about half the displacement of a two-liter engine) one degree.

When the Radiator Runs Dry: Dehydration

On a normal day each of us loses about three quarts of water through sweat, excreted wastes and the moisture in exhaled breath. Under strenuous conditions the body can lose nearly that much in an hour. A race driver or crew member easily can lose one to two gallons of water a day.

If adequate fluids are not consumed to replace the losses dehydration will result. Dehydration can result from intense, short-term exposure to heat, such as driving in a race. It also may develop slowly over hours or days without proper rehydration. In arid conditions -- in deserts or at high elevations -- sweat evaporates so quickly that people can lose great quantities of fluid without realizing it.

The first consequence of dehydration is reduced blood volume. Thickened blood requires higher blood pressure to force it through the body. Impaired blood circulation, in turn, diminishes the supply of oxygen and nutrients to muscles and the brain.

A fluid loss of two percent of body weight (three pounds for a

150-pound person, four pounds for a 200-pound person) can initiate fatigue and impair endurance and mental alertness -- capabilities upon which the racer's success and life depend.

A three percent weight loss causes the pulse rate to increase. A four percent loss reduces blood volume as much as 16 to 18 percent, causing dizziness, nausea, weakness, impaired strength and diminished coordination.

As blood volume falls so does the ability to dissipate heat. As weight loss reaches six percent (9 to 12 pounds) the victim begins panting like a dog in a frantic effort to blow off heat.

When nine to 10 percent of body weight (13 to 20 pounds) is sweated away, heat stroke is almost inevitable. At this severe level of dehydration the brain makes a last-ditch effort to preserve a minimum blood volume and orders the body to stop sweating. Internal body temperatures soar and cells in the critical organs -- the brain, kidneys and liver -- begin to die.

As we grow older -- and many race participants are mature adults -- more time is needed to rehydrate our blood systems after fluid losses. That is another reason it is extremely important to be aware of the consequences of ignoring the fluid needs.

Heat Illnesses

Muscle cramps are sustained and highly painful contractions of heavily-used muscles, most often in the legs and abdominal wall. These cramps result from inadequately replaced water and minerals lost through sweat.

The best cramp prevention is water. Once cramps occur the best treatment is the strain/counter-strain maneuver. Passively flex the muscle to maximal relaxation until the muscle relaxes, usually within 90 seconds. For example, if a calf muscle cramps have someone gently push the toes downward as far as possible and hold until the cramp subsides. Rubbing a cramp can bruise tight muscles. Applying balm just creates heat in the muscle -- which is what caused the cramp.

Heat exhaustion is a more serious response to dehydration. Due to the loss of blood volume the victim may become dizzy, weak and confused. Heart palpitations, headaches, intense thirst, nausea, vomiting and diarrhea may arise. The body continues to sweat, so the sufferer may feel cool and clammy despite having a fever.

Symptoms of heat exhaustion are cause for alarm and prompt

treatment to prevent the condition from escalating to heat stroke. The victim needs to drink cold fluids; have wet towels applied to the neck, groin and armpits; and possibly receive intravenous fluids. Place the victim in a shady environment, preferably off the ground. Hot soil or pavement can radiate additional heat into the body.

A heat exhaustion episode is proof one needs to learn more about hydration before the next race.

Heat stroke is a life-threatening emergency that can occur suddenly and sometimes without the warning of heat exhaustion symptoms. A heat stroke victim typically collapses into unconsciousness. Sweating may continue, but if the skin becomes hot and dry that indicates sweating has halted and body temperature is rising dangerously. Hyperventilation -- rapid, panting breathing -- can be present.

Once sweating halts, body temperature may soar to or over 106 degrees in as little as 20 minutes. Only minutes of exposure to that temperature can put critical organs at risk.

The central nervous system also is impaired by such temperatures and may cause bizarre, inappropriate behavior or a coma. Racing drivers who are approaching heat stroke may exhibit highly inconsistent lap times or altered driving lines.

Heat stroke symptoms require immediate medical treatment and efforts to lower body temperature. The risk of death from heat stroke depends on the level and duration of body temperature and the promptness of treatment.

When medical personnel and facilities are available the victim may be immersed in ice water. If immersion is not possible, an excellent alternative is applying ice wrapped in towels to the groin, armpits and back of the neck -- the key pathways of blood flow. If core body temperature has reached 105 degrees intravenous fluids should be started immediately.

Ounces of Prevention

The key to preventing heat illnesses (and increasing the odds of success on the track) is good old-fashioned water. In the heat of competition the body absorbs water more quickly than any other fluid.

Research has shown that water passes through the stomach to the intestine, where it absorbed into the blood, more quickly if it is cold (40 to 50 degrees Fahrenheit). Cold drinks also help cool the body by absorbing heat within the body.

In addition, people exercising or working in heat are more inclined to drink enough water if it is cold. Cold fluids do not cause stomach cramps, but drinking too rapidly may. Doctors therefore recommend that small amounts of water -- a 10-ounce cup, for example -- be taken at 15- to 30-minute intervals.

It is impossible to provide precise recommendations for water consumption because so many variables affect the body's sweat rate and ability to cool during exercise and heat exposure.

High humidity slows sweat evaporation and leads to higher heat retention. Breezes or air directed through the cockpit speed evaporation and help the body stay cool. Surrounding surfaces, such as pavement, seats and floorboards, can either radiate heat to the body or absorb heat from it. In the end, however, fluid loss is more a function of exertion and time at work than of temperature.

Drivers in races shorter than 20 or 30 minutes should do well without water during the race -- as long as they drink enough before and after driving.

Drivers competing in longer races should drink a cup of water at every opportunity and experiment with volume to determine the maximum amount their bodies can handle without stomach distress. Drivers who can carry water jugs equipped with tubes in their cars can achieve excellent results by continually sipping water. Again, experience will tell how much can be consumed comfortably.

Squeeze bottles are good accessories at the track. They enable us to keep cold drinks at hand and sip throughout the day, the most efficient way to hydrate the body.

Sports Drinks

Sports drinks are somewhat controversial. A sweet drink may be more appealing to a hot person, who then may consume more of it. However, sports drinks contain carbohydrates (sugar) and minerals intended to provide energy and replace minerals (mainly sodium and potassium) lost through sweat. Solutions that contain too much mineral and carbohydrate cannot be absorbed by the intestine as quickly as pure water can be.

While a good diet should provide all of a body's nutrient and mineral replacement needs, sports drinks and other tasty fluids are acceptable at some lengths before and after hot workouts. Athletes in endurance sports, such as bicycle racing, routinely consume sports drinks, fruit juices and cola soft drinks for energy during competitions but are advised not to take them at full strength.

BEATING THE HEAT

During competition or intense heat exposure these drinks should be diluted enough to reduce the carbohydrate content to 2.5 grams per 100 milliliters of water. At that level the intestine absorbs them as quickly as water. Sugared soda should be diluted with three parts water; fruit juices with five parts water; and sports drinks with one to two parts water. At those levels there is not sufficient carbohydrate remaining to provide significant amounts of energy, but the muscles burn far more energy during intense exercise than drinks can replace anyway.

Most soft drinks include caffeine that can contribute to dehydration. Diet soft drinks contain no sugar and are more quickly absorbed than sweetened drinks. Water remains the beverage of choice during the race. After a race the first couple of pints of cold drink should be water, too. Fruit and vegetable drinks can replace lost minerals naturally. Unsweetened fruit juices contain fructose which is absorbed more readily than sucrose.

It is best to avoid drinks containing alcohol or caffeine (tea, coffee and most sodas) in the days before and after hot-weather races. Alcohol and caffeine have a diuretic effect, meaning they may cause the body to urinate as much or more fluid than they provide. In addition, tea may have a laxative effect which is definitely unwanted during a race.

Preparing for Heat

Preparation for a warm-weather race, whether we drive the car, work on it, flag it, score it or watch it, should begin two days in advance. Drinking two quarts of water daily in small doses gradually accustoms the body to holding more fluid. Drinking too quickly tricks the body into excessive urination. Fluids containing some salt, such as sports drinks, may be retained better than water.

Hyperhydration -- drinking a pint of cold water 15 to 30 minutes before the green flag -- is a good way to start a race.

Your Personal Hydration Gauge

When possible, race drivers, pit crew members and track and safety workers should weigh themselves before and after races to measure fluid loss. For every pound of weight lost they should consume one quart of an acceptable drink. Any loss exceeding five pounds is proof that inadequate fluid was consumed.

The body's water balance also can be accurately gauged by observing the color of urine after races or exercise:

-- Clear urine indicates excellent water balance.

-- A slight straw color indicates slight dehydration.

-- The color of straw indicates mild dehydration.

-- Dark yellow warns of possibly serious dehydration. If you are still standing and alert enough to make a mental note, remember to do a much better job of rehydration next time.

Conditioning & Acclimatization

Heat stress is yet another reason drivers, crew members and track workers should get in top physical shape. Regular exercise and heat exposure cause a number of helpful physiological adaptations.

Exercise conditions the body to sweat more while losing fewer minerals in the sweat. Fit people have more blood fluid volume, further increasing heat tolerance. The muscles become more efficient and produce less heat while they work. Blood flow to the skin increases, improving heat loss.

People who exercise enough to increase their cardiovascular output are better able to maintain normal operating parameters during heavy work and modest dehydration. Their blood systems are better able to supply oxygen to hard-working muscles and organs after fluid levels start to drop.

If one lives in a cool climate and is heading for a hot-weather race, allow as much time as possible to adapt to the new environment. Arriving a week early may be out of the question for race teams, but that is considered the optimal period for heat acclimatization.

After arriving at a hot race destination, avoid air conditioning. The body will adapt better if it spends most of its time in the heat.

Replacing Salt?

One of yesterday's common fallacies was belief in the use of salt tablets. While the human body rarely can survive more than three days without water, it can go more than 30 days without replacing salt. When the body sweats the blood loses proportionally more water than salt, leaving a higher salt level in the blood. Giving salt without adequate water makes the situation worse and may increase the risk of heat stroke. Swallowing salt tablets also can irritate the stomach and cause vomiting or diarrhea which further dehydrate the body.

Normal foods can replace salt losses if less than six pounds of body weight has been lost to sweat. If sweat loss exceeds six pounds some experts recommend replacing it by drinking sports drinks or water containing one teaspoon of salt per gallon.

The exercising body actually needs more potassium than salt. Potassium comes into use during exercise by being released into the blood stream to open the veins to increase blood circulation. Foods rich in potassium (bananas, vegetables, whole grains, beans, nuts and citrus fruits) maintain the body's balance of this important mineral.

A Splash of Fuel and a Splash of Water?

We often see hot, weary drivers and crewmen splash themselves with cold water during breaks in activity. That feels good for a few seconds but, research has shown, spraying water on the body does not lower body temperature, heart rate or sweat loss.

Splashing water on a sweat-soaked driver's suit might be counterproductive. If the suit already is so wet that evaporation and heat loss are stifled, more fluid will, if anything, worsen the situation. If there is time to hand a driver a cup of water, he or she will gain the best benefit by drinking it.

(Dr. Hunter once treated a Trans Am driver for second-degree burns of the buttocks resulting from the steam-heating of water spilled in his car's seat.)

Equipment Colors?

An automotive paint analyst told us the interior of a black passenger car can get 50 to 60 degrees hotter on a sunny day than a white car. One can't predict the temperatures that may be experienced inside race cars, which have varying degrees of ventilation, but it is something to consider. Likewise, common sense suggests that drivers of open-cockpit cars select light-colored driving suits and helmets if they race under sunlight.

Track and Pit Crews at Risk, Too

People working around race cars face heat and dehydration risks, too. Plenty of cold water needs to be kept on hand and consumed continually in safety vehicles, paddocks, pits and corner stations.

Moderate dehydration has not been found to adversely affect performance in intense, high-power activities lasting less than 30 seconds -- pit stops, for example. But safety crews responding to an accident or crewmen toiling during a non-routine pit repair stop may need maximum effort for several minutes. They should not put their well-being or someone else's at risk through a lack of conditioning or hydration.

Medications

Some medications impair thermoregulation, so be sure to ask a physician or pharmacist about the side effects of any that are being taken. Potential culprits include antihistamines, antidepressants, sedatives, tranquilizers, and thyroid and ulcer medications.

Cool Suits

Even with peak fitness and preparation the human body cannot be expected to fully withstand 100 to 200-degree environments for hours. Cool suits are a great driver aid -- if they work. Know the limitations of this equipment and carefully install, maintain and operate it.

Official Action

Race officials can help prevent illnesses resulting from heat and dehydration as well as injuries resulting from accidents caused by skill impairment.

Race tracks and sanctioning bodies must equip employees and officials with plenty of ice and cold drinks and provide ample opportunities -- if not orders -- for them to be consumed heartily.

The National Weather Service or a wet bulb thermometer should be consulted to determine the heat index during race meets. Repeatedly remind drivers, crews and fans of the risks and warning signs: Chills, shivering, dry skin, throbbing sensations in the head, nausea, disorientation, unsteadiness and piloerection (goose pimples) on the chest and upper arms. Stress the need for fluid replacement and point out that people who insist on chugging beer on hot days could give themselves brain and organ damage even if they don't fall out of the bleachers.

During warm weather, track officials and pit crews should carefully monitor lap times -- broad fluctuations are a good sign of driver impairment. We have seen variations of seconds a lap toward the end of tough races. Officials shouldn't be afraid to use the black flag to determine whether an erratic driver is able to continue. Heat

BEATING THE HEAT

illness at racing speeds can be as dangerous as drinking on the highway.

Track medical personnel must have an ice supply handy and reserved for emergency use. If anyone exhibits symptoms of heat stroke in the absence of medical personnel (such as in a testing situation) an ambulance should be called at once.

Typical race track snack shack foods are high in fat and high in sugar -- and not particularly nutritious. But with a little knowledge and advance planning you can maintain healthy eating habits even if you seem to live at race tracks.

Chapter 7

EAT FOR SPEED:
NUTRITION AND THE RACER

"Probably the biggest problem with Kyle (Petty) was that he was not eating enough and not eating on a schedule that would help his body store up energy to last him through a race . . . He's now on a very, very high carbohydrate diet, low in fat with a moderate amount of protein."
-- "These Racers Really Are What They Eat," Winston Cup Scene, Nov. 14, 1991

You wouldn't dream of dumping kerosene into your race car's fuel tank. But most people inflict equal indignity upon their bodies by stuffing their stomachs with similarly low-grade fuel. The typical American diet is low in healthful energy and high in clogging fat.

Diet alone cannot turn a losing driver into a winner, but it can determine which side of the finishing line a contender may occupy as the checkered flag falls.

Race drivers are endurance athletes who require nutrition that is long on basic energy sources and short on worthless calories from fat and sugar. Crew members, track workers and race fans also can feel healthier and more energetic by forsaking the burgers-fries-chips-soda-beer-candy bar meal plan.

Eating properly does not require living on nuts and berries or gobbling expensive dietary supplements. All that is necessary is learning the simple basics of nutrition and choosing sensible -- and enjoyable -- items from the traditional four basic food groups. A nutritious diet still can include sweets and other favorites -- these just need to be eaten in moderation as treats rather than staples.

The human body requires the same basic nutritional building blocks whether it is watching races or contesting them. The only difference lies in the amount of food -- measured in calories -- that is burned.

EAT FOR SPEED

Sometimes overlooked in our slim-conscious society is the fact that hard-working people must eat enough to meet their high energy needs. Skipping meals is a leading cause of that tired, run-down feeling many of us experience from time to time. If the body runs out of gas it cannot think clearly or work efficiently. For a peak energy level one should eat healthy foods at four- to six-hour intervals through the day. The body uses food more effectively in small doses than in one daily mega-dose.

The "average sedentary American" might down 3,000 calories a day. That's too much. The typical adult male needs about 2,700 calories a day while a woman needs 2,000 calories. People undertaking a moderately serious exercise program, meanwhile, may need 3,000 to 4,000 calories daily. (That means people who exercise just about every day actually can eat MORE and still control their weight!) The daily diet must include all the basic nutritional ingredients that keep the body purring.

Human Racing Fuel

Carbohydrates should make up 60 to 70 percent of the calories consumed each day. The percentage should be higher for people following intense exercise programs.

Fats should cover 20 to 30 percent of one's daily caloric intake and protein only 10 to 15 percent. Unfortunately the typical modern man and woman eat too much fat and protein at the expense of carbohydrates. The average American derives less than 50 percent of his or her calories from carbohydrates.

Fatigue during exercise -- or races -- results from depletion of the glycogen stores in the muscles. Glycogen, the body's basic fuel, consists of long chains of glucose molecules and is stored in the liver and muscles. A diet high in carbohydrates increases the glycogen stores of muscles as much as 65 percent. A diet heavier in fats and proteins conversely reduces glycogen and endurance.

The body's ability to synthesize glycogen is directly proportional to its consumption of carbohydrates. Athletes in long-distance sports such as marathon running and bicycling have long practiced a tactic known as carbohydrate loading.

In preparing for races these competitors exercise their muscles to exhaustion and then consume meals consisting largely of carbohydrates. This creates "glycogen supercompensation," an increase in the glycogen content of the heavily-worked muscles.

More than 50 years ago a study showed that exercise could be sustained longer when preceded by such high-carbohydrate consumption. When comparing athletes who had eaten high-carbo diets and low-carbo diets for three days, the high-carbo eaters could exercise an average of 210 minutes before exhaustion while the low-carbo eaters lasted only 80 minutes.

The original form of carbohydrate loading included a preceding low-carbohydrate consumption phase which now is generally scorned because of its dangerous side effects. In this practice athletes exercised heavily but avoided eating carbohydrate-rich food to starve the muscles of glycogen.

The Four Food Groups

Each day, as a rule of thumb, one should eat two servings of foods from the dairy group, two servings from the protein group, four servings from the fruit/vegetable group and four servings from the cereal/grain group.

1. Cereals and Grains = Carbohydrates

Cereals and grains make up the most important food group for racers and athletes. Best of all, these foods are NOT fattening.

Carbohydrates consist of molecules made up of carbon, oxygen and hydrogen, which is how they get their name. This composition makes them an excellent source of fuel. Pasta, rice, potatoes and whole-grain baked goods are leading sources of carbohydrates.

Sugar is a carbohydrate, too, but a simple one that is absorbed by the body so quickly it provides negligible energy. The average American citizen eats his or her weight in sugar each year -- far too many wasted calories. And eating a sugary snack might make you hungrier, rather than satisfy hunger, by causing the body to produce insulin and lower the sugar level in the blood.

The complex, natural carbohydrates in fruits, fruit juices, vegetables and grains are a better grade of fuel than sweets. Natural carbohydrates also provide minerals and vitamins that keep the body in tune. Carbohydrates contain a trace of fat, too.

Carbohydrates provide only four calories per gram of food. Fats carry nine calories per gram.

2. Fruits and Vegetables

Fresh fruits and vegetables are an excellent, inexpensive source of carbohydrates for energy; vitamins and minerals essential to bodily chemical reactions; and fiber that promotes stomach and bowel health. Being high in bulk and low in calories, fruits and vegetables are excellent foods for people trying to control their weight.

3. Protein

Proteins provide many of the body's building blocks, such as the basic components of muscles, ligaments, skin, hair and nails. Hemoglobin, which carries oxygen through the blood, is a protein. Enzymes that control bodily chemical processes and antibodies that fight infections are proteins, too. Proteins also work as sensory receptors for sight, hearing, taste and smell.

The protein group includes meat, fish, poultry, eggs, beans and nuts. Just a few ounces of these foods easily satisfies the body's minimum daily protein requirements.

Proteins are made up of molecular units called amino acids. The body requires 20 different amino acids and can produce 11 of them. These are called nonessential amino acids because they do not have to come from food. The other nine amino acids must be derived from food, so they are called essential amino acids. Foods that contain all essential amino acids are considered "complete" proteins. These include eggs, fish, meat, poultry, milk and milk products. "Incomplete" proteins, which lack some essential amino acids, come from vegetables, fruits and cereals.

Vegetarians can get all the protein they need without eating meat but require a variety of foods to make sure they obtain all the essential amino acids. The best non-animal sources of protein are nuts and legumes -- beans, peas and lentils.

Protein sources that are high in fat -- red meats, eggs, butter and some cheeses -- should be limited to a few servings a week. Poultry, fish, beans and nuts provide protein with less fat. If chicken or fish is deep-fried, however, wads of fat will be hanging from it.

It is commonly but wrongly believed that athletes require massive quantities of protein to maintain muscle mass. In truth even the most muscle-bound bodies turn over little protein. The modern diet is rich in protein, averaging 17 percent of total consumption. That provides enough protein to take care of the most athletic people among us.

The body has no way of storing excess protein for future use. Eating surplus protein does nothing to improve athletic performance and may diminish performance by bogging the stomach, liver and kidneys with excess material to process and excrete.

Some jocks are convinced that high-protein diets will increase muscle mass. In the absence of exercise, high-protein foods are burned as energy, converted to fat or excreted.

In extreme cases the body can metabolize protein for energy. It is better to eat sufficient amounts of carbohydrate to do the job more efficiently.

4. Dairy Foods

Dairy foods provide protein and vital minerals and vitamins but also can be high in fat. Because most people consume far too much fat, low-fat foods such as 2% milk and yogurt are preferable to whole milk, cream, cheese, butter and ice cream.

A Word About Fats

The taste buds love foods containing fats -- butter, thick and marbled red meats, cheese, gravy, pastry, ice cream and the aptly-named "junk foods." That is unfortunate, because the palate leads us to eat far too much of this stuff at the expense of healthier foods.

Vegetarians who avoid meat still can eat way too much fat if they make cheese and butter their meat replacements.

Just 20 to 30 percent of our daily calories should come from fats, which basically are calories without nutritional value. Fatty foods do not replenish spent muscle glycogen, so muscle fatigue can result from eating too much fat and insufficient carbohydrates.

No more than one-third of our daily fats should be foods nutritionists designate as "saturated" fats -- those that contribute to high cholesterol levels and heart disease. Saturated fats are usually animal-based: meat, whole milk, cheese, butter. Fast-food hamburger meat is about 20-percent fat. Some vegetable fats -- coconut oil, solid margarine and hydrogenated vegetable oil -- also are saturated. Any fat that has a solid form at room temperature generally is saturated.

Polyunsaturated fats -- as found in liquid vegetable oils -- are more acceptable than the saturated fats. The polyunsaturated fats still carry empty calories.

Many foods contains fats. One means of determining how much fat a food has is leaving a piece on a napkin or paper towel. Fatty foods -- chips or cakes, for example -- will leave a grease stain proportional to their fat content.

Fat isn't all bad, however. Fat is used to build cell membranes and keep the skin in good shape. Some fat carries certain vitamins through the body.

While fat provides a much more concentrated source of energy than carbohydrate, the body requires oxygen to break it down. When we are exercising hard there is not enough oxygen available to adequately burn fat for fuel. That's why the body prefers to use glycogen during intense activity. People who exercise often, however, do become more efficient at transporting oxygen and using fat for energy.

Don't worry about getting enough fat. Most foods naturally contain small amounts, so even people who go out of their way to avoid it consume enough to remain healthy.

Cholesterol

Depending on its type, cholesterol can be one of humanity's leading health threats or a highly beneficial substance.

Some cholesterol is manufactured within the body. This "good" cholesterol is high-density lipoprotein (HDL). It contributes to useful body functions and carries "bad" cholesterol (low-density lipoprotein or LDL) to the liver, where it is broken down for excretion. The HDL cholesterol insulates nerves, repairs tissues and produces bile that helps digest food. This cholesterol also creates hormones, including those sex hormones that are so important to so many racers.

The bad LDL cholesterol enters the body in food and circulates in the blood. When present in excess, LDL is deposited on artery walls and forms plaque that, over time, causes the narrowing or blockage of arteries (atherosclerosis) and, possibly, heart attacks. Dietary cholesterol is found in foods bearing animal fat. Foods high in cholesterol include whole milk, cheese, egg yolks and organ meat (liver and kidneys). The average American adult carries too much of this cholesterol. A low-cholesterol diet and exercise can reduce total cholesterol and the risk of heart disease. Here's another advertisement for exercise: Regular, intense exercise slightly raises the body's HDL level. Unfortunately, the HDL boost is not enough to compensate for poor nutritional practices.

The Humble Fiber

Dietary fiber is a part of food people can't digest. While providing no nutritional value, fiber still does considerable good work. Fiber helps keep bowel movements regular, dilutes bile acids

Comparative Cholesterol Content of Common Foods

Liver, 3.5 oz.	300 milligrams
Egg yolk, 1	250 milligrams
Lean red meat, 3.5 oz.	94 milligrams
Poultry, 3.5 oz.	75 milligrams
Fish, 3.5 oz.	70 milligrams
Butter, 1 tablespoon	30 milligrams
Margarine, 1 tablespoon	0 milligrams
Ice cream, 1 cup	53 milligrams
Ice milk, 1 cup	26 milligrams
Whole milk, 1 cup	30 milligrams
2% milk, 1 cup	18 milligrams
Skim milk, 1 cup	7 milligrams
Yogurt, low-fat, 8 oz.	17 milligrams
Buttermilk, skim, 1 cup	5 milligrams
Cheddar cheese, 1 oz.	27 milligrams
Swiss cheese, 1 oz.	25 milligrams
Cream, 1 tablespoon	20 milligrams
Plain pasta, 1 cup	0 milligrams
Whole-wheat bread, slice	0-5 milligrams
Brown rice, 1 cup,	0 milligrams
Baked potato	0 milligrams

and reduces risks of colon cancer and constipation. Whole grains, corn meal, brown rice and fresh fruits and vegetables are good sources of fiber.

Hit the Bulls-Eye!

Dr. Hunter uses a bulls-eye target created by Covert Bailey of Oregon for his video "Fit or Fat for the 90s" and reproduced at the end of this chapter, to help patients distinguish desirable foods (high in energy, fiber, vitamins and minerals) from those that are less nutritious (high in saturated fats, sugar and preservatives). Eating foods closer to the center of the target assures a daily diet that is on the right track.

The Pre-Race Meal

Sports researchers long ago black-flagged many traditional beliefs about pre-game meals. The legendary huge meal loaded with steaks, eggs and fats is the last thing any one -- driver or crew member -- needs before the stress of competition.

Proteins and fats contribute little energy for endurance activity. Meat and greasy foods take too long to digest, too. The stomach requires significant blood flow to digest food. If food remains in the stomach when competition starts, the body has to divert blood flow from working muscles, the brain and other critical organs. If demands from other parts of the body over-ride the stomach's pleas for blood flow, painful and distracting cramps may result.

The stress preceding a race, which most of us recognize as the sensation of "butterflies," may slow the passage of food through the stomach. Plan accordingly.

People who encounter difficulties digesting milk products obviously should avoid them before competition. Spicy foods also should be avoided. Pre-race butterflies are one thing -- making them worse by inducing gas and cramps is another.

Another no-no is taking a large dose of sugar, such as a candy bar, just before competition or training. A sugar jolt paradoxically may decrease the body's energy level by spurring an over-reactive release of insulin. This insulin inhibits the body's use of the energy that is stored in fats, forcing it to deplete blood glucose and muscle glycogen supplies sooner. As a result, fatigue is hastened. One study found that distance runners reached exhaustion 25 percent sooner if they consumed a sugar-charged drink before exercising.

What the body needs just before a race is 500 to 1,000 calories of (no surprise) easily digested carbohydrates. Spaghetti (light or no sauce), bread, muffins, bagels, baked potatoes, pancakes or waffles (little butter and syrup), cereal (with low-fat milk) and fruit are pre-game choices of many knowledgeable, successful athletes.

A couple of glasses of fluid, preferably fruit juice or water, should be part of the pre-game meal. Avoid caffeine -- it creates excessive urination that can contribute to dehydration.

Caffeine is touted by some sports nutritionists as a means of promoting the use of fat for energy, thus stretching glycogen supplies and endurance. Some marathon runners drink two cups of coffee or tea an hour before races to maximize fat metabolism, but caffeine adversely affects some runners. Its diuretic effect and racing's propensity for dehydration probably make caffeine consumption unwise for motorsports participants. People who rely upon coffee to stay alert would be better off getting more sleep.

Avoid salty and bulky foods, too. Salt can prompt excessive urination just when body fluids are needed most. Bulky foods can digest too slowly.

Another tip -- don't try out a new meal plan on race day. Give it a shot on a training day to determine how it affects you.

The pre-race meal should be eaten at least three hours before the green flag to give food plenty of time to clear the stomach and the body plenty of time to complete resulting bowel movements.

Maximum blood stream efficiency is the leading benefit of an empty stomach, but there is a more sobering potential benefit. If a crash causes unconsciousness and vomiting, asphyxiation and respiratory arrest might result if the stomach is full. Vomiting also may cause aspiration pneumonia -- the inflammation of the lungs from stomach acids and infection by intestinal bacteria. That's the same reason people are denied food and drink before surgery.

After the Race

A high-carbohydrate diet helps the body recover from races and strenuous training sessions. The same good foods that help the body compete also replenish its energy stores, help it feel rested and minimize muscle soreness. The post-work meal needs to include plenty of water and light fluids, too.

Food and Training

When participating in a vigorous physical training program -- one sufficient to achieve significant aerobic benefit -- it is best to schedule meals after rather than before workouts. Eating after exercise will help with weight control. Vigorous exercise boosts the body's metabolism, making it burn food more efficiently while converting less food to fat. Also, since exercise decreases the body's glycogen stores, carbohydrates can be converted directly to glycogen instead of fat.

Eating heartily before hearty exercise can cause illness -- the body cannot provide enough blood flow to power the stomach and the muscles at once.

Eating on the Road

Spending a lot of time on the road and trying to stay within a budget does not preclude good nutrition. Careful planning can keep supplies of good food in the car, trailer and hotel room. Careful choices can make even a fast-food pit stop healthy.

At breakfast lean toward pancakes, french toast, muffins, cereal, fruit and juices. Avoid butter and go light on syrup. Use jam instead of butter and syrup. Use low-fat milk for cereal, hot chocolate and chocolate milk. Avoid hash browns, bacon, eggs, sausage, doughnuts and sausage-egg-biscuit sandwiches that will keep you floating in fat all day.

EAT FOR SPEED

Whether racing or training, breakfast is the most important meal of the day. Many people would be better off if they ate more at breakfast and less at dinner.

At lunch, eat the bread and carbohydrates and avoid much of the stuff that gets stuffed in sandwiches. Hold the mayo (loads of fat) and throw back the hamburgers and fries. Go for things liked baked potatoes, pasta with little sauce, chili and salads.

Don't, however, assume that anything at a salad bar is healthy. Skip cheeses, hard-boiled eggs and thick dressings while loading up on the garbanzo beans, toasted croutons, vegetables, bread and crackers. A slurp of some salad dressings can carry as much as 400 calories, mostly fat.

At dinner time, think carbo: Pasta; baked potatoes; rice; bread and rolls with jam or jelly instead of butter; and thick-crust, vegetable-laden pizzas (no fatty pepperoni).

Before leaving on a race trip, pack up apples, oranges, dried fruits, canned fruits packed in water (no syrup), fruit juices, whole-wheat pretzels, breakfast cereal, wheat crackers, granola bars, fig newtons, oatmeal-raisin cookies and herbal teas. These items provide great snacks and quick breakfasts or lunches. Packing your own provisions also is a good way to cut expenses.

Watch out for fast foods -- a big cheeseburger, greasy order of fries and a shake can provide as many as 1,000 calories, many of them fat and most of them salty.

Typical Fast Food Calories

Hamburger	200-350
Cheeseburger	300-410
"Super" Burgers*	450-1040
Fried fish sandwich	390-570
Roast beef sandwich, regular	300-350
French fries, regular order	200-260
French fries, large order	320-400
Chocolate shake	340-385
1/2 cheese pizza, 13"	680
1/2 supreme pizza, 13"	800
Plain cake doughnut	275
Breakfast biscuit,	
sausage & egg	521-585
bacon, cheese & egg	480
2 pieces fried chicken	395-545
1 tablespoon mayonnaise	100

* The big doubles and triples, with cheese, bacon, dressing, etc.

Vitamins?

There are more than 60 chemical substances known as vitamins and minerals that are essential to the functioning of the human body.

Vitamins are components of natural foods that cannot be made in sufficient quantities within the body, so they must be delivered by food. (An exception is Vitamin D, which the body can produce when exposed to sunshine.)

There are 13 vitamins that are essential to life and peak performance. Vitamins work in conjunction with proteins to regulate body functions. Vitamins are vital to energy metabolism; the excretion of carbon dioxide; fat and glycogen formation; blood clotting; bone growth; vision; and the maintenance of skin, bone and cell tissue.

Vitamins only work in conjunction with nutrients found in food. On their own they are as useful as fuel without a race car, so taking vitamins in the place of meals is a waste of money and health.

A good, basic, daily diet holds enough vitamins for even the hardest-driven athletes. Serious exercisers tend to get more vitamins and minerals than needed because they are eating more good food to compensate for their higher caloric expenditures.

The medical literature universally argues that athletes who eat a good variety of foods should not need supplements of vitamins, minerals or miracle mystery elements. While there are Recommended Daily Allowances (RDAs) for each vitamin and mineral, it is not necessary to know them -- just eat the right number of helpings of each of the four food groups each day and you will do fine.

Repeated responsible medical studies of nutritional "trick set-ups" and miracle substances have found them lacking in benefits. What good they do accomplish, if any, is psychological.

Swallowing excessive doses of vitamins actually can be harmful. Too much of Vitamins B6, D or A can lead to liver disease. Excessive Vitamin C destroys Vitamin B12. Overdoses of Vitamin E can prompt headaches, fatigue, blurred vision, muscular weakness and stomach ailments.

A doctor's advice should be sought before consuming any nutritional miracle. Don't necessarily believe advertisements. As Dr. Susan M. Kleiner, a registered dietitian, wrote in the journal Physician and Sportsmedicine, "Many people believe that false advertising is unlawful and that nutrition and health claims are regulated by the government.

"Unfortunately, this is only partially true. The FDA (U.S. Food and Drug Administration) does not have the money or staff to pursue the many claims that are made. Generally, only the most outrageous or life-threatening claims are acted upon."

The travel and long track days that accompany racing can, on the other hand, make eating right difficult. If road food may not be getting the job done, some nutritionists recommend the daily consumption of an inexpensive, basic multivitamin.

Minerals

The body requires some natural elements to function, too. These are categorized as major minerals and trace elements. These aid in the control of cellular functions such as water distribution; energy conversion; electrical activities such as the nerve impulses that keep the heart beating and control muscle contractions; and construction of bones, teeth, hemoglobin, cartilage and tendons.

The major minerals are sodium, potassium, chlorine, calcium, phosphorous, magnesium and sulfur. The trace elements are fluorine, chromium, manganese, cobalt, copper, iron, zinc, selenium, molybdenum and iodine.

Potassium is one of the athlete's best friends. In addition to reducing the risk of high blood pressure, potassium keeps arteries strong and minimizes the likelihood of muscle cramping. Whole grains, vegetables, potatoes, fruits and fruit juices are good sources of potassium. The minerals and trace elements are found in dairy foods, whole grains, vegetables, red meats and cereals. They are another reason to eat a varied, balanced diet.

There is no evidence that consuming mega-quantities of minerals helps the body. As with vitamins, excess quantities merely get excreted and make one's urine more expensive.

Salt?

People who eat nutritious, balanced meals do not need to take salt tablets. The bountiful modern diet, again, contains more than enough sodium to replace that which is lost through sweat -- about six to ten times the amount we actually need. We need to consume only one-fifth of a gram (.007 ounce!) of salt each day.

Salt supplements are counterproductive. Active people adapt to heavy sweating by excreting less salt in sweat. If they consume too much salt, this adaptation does not occur and the body can be at higher risk of heat illness during exercise or hot weather.

Dieting

The way to lose weight is to eat sensibly and exercise regularly. Dieting alone doesn't do the job. When food intake is reduced, the metabolism simply adjusts to do a better job of hoarding fat. If you try to lose weight only by sitting on your rear-end, you will keep enough padding there to make sitting comfortable.

Alcohol

Forget the myths about nutrition and alcoholic beverages. They do not contain much nourishment. A 12-ounce beer contains about 150 calories. Only one-third are carbohydrates. The rest primarily are alcohol, which are poor for nutrition and fluid replacement. Alcohol (particularly in excess) can affect the body for some time. Food and drink do not completely metabolize for five days. Alcohol is a diuretic, so it should not be consumed during or immediately before or after strenuous and potentially dehydrating activity.

Drunkenness is highly detrimental to health and performance. But if one does slip, drinking two quarts of water before bed is recommended by nutritional experts. Aspirin alleviate the well-deserved discomfort. Caffeine also may assist. Bland food can settle the stomach. Some people insist B-complex and C vitamins help metabolize lingering alcohol. A swim, long run or brisk walk can calm the nerves. And keep drinking fluids.

The Nutrition "Bulls-Eye"

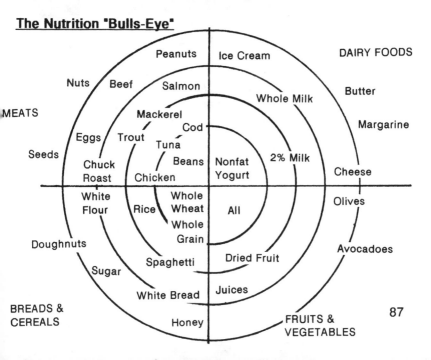

87

MEN WHO WEAR GLASSES <u>DO</u> MAKE PASSES: Poor vision can impede the coordination and reaction times required for successful and safe racing, so detecting and correcting visual defects is a critical responsibility. While Indy-car champion Bobby Rahal has poor natural vision, corrective measures have helped him become one of the most successful drivers of our times.

Chapter 8

VISION FOR RACING

"You can't hit what you can't see" is a cliche applied to many sports. In racing the predicament is seriously reversed: You CAN hit what you can't see.

Vision is liable for survival and success in racing. Good sight consists of more than sharp focus -- about a dozen visual functions make up the total package.

Dr. Michael Henderson, a trailblazing motorsports medicine researcher, wrote more than two decades ago, "There is no evidence that first-class drivers need supernatural eyes. The ability of a driver wearing glasses -- as long as by so doing his visual defect is fully corrected -- need not suffer in the slightest."

Recent research indicates that drivers with better visual skills should be able to perform at a higher level than those with lesser vision. Seeing further down the track allows more time to react; identifying objects more quickly allows the eyes and brain time to scan more of their surroundings.

Racing drivers should have at least 20/40 vision, corrected or uncorrected, and a 170-degree field of vision (the width of the view seen by the eyes when looking straight forward). Most optometrists begin prescribing corrective lenses at 20/40. Although racing organizations may not have specific vision standards, those are the U.S. Department of Transportation's requirements for professional truck drivers.

A state driver's license is not sufficient evidence of suitable vision for racing. Some state motor vehicle licensing departments do not consider a motorist legally blind until vision falls under 20/200 and visual field is as narrow as 15 degrees. The 20/40 level, however, is generally accepted as the minimum required for an unrestricted state license.

Racers should undergo a thorough vision test every year, especially after the age of 40. That's when eye diseases and visual changes are more likely to occur. The professional administering eye examinations should be aware that a thorough examination is needed to evaluate the skills required for motor racing.

Some visual shortcomings can be overcome by corrective lenses or training exercises, some of which are offered at the end of the chapter. To start, let's learn how to make the best use of vision by understanding its components.

STATIC VISUAL ACUITY, the ability to focus on objects immediately in front of the eyes, is the cornerstone of other visual skills. When one can identify at 20 feet an object which the typical person also can see from 20 feet, vision is rated 20/20. A person who can see at 20 feet what the normal population sees at 80 feet is classified 20/80.

Some people can see objects farther away than the normal person, so superior 20/15 and even 20/10 ratings are not unusual. These mean one can clearly see at 20 feet what most people must be within 15 or 10 feet to see.

Better visual acuity permits faster responses to environmental conditions. A person with 20/10 vision should react twice as fast to a visual cue as someone who is 20/20 and four times as quickly as someone who is 20/40.

Static visual acuity covers a range of vision only about six degrees wide -- 1/60th of a full circle -- extending directly in front of the eyes. It takes about a quarter of a second for the eyes to focus on and identify an object, so at only 60 m.p.h. the central vision can take snapshots only at 22-foot intervals.

Racers need to see more than that. The PERIPHERAL VISION supplies supplementary images which the brain merges with pictures from the central visual field. The result is a broader, smoother moving picture of things happening outside of the car.

People with superior peripheral vision are able to see more of their environment -- such as a car pulling alongside -- while remaining focused ahead on the track. Peripheral vision also makes objects going past appear to move more slowly and clearly.

Women have been found to have better peripheral vision than men. On the other hand, the stress of competition can cause the field of vision to narrow and women tend to experience more stress narrowing than men.

When designing a race car or selecting helmets and glasses it is important to keep the peripheral vision field clear of obstructions.

DYNAMIC VISUAL ACUITY is the ability to follow and focus on moving objects. Sports performance requires more than the ability to simply focus on stationary objects while sitting still. The eyes must move quickly and in coordination to track things that are in motion. Racing demands greater skill yet because the driver is moving rapidly, too. Training drills can improve this ability.

NIGHT VISION is almost a separate skill from day vision because it uses different light-sensitive receptor cells on the retinas at the back of the eyes. Much of America's racing occurs at night on marginally-lighted tracks so good night vision is a necessity to many competitors.

Night conditions diminish the quality of vision because less light reaches the eyes. It is more difficult to focus, so it takes longer to identify things and the brain receives less information to analyze. Contrast drops at night too: Objects that appear almost the same color as their surroundings -- such as a dirt track guard rail caked with mud -- might be impossible to see at night.

The intensity of light is expressed by the foot-candle -- the amount of light created by a one-inch-thick candle, measured at a distance of one foot. The brightest sunlight at noon on the clearest day of summer creates about 10,000 foot-candles. Using a photographic light meter to measure the lighting conditions at a typical dirt track, about 8,000 foot-candles were present when the track opened late in the afternoon of a June day. By dusk, the ambient lighting had fallen to about 2,000 foot-candles. At the end of the evening the meter measured 32 foot-candles on the track immediately under the track lights and as little as 8 foot-candles between lights.

The eyes need 30 to 60 minutes to fully adjust after sunset. It can take 24 hours of darkness for the eyes to achieve maximum night vision capability. Some experts advise wearing sunglasses late in the day to advance the process. Looking at bright light even briefly can interrupt night vision adaptation, so avoid looking directly at track lights and headlights. Track officials also should monitor the portable spotlights used by mechanics to make sure they do not endanger drivers on the track.

DEPTH AND SPACE PERCEPTION permit the mind to compute the locations and distances of objects. Stereoscopic vision is a major source of this facility.

VISION FOR RACING

The brain also relies on other cues for depth perception. The light reflected by a close object is brighter than the reflection from a distant object, so the brain can use this cue to estimate distance. Perspective, distinguished as the narrowing of receding roadways or railroad tracks, is another cue. The brain may judge distance from the size of cars, signs and buildings. While the eyes literally see far-off objects as simply small, the brain interprets the smallness as an indication of distance.

Moving the head, as cats and snakes do before striking, provides differing images that the brain compares to compute distance. The additional time needed to execute this function makes it less useful than stereoscopic perception in racing conditions.

STEREOSCOPIC VISION, the ability to see three-dimensional images, is critically important to racers since it permits distances to be measured most accurately and quickly. The brain computes distances by comparing two slightly differing images, so seeing in stereo requires two good eyes. Stereoscopic vision is most effective at distances under 75 feet; at greater distances the eyes provide nearly-identical images.

Some people may suffer visual defects, such as poor eye muscle coordination, which impair their stereoscopic vision even when both eyes are functional. Exercises can correct some of these problems. One-eyed drivers are, to say the least, at a serious disadvantage and pose a potential hazard to themselves and others.

VELOCITY JUDGMENT uses visual images to tell us how quickly objects are approaching or departing. When the brain detects an object growing or shrinking in size, it determines how fast the object is coming or going by the rate of change.

An object appears to double in size when its distance is reduced by half. The brain can be deceived, however, by the actual size of the article in question. A full-size stock car traveling 100 m.p.h. may seem to approach more quickly than a midget or Formula Vee coming at the same speed. Research suggests that highway motorists may not attempt a pass when a large truck approaches in the oncoming lane but will pass when a motorcycle or small car is coming at the same speed from the same distance.

ACCOMMODATION is the ability of the eyes to shift focus from one object to another. The average person takes half a second to switch focus from an object a couple of thousand feet away to an object within inches, and vice versa.

At 200 miles per hour, then, normal eyes can be out of order for up to 150 feet -- half the length of a football field -- while they move from the tachometer to the end of a long straightaway. At 100 m.p.h., a speed well within the reach of the most basic racing machines, 73 feet can be covered during this extreme visual accommodation. For this reason, dashboard instruments should be placed as far from the driver's eyes as possible and bear large, easy-to-scan markings.

COLOR VISION is abnormal, to some degree, in 8 percent of men and 0.5 percent of women. Some forms of color blindness make it difficult to tell the difference between traffic signal lights and racing flags. A driver with color vision deficiency may need twice as much time as a normal person to process and respond to color signals. It may be necessary to use other cues, such as position or shape, to identify a signal. The wrong decision still may be made.

Considering that one in a dozen male racers has a color vision defect and many races occur under poor lighting conditions at night, we wonder how many racing accidents are caused or worsened by slow driver responses to yellow flags and lights.

We suggest tracks would be safer if yellow warning lights were equipped to flash so they could be distinguished from steady green lights. Motion is one of the strongest visual stimuli, so flashing should make caution signals more easily detectable by drivers with normal vision, too.

Because color blindness may make yellow and green flags indistinguishable, might it be helpful to place a warning symbol on yellow flags, particularly for night racing?

REACTION TIME is highly dependent upon vision. A normal person can take half a second to detect a signal light change and begin to apply a car's brakes. Our standard 100-m.p.h. race car covers 73 feet (nearly a basketball court) before a person of normal color vision and acuity can evaluate a warning signal and initiate braking. Poor vision sometimes might mean the difference between a serious accident and no accident.

Reaction times are delayed when light transmission to the eyes is limited or confused by glare; low levels of light; light absorption by windshields, face shields and goggles; illness; or medications. Visual reaction can be practiced and improved.

EYE-HAND-FOOT coordination, another motorsports necessity, also is impossible without good vision. The brain and muscles depend upon eyesight for leadership. This skill also can be largely improved through training exercises.

THE SENSE OF BALANCE and perceptions of movements affecting the body are among the environmental cues upon which drivers depend. While the inner ear is mainly responsible for balance, vision contributes some information. About 20 percent of the nerve fibers departing the eyes are connected to parts of the brain responsible for balance.

LIMITATIONS IN VISION: Racers must be aware of a number of natural and environmental phenomena that can or do limit vision:

BLINKING is a reflexive action that washes tears across the surface of the eyes to keep them clear. Each blink lasts about .3 second and people typically blink 20 times per minute -- so our eyes are closed 10 percent of the time. That means it is important to make the best use possible of the vision that is at our disposal.

WINDSHIELDS, GOGGLES, FACE SHIELDS and TEAR-OFFS can absorb or reflect light and limit the eyes' efficiency. Light losses can be worse when windshields are slanted backward at sharp angles or covered with bugs, oil and sandblasting. When light transmissions are weaker, the eyes and mind take longer to analyze and respond to the environment.

Clear glass absorbs about five percent of light striking it at a 90-degree angle. Light hitting acrylic resin windscreens or face shields at this angle suffers a six- to seven-percent loss. Dirty surfaces rob another two or three percent of light's strength.

When windshields are angled, additional light is reflected rather than transmitted. At 30 degrees, light transmission is reduced 10 percent by a glass windshield, 20 percent by a clean acrylic windshield and 30 percent by a dirty acrylic windshield. A severely streaked windshield raked at an acute angle may reflect half the light striking it. Face shield tear-offs absorb additional light, too.

ACCOMMODATION TO LIGHT AND DARK: The eyes can require several seconds, sometimes minutes or hours, to fully adjust to changes in light levels. The pupil changes in size to control the amount of light that enters the eye. When light shines on an eye the pupil starts to contract to reduce the brightness to a tolerable level, but only after 0.25 second. The pupil may not reach optimum size for five seconds. A racer driving on a dim track at night, in our standard 100-m.p.h. machine, could cover more than 1/8-mile while her or his eyes adjust to a bright light at the edge of the track.

GLARE, a related problem, is defined as scattered or unwanted light entering the eyes and interfering with light reflected from objects we do want to see. Bright flashes of light or dirty, scratched windshields, goggles and face shields may multiply glare difficulties.

When driving at night one should attempt to keep bright lights in the peripheral visual field if it is necessary to pass them or monitor their positions. Taping the upper portion of the helmet face shield or windshield can overcome some of this effect, except late in the day when the sun is low in the sky.

SNOW BLINDNESS is a longer-lasting impairment of vision caused by bright ultraviolet light. This condition often occurs in the presence of snow, desert sand or open water, at high altitudes or while welding. The corneal epithelium, or outer skin of the eye, can be painfully burned, causing photophobia -- intolerance of light. Most people involved in racing spend considerable time outdoors during daylight, so consider good sunglasses and hats a medical necessity.

DRUGS OR MEDICATIONS, including some available without prescriptions, can affect vision by enlarging the pupils, slowing accommodation and drying the eyes. Culprits include cold and asthma remedies and some laxatives and suppositories. It may take weeks for some drugs to fully pass from the body. Always consult your doctor before taking any medications during the racing season.

DISEASE AND ILLNESS can diminish vision, too. Thorough vision testing can reveal previously-undetected medical problems. Likewise, any disease or illness warrants a discussion with your physician to determine the wisdom of racing participation.

VISION FOR RACING

EYEGLASSES, of course, are essential to people with slight visual defects. However, remember that glasses with thick frames or side shields can block portions of the visual field. Seek glasses with large lenses and slim frames. Aviator-style glasses are popular with pilots for that reason. Because of the possibility of breakage in an accident, investigate the tough, plastic glasses offered for athletic wear.

CONTACT LENSES are perfectly acceptable for racing. While contact lenses were not considered suitable for racing use many years ago, today lenses are used by many top drivers.

TRAINING DRILLS: There are countless sports, games and exercises that can boost visual skills.

-- Play video games, wiffleball, paddleball, tennis and other sports requiring eye-hand-foot coordination.

-- Draw letters on a ball; bounce it off a wall and floor, watch for the letters to appear and call as many of them as you can before catching the ball. Bounce the ball faster as you get better.

-- Suspend a ball from a ceiling. Swing it, lie underneath and try to track while looking through a soda straw with one eye.

-- When walking, sitting or riding in a car, keep the eyes focused straight ahead and try to absorb as much detail as possible through the peripheral vision.

-- Visualize a tic-tac-toe grid in front of you. Move the eyes in all nine possible line directions.

-- Stand over a phonograph and try to read the labels on rotating records.

-- While driving or riding on the highway try to read approaching signs and license plates at the greatest distances possible.

Dr. William Feldner of the Hunter Trauma Team tests the sight of Trans Am racer Tommy Kendall. A vision test should be part of every driver's annual physical exam.

A successful career in racing doesn't need to end at 30, 40 or even 50! Drivers like Richard Petty (above) and Harry Gant, who continued driving in the high-G, high-mileage realm of the NASCAR Winston Cup Series after age 50, are proof that your body will take care of you if you take care of it.

Chapter 9

AGING AND RACING

"I am proud as hell that I have done what I have done, but it isn't going to win me another race or another championship. I am going to have to work hard . . . I am a believer that age is not a factor unless you let it become a factor. Your proof is Harry Gant and Richard Petty. It is easy to get caught up in the fame and fortune and drink wine and eat the wrong foods. If you take care of yourself, you are going further down the road than the guy who abuses his body."
-- Dale Earnhardt, 39,
Speedweeks, 1992

What Is Age?

Aging is not as bad as most people think. While there is no evidence aging can be prevented, physical fitness and enthusiasm can compensate overwhelmingly for its ravages. This knowledge is extremely important in motorsports because so many competitors remain in -- or even enter -- the sport in what used to be popularly considered "middle age."

Research has shown that athletic life does not end at 40 or 50 or even 60. Top "masters" athletes perform nearly as well in their 40s as they did in their 30s. Well-conditioned athletes decline only gradually through the 50s and 60s.

Up to 50 percent of the physical decline blamed on aging can be postponed by regular exercise. It is now apparent that many parts of our bodies go to pot from disuse, not birthdays. Some diseases historically associated with aging can be avoided completely.

Racers must be aware, on the other hand, that age <u>does</u> cause inevitable deterioration in many bodily functions. Some abilities begin to fall during our 20s. That is further reason to get off our rear ends to keep as much ability as we can and make the most of it!

AGING AND RACING

Why Do We Age?

Scientists are still trying to understand the causes and reasons for aging. There are several theories; possibly all play a role.

The "wear and tear," "error" or "stochastic" theories hold that we simply get used up and worn out after years of use. As our bodies wear down, the cells that repair the damage aren't exactly factory-quality replacement parts so functional ability gradually is lost.

The "program" or "clock" assumption states that our genes are programmed to keep the body going a specified period of time. Then that's it. There is strong scientific evidence that our cells, most of which are continually replaced during life, are designed to reproduce only a certain number of times. Some cells, such as in the nervous system, may not reproduce at all, while others seem to reproduce 50 times. Cells also show signs of age in later generations. Research has pointed to the first chromosome of our DNA as the home of a potential aging gene.

The "free radical" theory holds that people in most societies speed their demise by eating too much food. That accelerates the metabolism and boosts exposure to free radicals -- unstable parts of molecules that are by-products of physical processes. These unstable radicals are highly reactive, combining with and damaging cells in the body. This theory is supported by knowledge that people and laboratory animals who consume very small amounts of food live longer.

How Old Can Racers Be?

Current statistics suggest that people who stay fit should be able to race well into their 50s. A few lucky individuals today are driving competitively after the age of 60. It might be possible for today's 20-year-olds to push those thresholds even further by staying healthy, firm and trim for the next four or five decades.

While racing is very much an endurance sport, the benefits of experience and wealth can give drivers over 30 or 40 an equal shot at success, if not an advantage.

In the NASCAR Winston Cup series, drivers under 30 represented 16 percent of the drivers who finished in the top 20 in points from 1987-1991. Drivers in the 30-34 age group made up a large portion of the top 20; a full quarter of the leading NASCAR drivers were over 40 -- and 14 percent were over 45.

Top 20 NASCAR Winston Cup Drivers: 1987-1991

Under 30	16%
30-34	39%
35-39	20%
40-44	11%
45 and over	14%

Top 20 IndyCar (CART) Drivers: 1991

Under 30	5
30-34	5
35-39	4
40-44	3
45-49	1
50+	2
Range: 26-55 years	

The points standings for other professional U.S. racing series also reflect the domination of drivers over 30.

Top 20 SCCA Trans Am Drivers: 1991

20-29	5
30-39	6
40-49	7
50 and over	1
Not available	1
Range: 22-50 years	

Top 20 USAC Silver Crown Drivers: 1990

Under 20	1
20-29	4
30-39	6
40-49	7
50 and over	2
Range: 19-53 years	

Top 20 USAC Sprint Car Drivers: 1990

Under 20	2
20-29	4
30-39	6
40-49	8
Range: 19-46 years	

Top 20 USAC Midget Drivers: 1990

Under 20	1
20-29	6
30-39	8
40-49	4
50 and over	1
Range: 19-57 years	

Sports Car Club of America membership peaks between 30 and 40 years, according to a 1990 survey. Drivers make up 49 percent of members:

SCCA Membership

Under 18	1%
18-24	7%
25-29	11%
30-34	19%
35-39	21%
40-44	18%
45-49	13%
50-54	6%
55-59	4%
60-69	2%
70-79	< 1%

A computer analysis of thousands of racing driver injuries reported to North American Racing Insurance (NARI), mostly on short oval tracks, shows that the majority of drivers at that level of the sport probably are 20 through 40 years old. Significant numbers of drivers are over 40. Racers over 50 also are common and a few even have passed their 65th birthdays. While these ages are for drivers involved in accidents rather than the total racing population, they do reflect the broad range of ages seen on the track.

Ages of Drivers Involved in Accidents
Reported to North American Racing Insurance, 1988-1991

Under 20	7.6%	45-49	3.5%
20-24	19.0%	50-54	2.1%
25-29	25.9%	55-59	0.8%
30-34	20.2%	60-64	0.2%
35-39	14.4%	65 and over	0.2%
40-44	6.2%		

How many drivers in the U.S. are your age? Let's apply the percentages listed above (imprecise though they may be) to an estimate of the U.S. racing population. In 1990 the respected trade publication Performance Racing Industry surveyed hundreds of racing organizations and tracks in an attempt to determine the number of people who drive a racing machine at least one time each year. The total the magazine reached, believed accurate within 50,000, was 350,000 drivers.

Applying the NARI data to the magazine's estimate, we projected the numbers of drivers who may occupy each age range. We found that the U.S. may have 11,550 racers who are over 50 years old and 1,400 who are over 60:

Estimated Age Distribution: U.S. Racing Drivers

Under 20	26,600
20-24	66,500
25-29	90,650
30-34	70,700
35-39	50,400
40-44	21,700
45-49	12,250
50-54	7,350
55-59	2,800
60-64	700
65 and over	700

How Does Age Affect Performance?

To determine how aging may affect performance over careers and seasons, a computer was used to analyze the driver age distribution and finishing results of NASCAR Winston Cup races from 1987-1991. This series was chosen because data were readily available from the annual NASCAR Yearbook and Press Guide; races are held from February through November in a variety of weather conditions; most races are held on oval tracks with which drivers can become familiar; and the series is highly competitive. Many cars are capable of winning races, making driver ability and fitness a potentially significant factor in the outcome of races -- 23 drivers won during the span of 144 races.

When victories, top five finishes and top ten finishes were examined, drivers who attained the ages of 35 to 39 during the years studied emerged as the group most successful in claiming more than its share of top finishes. While making up 20 percent of the top 20 points finishers over the five seasons, they earned 29.9 percent of all victories; 24.2 percent of top fives; and 21.4 percent of top tens. These drivers finished first in 37.5 percent of the short track races and 30.4 percent of the superspeedway (tracks one mile or longer) races. They were shut out on the road courses mainly through the domination of Ricky Rudd and Rusty Wallace, both under 35 during the period studied.

The 30-34 age group appeared to be the next most successful. These drivers represented 39 percent of the top 20 in points and won more than their share, too, taking 43.7 percent of victories; 40.3 percent of top fives; and 39.7 percent of top tens. This group excelled, thanks to Rudd and Wallace, on the road courses, winning 100 percent of all races, and on the speedways, winning 44.6 percent of the time.

How about the older drivers? The drivers 40 to 44 years old held their own through the five seasons analyzed. Comprising 11 percent of the leading drivers, they won 11.8 percent of the races and earned 10.3 percent of top fives and 11.2 percent of top tens. They grabbed twice their share of short track victories -- 22.5 percent -- and did pretty well on the superspeedways, too, winning 8.7 percent of those races.

Statistics for drivers 45 and older indicated a drop in performance. Representing 14 percent of the leading drivers, they won 7.6 percent of races and collected 13 percent of top fives and 14.5 percent of top tens.

Still, the older drivers performed better than those under the age of 30, whose superior physical endurance probably was offset by lesser experience and less capable equipment. The under-30 crowd occupied 16 percent of the top-20 points positions during the five-year period but took only 6.2 percent of the victories; 8.7 percent of the top fives and 11.8 percent of the top tens.

Finally, it was hypothesized that age-related declines in driver endurance could affect performance over the course of a season. Might older drivers be less successful during stretches of the season contested in hot weather? Might younger drivers do better in hot weather when their superior endurance becomes a more significant factor? The computer suggested that such phenomena do occur.

The NASCAR drivers 45 and older encountered a series of peaks and valleys through the seasons. They won more than their share of races in February and September and earned about their share in May and November. From March through April and June through August, however, their success rate dips below their average.

Drivers 40 to 44 years old do best in races held from February through May and in September-October. This group of drivers won 14.3 percent to 19 percent of the races held in those months but only 0.0 percent to 6.7 percent of races contested in the hot summer months of June, July and August. While they won none of the November races during the five years, they did earn 16 percent of the top fives and top tens.

The 35- to 39-year-olds exhibited little seasonal variation in performance. They won less than their share of races only in February, May and October -- relatively cool months rather than months in which endurance could be a significant factor. In fact, this age group does quite well through the heat, winning 26.7 percent to 40 percent of June-September races. Could it be that cool weather helps the guys over 40 beat their younger competitors?

Hot weather proved to be a definite advantage for the 30- to 34-year-old racers, who performed well throughout the year and had most of their best performances in summer. They won 61.1 percent of June races; 40 percent of July races; and 60 percent of August races. They also hit peaks in February, October and November. In fact, they slipped only in the cool months of April and May and the transitional month of September. Could that, too, have resulted from the older drivers re-asserting themselves through advanced experience?

The drivers younger than 30 also are consistent through the year, or at least in races held after February. Their statistics show a meaningful peak only in May, when a grueling 600-mile race is held at Charlotte Motor Speedway and a similarly brutal 500-miler is held at Dover.

While it appears there might be an age/endurance factor in racing, we do not see it as a reason older drivers should accept reduced likelihood of success when the going gets tougher. Instead we see it as an indication that more drivers need to be working harder to stay in shape.

Effects of Age -- And Ways to Give Them the Caution Flag

The body inevitably becomes slower and weaker with age. But

fitness waves a yellow flag that can make age travel the track of life at a slower pace.

VO2 MAX

The body's maximum volume of oxygen utilization, or VO2 max, determines our athletic performance and endurance capacities. This function declines about one percent annually, starting in the mid-20s, in people who are not active. At age 20 the body can boost its oxygen flow during exercise to about 12 times the resting rate. By age 70 the reserve is only three to four times the resting level.

Exercise can slow or reverse the rate of decline. A study of 30- to 50-year-old men found that physical activity nearly erased age-caused V02 decline over 10- and 18-year periods. Elite senior athletes are known to lose only one to two percent of their work capacity per DECADE. A study found that exercise could bring an eight-percent gain in VO2 max in active men 52 to 88 years old. Another project brought a 14-percent boost to men 67 to 76 years old.

CARDIOVASCULAR FITNESS

While the heart grows larger in capacity with age, its maximum beating rate begins to decline at age 25. The heart also needs more time to return to resting rate after exertion. Cardiovascular conditioning is highly responsive to exercise, which also boosts the efficiency of the body and enables it to make more efficient use of the available supply of oxygen.

Aging affects blood vessels, too. As deposits accumulate on vessel walls and obstruct blood flow, greater cardiac effort is required to move blood through the body. Aging also brings a decrease in the blood vessel network to body tissues and organs, making it more difficult to supply them with oxygen.

BLOOD PRESSURE

An 18-year comparative study of active and inactive groups of men from their 40s through 60s found that exercise offsets the blood pressure boost that can accompany age. During the study a group of inactive men experienced an increase in blood pressure from 135/85 to a hypertensive level of 150/90. In the meantime, men who exercised regularly experienced no increase in blood pressure over the 18-year period. In fact, their blood pressure dipped from an already healthy 120/79 to a slightly better 120/78.

LUNG FUNCTION

The lungs become somewhat stiffer and surrounding muscles weaken. Small blood vessels within the lungs become more dense and resistant to blood flow. The body tries to compensate by taking more frequent breaths but older athletes nonetheless may feel breathless during competition because their bodies are not absorbing enough oxygen.

The lungs begin losing capacity in the mid-30s. By age 70 the lungs must work 20 percent harder to overcome inflexibility. Lung function will fall more quickly in people who smoke or have encountered long-term exposure to air pollution.

Exercise offsets lung aging by keeping chest muscles strong and encouraging efficient use of oxygen.

MUSCLE STRENGTH

The typical person achieves peak muscle strength in the 20s and retains it into the late 30s. Muscle strength, mass and blood flow start to decline then, but the rate is fairly slow until about 50. Even at 60 years of age most people have 80 percent of their strength. People who haven't been active, however, can lose 40 percent of their strength by 60.

People who keep working their muscles can experience no significant decrease in strength as late as the 60th birthday. It is never too late to start or continue training -- exercise has been proven to boost strength in people over the age of 90.

FLEXIBILITY

The connective tissues, such as cartilage, ligaments and tendons, stiffen with age as their water content decreases and their basic material, collagen, is transformed into a tougher and thicker molecular form. Unless exercise stimulation is provided, the joints will lose flexibility and become more prone to injuries. This phenomena applies to racing in particular -- collisions and spins can create centrifugal forces capable of stretching the joints beyond their limits.

Exercise preserves, even extends, range of movement and appears to speed the turnover of collagen cells so connecting tissues remain pliable.

BONE MASS

The loss of bone mass, or osteoporosis, strikes men in the 40s or 50s. They can lose 10 to 15 percent of their bone content by age 70. Women are affected by osteoporosis after approximately 35 years of age and can lose one percent of bone mass per year.

Daily exercise can largely counteract osteoporosis. Activity causes bones to gain strength, thickness and mineral concentration.

NERVOUS SYSTEM

Reaction times, stimuli recognition and muscle movements depend upon billions of cells, called neurons, that make up the nervous system. During the 40s the quantity of neurons present in the nervous system, including the brain and spinal cord, begins to drop. The quality of chemical interactions between neurons fades, too, so reaction speeds slow.

Nerve conduction velocity slows 10 to 15 percent over the course of life. About three percent of nerve velocity is lost during each decade after age 30. As conduction velocity slows, information takes longer to reach the brain, which then needs more time to analyze situations and make decisions. Commands take longer to reach the muscles.

Studies have found that reaction times are fastest in people who are in their 20s. Reaction times decline gradually after 30.

A test (using apparatus consisting of electrical buttons pushed in response to light cues) indicated that reaction times as quick as 120 milliseconds are about as good as anyone can expect. The average reaction time for people 10- to 19-years-old was about 260 milliseconds; from 20-29 years the average fell to about 240 milliseconds and rose gradually to about 265 milliseconds by the age of 50 and nearly 280 milliseconds by 60.

A study using a different test device (tones emitted through headphones) established a 133-millisecond mean reaction time for men aged 19 to 44 years and 136 milliseconds for men 45 to 64. Women were measured at a 137-millisecond mean for the 19-to-44 age group and 145 milliseconds for the 45-to-64 group.

Again, physical fitness and exercise keep this bodily function in tune longer. Aerobically-fit 60-year-olds can be as mentally alert as 20-year-old couch potatoes. People who begin to exercise, even over the age of 65, can improve their mental performance.

SWEATING AND HEAT TOLERANCE

The body's water content, from blood volume down to the cellular level, decreases with age. Kidney function is reduced also. This limits the body's ability to control fluid volumes and increases the risks of dehydration or over-hydration. People older than 50 face a markedly increased incidence of heat-related illness and death. Lower sweating rates have been identified as a cause. Training, however, can spur the body to begin sweating sooner and in greater volume. Exercise and close attention to hydration and heat acclimatization are even more important for motorsports participants and fans as they get older.

VISION

As we age the lenses in our eyes become denser and transmit less light to the visual receptor cells. Metabolic changes, the slowing nervous system, reduced pupil diameter and diminishing blood flow make the eyes less efficient, too.

Visual acuity increases from about six to 20 years of age -- that's when the lenses starting getting denser. Vision remains constant or declines only slightly until about age 45. Marked decline commences at about 45; the rate of deterioration accelerates again at around 60 and 70 years of age.

There are individual variations in rate of visual deterioration. Some 80-year-olds who are in good health and free of eye disease see as sharply as the typical 20-year-old.

As a result of reduced visual abilities, eye-hand coordination and visual reaction speed may drop 8 to 10 percent for every five years of age between 20 and 40.

The eye lenses become slightly yellow with age, so color vision is affected, too. White shifts to yellow; blue objects appear darker. It may become difficult to tell some colors apart, particularly in dim light.

Glare sensitivity becomes higher at around age 40 because the lenses increasingly scatter, dim and alter the color of passing light. Dark adaptation slows due to reduced light transmission resulting from lens density and reduced pupil diameter.

Field of vision begins to decline at about 35 years of age, too. Lens yellowing and density again are factors.

Accommodation, the eyes' ability to handle shifting focus distances, declines after 40 to 45 years of age. The lenses steadily become less flexible and less responsive to the muscle contractions which alter their shape to focus light on the back of the eyes.

Stereopsis, a major source of depth perception, improves from childhood through the 20s and holds relatively steady through the 30s and 40s before entering marked decline.

GENERAL HEALTH

People who exercise vigorously obviously enjoy better general health than lazy men and women of similar ages. When the body is exercised good things happen throughout it. Even the cells, because of increased blood flow, get more nutrition and grow in size and efficiency.

One of the metabolic effects of exercise is an increase in the body's level of high-density lipoprotein cholesterol (HDL), the so-called "good" cholesterol that reduces the risks for hardening of the arteries. One study found that fitness can bring a 64-percent decrease in the risk of heart attacks and may add one to two years to life. Another research project attributed 33 percent of the heart attack risk facing non-active people to their lack of exercise -- not their age.

Regular exercise also boosts one's mental outlook. Fit people feel better about themselves. That may avert the psychological depression that can plague the elderly.

THE STEERING WHEEL IS IN YOUR HANDS

It is unfortunate that many people believe life, at least one that is active and productive, ends at 30 or 40. People who remain physically fit should not even begin to think about slowing down until at least 50. Up to then, evidence suggests, lifestyle more than aging determines athletic ability.

There is ample proof that even a moderate degree of fitness can vastly enhance the quality of life and ward off cardiovascular diseases which claim many lives prematurely. Activity also encourages good nutrition and the avoidance of bad habits like smoking and drinking. The National Institute on Aging has reported that 80 percent of the health problems of the elderly might be preventable rather than inevitable.

A couple of studies which examined the effects of exercise on thousands of working-age people found dramatic changes: Sick leave from jobs plummeted 82 to 87 percent after one to two months of exercise.

People of similar chronological ages can have vastly different functional and biological ages. Much of the difference between individuals can result from mental attitudes.

Dr. Ken Dychtwald, in his intriguing book <u>Age Wave</u>, examined the harmful effects of what he termed "gerontophobia," or fear of aging, in our society. He argues that our minds program our bodies for decline by harboring an "elder within" who provides a role model for our advancing years.

"If we envision these later years as a time of boredom, social isolation, and ill health, we may consciously or unconsciously aim ourselves in these directions," Dychtwald wrote. "But it may well be that one of the most powerful limits is inside us, in the visions we hold of tomorrow and next year, of ourselves as we grow older. If our 'elders within' are healthy, involved, active and full of life and learning, then the gift of extended life might hold the promise of a dramatic and unprecedented expansion of our opportunities for growth, adventure, wisdom, experience, and love."

EXPERIENCE

Experience can go a long way in offsetting the physical deficits of aging, especially in motorsports because skill, composure and technical knowledge are big parts of the performance equation. Even in highly aerobic sports such as swimming some people actually get faster with age.

Consider the dramatic multi-race NASCAR winning streak enjoyed by a 51-year-old Harry Gant in the fall of 1991 and Emerson Fittipaldi's 1989 Indianapolis 500 victory at the age of 42. There are examples in other sports, too. Gordie Howe played in his 22nd National Hockey League All-Star Game at 52. Carlos Lopez won an Olympic marathon gold medal at 42.

A POSITIVE ATTITUDE

How long can people remain active in racing? As long as their physical abilities hold out, they love the sport and they are willing to work for it. The calendar shouldn't tell us when to stop racing -- only mental sharpness, vision, endurance, coordination and reaction times should do that.

Richard Petty, Harry Gant, A.J. Foyt, Paul Newman, Hershel McGriff, Hooker Hood, Jim McElreath and Ralph Liguori raced, literally and figuratively, into their 50s and 60s. Today's retirees are playing tennis and running marathons. Enthusiasm, positive thinking and hard work can keep us young years after less courageous folks have surrendered to their birth certificates.

AGING AND RACING

Bill Seebold is still one of the nation's top powerboat racers at the age of 51. He credits a daily fitness regimen with keeping him competitive in a sport in which 50 laps of neck-snapping 4.5-G turns on choppy water at over 100 m.p.h. can physically drain drivers of any age.

The trim Seebold exercises daily, especially for neck, arm and back strength, and plays racquetball. "When I was 30 years old I didn't have to exercise. Now I'm 51 and racing 30-year-olds," he said. "The older I get, the more I have to pay attention to keeping my body tuned up."

Age-Related Changes in Physical Status

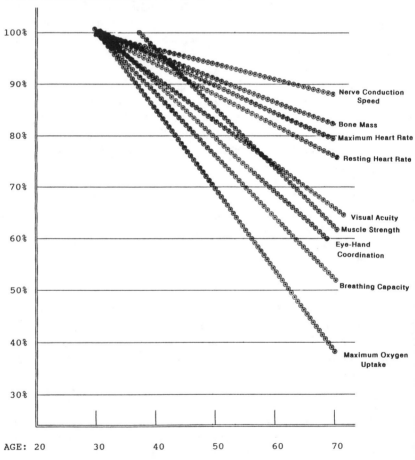

<u>Seasonal and Age Variations in Driver Performance</u>

Performance on short tracks, speedways, road courses and all races combined; performance by month.

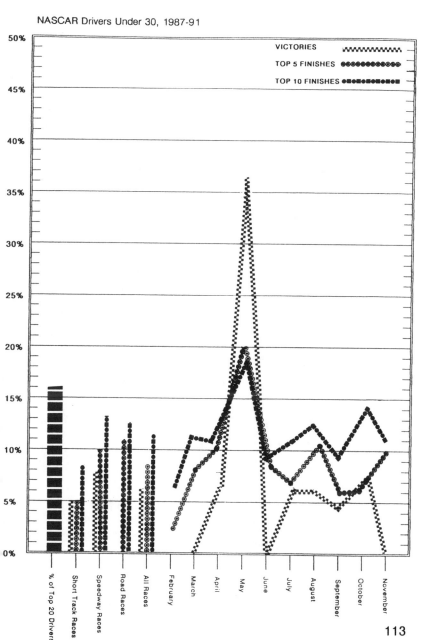

NASCAR Drivers Under 30, 1987-91

VICTORIES
TOP 5 FINISHES
TOP 10 FINISHES

Seasonal and Age Variations in Driver Performance
Performance on short tracks, speedways, road courses and all races combined; performance by month.

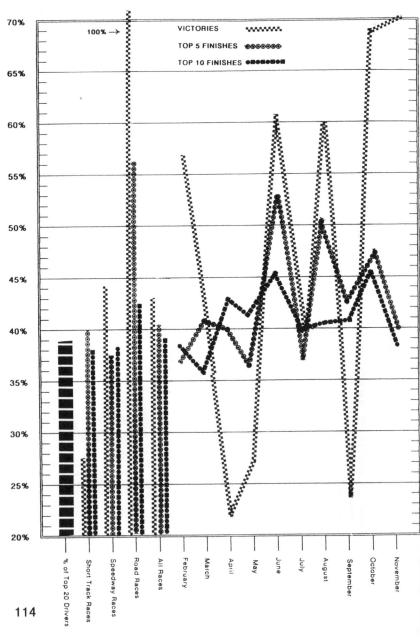

NASCAR Drivers 30-34, 1987-91

Seasonal and Age Variations in Driver Performance
Performance on short tracks, speedways, road courses and all races combined; performance by month.

NASCAR Drivers 35-39, 1987-91

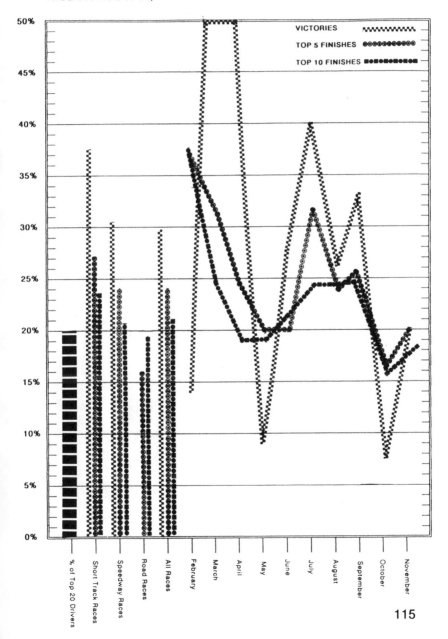

Seasonal and Age Variations in Driver Performance

Performance on short tracks, speedways, road courses and all races combined; performance by month.

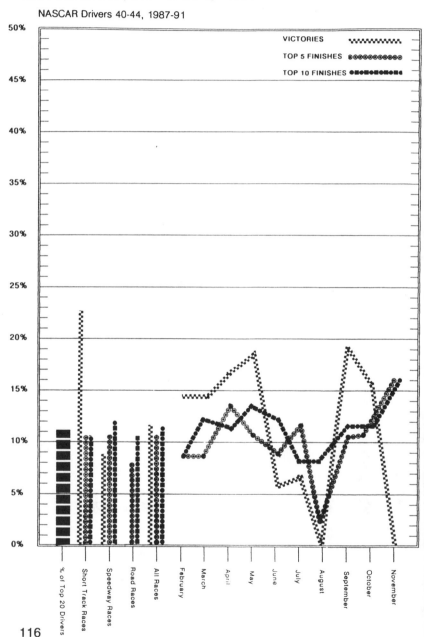

NASCAR Drivers 40-44, 1987-91

Seasonal and Age Variations in Driver Performance

Performance on short tracks, speedways, road courses and all races combined; performance by month.

NASCAR Drivers 45+, 1987-91

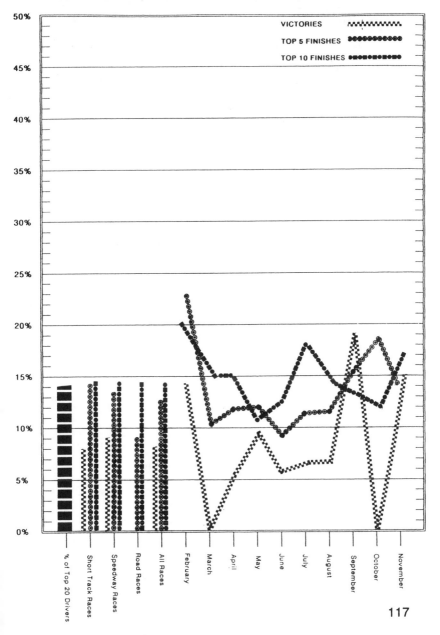

Mental skills, leadership and teamwork are the keys to making a racing organization more -- or less -- than the sum of its individual human parts.

Chapter 10

THE PSYCHOLOGY OF WINNERS

"It doesn't take much to psych me up for a race. When you get in and hit the switch, I'm turned on and ready to go, just like the car is. If I had to psych myself up to race, I don't think I would be as good as I am."
                                        -- Dale Earnhardt

Competitive success depends upon mental superiority and conditioning as well as upon physical ability. Racing certainly demands the highest levels of intelligence, alertness and composure.

The mind has more control over the body than a driver has over a car. Attitudes and emotions influence even automatic body functions such as heart rate, blood pressure, lung expansion, muscle tension and nerve conduction. The mind is driver, voltage regulator, rev limiter, thermostat and fuel pump. Racers, like all athletes, must overcome themselves before they can overcome the competition.

"Race car driving . . . demands a high standard of physiological performance and information processing, but in the whole man the personality will still play a crucial part in the determination of the driver's ability," wrote motorsports medicine pioneer Dr. Michael Henderson in his 1968 book, Motor Racing in Safety: The Human Factors.

A surprising amount of research has been dedicated to motorsports psychology and the mental attributes of successful racers. Some abilities are hereditary; others can be learned.

Attributes of Successful Racers
"Professional race drivers tend to score higher with regard to several critical personality variables. This likely reflects the rather incredible demands made upon such men to perform precisely under conditions of great stress and risk. They are a very select

group," wrote Keith Johnsgard, a psychological researcher who studied hundreds of racers in the 1960s and 1970s.

Psychological testing has identified successful racers as leaders who are independent, aggressive, competitive and compelled to dominate. They are highly intelligent and quick-thinkers. They are self-controlled; self-reliant; persevering and tough-minded; experimenters; realistic; decisive; reserved; and detached. They are not shy about expressing opinions. Good racers have been found to be creative, abstract thinkers, meaning they are quite capable of learning new things.

Obviously no one of low intelligence or slow thought belongs in a race car. Racing demands a mind that processes information rapidly and selectively. Even at street speeds, the eyes, ears and other senses send the brain far more input than it can fully absorb.

Good racers must excel at maintaining an unwavering focus under demanding conditions. Superior mental abilities allow drivers to process more incoming data and prolong their physiologic endurance. Drivers with higher intelligence, innate ability and composure will face races with less mental stress, thereby stretching their energy reserves longer into a race. As endurance does dissipate, intelligence and self-control provide a measure of compensation.

Race drivers enjoy attention, ranking high in exhibitionistic and heterosexual tendencies. On the other hand, exceptional racers have low needs for interpersonal relationships, joining groups or having many close friends. While they may have many friends, the relationships may not be deep. They don't mind receiving emotional support but are not particularly prone to nurture in return.

Highly-ranked drivers also have low tendencies to feel guilt or blame. They can tolerate a poor performance and get on to the next race without self-punishment.

While many people view race drivers as crazies with death wishes, psychologists have found them quite the opposite. Racers willingly take risks, of course, but are nonetheless well-controlled, emotionally stable and bear a high sense of responsibility for their actions. Nor are they impulsive: They can refrain from acting when action would be inappropriate.

Speaking of taking risks, drivers who make a lot of mistakes early in their careers may excel later because they are more aggressive and try harder.

What separates winners from runners-up? Better drivers have

been found less independent and more aggressive than merely good drivers. Some believe better drivers also may be a bit more receptive to criticism and suggestions, but this finding is disputed.

Top amateur racers differ in some respects from top professionals. The amateur must spend considerable time working on his car and earning money for racing. Successful amateurs, therefore, are likely to be more orderly and less domineering and aggressive than their pro counterparts.

An overwhelming component of success in any endeavor is a winning attitude. Dr. Denis Waitley, an outstanding motivational speaker and author, wrote in his best-selling book The Psychology of Winning:

"Winners focus on past successes and forget past failures . . . high self-esteem seems to be the common denominator . . . In the face of discouragement, mistakes and setbacks, their inner drive keeps them moving upward toward self-fulfillment. Winners see risk as opportunity. They do not fear the penalties of failure."

The Mental Skills of Success: Concentration

A leading component of performance is concentration. "Stirling Moss, one of the Grand Prix circuit's all-time great drivers, insisted that concentration was the hardest thing for a driver to develop. It appears that concentration may not be teachable but is largely self-developed," wrote Robert N. Green, M.D., in the textbook Sports Injuries: Mechanisms, Prevention and Treatment.

Concentration must be matched to the demands of competition. It needs to be focused like a flashlight -- broadened when many things must be absorbed and narrowed when selectivity is required. The skill can be learned and practiced.

Drivers must absorb critical data on the presence of other cars and guard rails; feedback from the pavement; and input from the eyes, steering wheel and seat bottom. Meanwhile they must ignore a blizzard of other stimuli -- roaring engine noise, movement in the crowd, wind-blown banners, sweat dripping down their foreheads. They cannot be so overwhelmed by surroundings that they forget they are controlling a car; nor can they be so intent upon their own driving that they overlook a car spinning ahead of them or a waving yellow flag.

Crew members also must keep their mental flashlights adjusted. When changing tires on a pit stop they must blot out the rest of the world; when devising late-race strategy they must soak up data on weather conditions, the competition and the readiness of their tools and supplies.

Performing Under Pressure

As explained in earlier chapters, racing creates enormous physical and mental stresses. The psychological and physiological reactions to stress are collectively termed "arousal." It is both a result of and cause of physical reactions affecting performance.

Arousal affects athletes in a continuum shaped like an inverted "U" because, initially, the phenomenon kicks the body into a higher gear that assists it in meeting challenges. After arousal exceeds a certain level -- the top of the inverted "U" -- the influence becomes negative. Performance deteriorates as the body and mind become overwhelmed; focus, concentration, coordination, timing and muscle control diminish. Another key to motorsports success is controlling arousal.

Arousal is an individualized factor. An experience one person approaches as a thrill may be seen by another as impending doom.

The degree of desirable arousal depends upon the particular demands of an activity. Sports low in complexity (weightlifting and sprint running) benefit from a high state of arousal and its accompanying adrenal surge. Difficult tasks that require fine control -- shooting free throws, playing quarterback or driving a racing machine -- need a much, much lower arousal state. The odds of success are with those who handle stress as a normal fact of life and avoid reactions that magnify it.

Physical Reactions to Arousal

Stress can generate a "fight or flight" response that prepares the body and mind for danger. This super-charged condition is desirable under some circumstances, but not driving race cars or executing pit stops.

The aroused body releases hormones (adrenaline and noradrenaline) that boost heart and breathing rates, blood pressure, blood flow, sweating, brain activity, blood sugar release and oxygen consumption. The pupils dilate and the muscles tense. Excessive arousal unnecessarily speeds the consumption of energy, wasting strength that could later determine the outcome of a race.

Optimal arousal level varies with experience and skill. To drive at the peak of one's abilities (or perform the best pit stop possible) one needs to become aware of his or her optimal arousal level and how to maintain it. Experienced competitors can remain focused in a high arousal state. Less experienced racers will be less able to handle such a load and need to strive for greater calmness.

Winners control or positively channel their arousal. Researchers have found that successful racers actually perform better under pressure. "The race driver appears to have some very special strengths which allow him to perform well under great stress and risk," wrote Johnsgard.

When you're too high, deep breathing, muscle relaxation and mental exercises can bring you down. When you're too low, feed on the sweet smell of gasoline, the roar of engines and the excitement of the crowd to become more excited.

Many people lose their control and focus under stress and experience the response eloquently known as "choking." Tension swamps muscles that need to flow gracefully. The brain is unable to cope with onrushing information and excitement; it compensates by narrowing its focus and creating tunnel vision. Mistakes result from insufficient recognition of environmental conditions.

People who are overly aroused can feel inadequate, out of control, fearful of failure or guilty. They experience disruptive physical symptoms like shortness of breath or stomach or bowel cramps. Other signs that too much stress is present are loss of appetite or difficulty in concentrating, falling asleep or enjoying sex. Many headaches, back pains and stomach upsets are stress-related. Recognizing these signs is part of learning how to control arousal.

Relaxation skills can be learned. Stress can be relieved by thinking positive, gentle thoughts, taking deep breaths and, when possible, diverting attention to activities that unwind tension.

Confidence
Self-confidence plays into the performance equation, too. You can't accomplish something if you think you can't. Start listening to the things you say to yourself. When negative ideas flow into your mind, chase them away and replace them with realistic, positive thoughts of what it feels like to do your best.

The body functions more efficiently when freed of self-doubt. Researchers have found that negative thoughts, even tiny ones, adversely affect muscle relaxation, nerve impulses and heart/lung function. Negative thoughts can be self-fulfilling, too. Dwelling on fear of error often creates it. If the mind plays mental videotape of incorrect actions as the body performs, the wrong commands can be issued to the muscles. So remember to think positive!

Realistic Goals

Setting realistic, achievable goals fosters confidence. A competitor who sees no hope for success generates little perseverance and drive. Shooting too high is sure to bring disappointment, particularly in motorsports where each match results in one winner and dozens of runners-up.

The outcome of competitive effort hinges upon ability, effort and/or luck. An outstanding effort that comes up short, if viewed in the proper perspective, should be more rewarding than an unearned lucky trip to the winner's circle.

Specific sub-goals, as opposed to one lofty mega-goal, provide increased opportunity to experience real success, gain confidence and progress as a team. Strive to accomplish fast, precise pit stops; finish on the lead lap; move up in the points. Achieving each small goal begets success that should lead to further success.

Physical Conditioning

Your body is like your race car -- keeping it in top condition will help it perform at maximum mental ability. If the body is fatigued in the decisive stages of a race, it cannot expect a crisp performance from the brain.

Visualization and Mental Imagery

The mind can prepare itself and the body for successful performance simply by thinking. This phenomenon is known as visualization or mental imagery. Research has demonstrated that people who mentally rehearse physical skills, such as shooting basketball free throws, improve as much as if they practiced the actual motions. Successful athletes around the world, including race drivers, prepare for competition by visualizing every motion they will make through a complete match or lap, mentally feeling each muscle precisely follow its movements.

Visualization is a highly effective training tool when thoughts exactly match required muscle actions. Research has proven that visualization causes detectable electrical impulses in the muscles. Mental imagery can build self-confidence, relaxation and preparation for difficulty, too. Imagine yourself driving under the checkered flag, holding the trophy and tasting the champagne. Do it often and you'll begin to adopt the experiences as realistic goals.

Tuning out the world to focus on happy occasions and quiet experiences can calm jittery nerves. How often have you seen photos of drivers snoozing in their cars? They know that shutting out the world and focusing within is a way to lower arousal before hitting the track. Simply diverting attention to things other than racing can let the body unravel. Look for attractive girls or guys in the grandstands. Mentally sing a song. Visualize a memorable walk along a beach or forest trail. Swim laps in an imaginary ocean surf.

By playing out roles and responses to potential circumstances, the mind also can help itself and the body prepare for adversity. How will you handle the media if the engine blows? What will you do if a tire goes down? What will you say if YOU cause a crash?

Muscle and Breathing Relaxation

By consciously controlling breathing rate and muscle tone the mind can control the body. A long, deep breath momentarily slows the heart. Take two or three deep breaths and tune into the sensations of the chest and diaphragm muscles rising and falling.

Muscle relaxation is easy to practice, too. Pick a muscle group -- the arm, thigh, or forehead -- and close your eyes. Concentrate on tensing that part of the body as tightly as you can then gradually relax it, letting yourself experience the differing sensations of tautness and looseness. Imagine each muscle feeling warm or cool and focus on those perceptions. By practicing this technique on different muscles you should learn how to recognize stress in any muscle group -- and unwind it.

Dialing In

Many outstanding athletes say their best performances occur when they are able to let go of their conscious minds and run on a subconscious cruise control. They describe the sensation as something like an out-of-body experience in which the brain goes in neutral while a mysterious force guides their actions. The phenomenon has been described as a flow state, peak performance, sweet spot, concentration cocoon or transcendence.

"Many athletes have experienced such moments, moments when everything comes together exactly right and every movement is fluid, sure and natural; at such times, the athlete is completely free from consciously thinking about what he or she is doing. It is as though they were being directed by a power much greater than themselves," wrote Dr. Charles A. Garfield in his book, <u>Peak Performance: Mental Training Techniques of the World's Greatest Athletes</u>.

In racing, this euphoric, omnipotent feeling is characterized by a sense of oneness between man and machine. The body responds to its environment, turns the steering wheel and works the pedals seemingly without active thought.

The late Jim Clark once said, "I don't drive a car, really. The car happens to be under me and I'm controlling it, but it's as much a part of me as I am it."

Finding this state of mind is a matter of achieving such high levels of experience, preparedness, confidence and relaxation that movements and reactions become automatic. Garfield's book describes comprehensive mental training techniques that can lead to such a state. Many competitors have intuitively unlocked this frame of mind.

"I suppose the good drivers automatically are in the frame of mind they need to be in," Earnhardt said. "They don't have to be tuned in or turned on, they're always tuned in. I think this is a big advantage for me or Bill Elliott or Rusty Wallace or any of these guys."

The Pre-Race Plan

Starting one's race routine the night before an event can minimize pre-race jitters. Mentally rehearse the next day's activities -- awakening, showering, dressing, eating, getting to the track, getting in the car -- and scheduling sufficient time to do them without rushing.

Think ahead to how you'll feel before race time and what you'll do to keep an even disposition. Practicing the stressful situation mentally will make you better prepared when it arrives.

In the hours leading up to the race, think positively. Don't let the mind dwell on risk or failure. Rather than agonize over the outcome, relish the opportunity to race. Preview the joy you'll feel if the race gods decide it is to be your day. Think realistically: Don't consider the race a do-or-die battle. Give it your best shot and let the checkered flag fall where it may.

In the final minutes, don't think too much. That overloads the senses and keeps the stress level high. Put the mind on idle and let the instincts assume command. Take slow, deep breaths and ignore the butterflies. They'll fly away when they see the green flag.

Team Work

A racing team truly is more than the sum of its parts. People working together accomplish far more than a like number of individuals. Teammates pool their strengths to offset their individual weaknesses; they merge competitive fires to incinerate individual doubts. Team members persist, through bad times or good, if the group is cohesive and supportive. Cohesion and success are circular: Each encourages the other.

Group feedback can shape individual self-esteem and confidence. Motivation thrives if individuals strongly identify with the team and derive satisfaction from being part of it. Social cliques can harm team unity by making some members feel second-class. As often as possible, activities should include all members.

While individuals must, of course, fulfill personal needs, the team will be most successful when members place team achievement above personal goals.

Leadership

Leadership is crucial to any human undertaking. Leaders do not have to be crew chiefs, car owners or drivers. Any member of a crew can contribute leadership to the overall cause by setting good examples and encouraging cooperation and cohesion. Effective leaders recognize that individuals respond to differing leadership styles -- some need a pat on the back, others occasionally an iron fist. Motivation is task-specific, too. Getting people "up" for a pit stop requires less leadership than getting the shop cleaned.

When the chips are down, people tend to revert to dominant personality traits. Aggressive people take charge. Impatient people become restless. Critical people complain. Nervous people go up in flames. Good leaders anticipate these reactions and plan ahead, making team assignments based on personal tendencies and promoting group communications to foster understanding.

Leaders also realize that teams and individuals experience wide ranges of emotions (joy, disappointment, pride, shame, boredom) that must be addressed or sometimes simply accepted. Even an enthusiastic team needs someone to channel its energy, so organizational skills must be part of the leader's tool chest.

Leadership Styles

There are many leadership styles. Some are considered ineffective except in specific situations and individuals.

One style might be termed "Dictator." Discipline, control and fear are viewed as the primary motivational tools. Leaders may have to exercise discipline occasionally, but most people do not respond to fear over the long haul. If over-used, this style diminishes confidence and motivation.

The "Buddy" style generally permits the team to run on a consensus basis. A buddy can be pleasant company but probably won't lead troops to victory.

The "Persuasion" style encourages the crew to believe in the team's plan and themselves. Individuals are encouraged to contribute ideas without concern for retribution, knowing their thoughts can contribute to the good of the cause. The persuader allows members of the crew to share responsibility for successes as well as failures.

While the good of the team depends upon cooperation, research has found that members of winning teams feel highly positive about themselves as individuals, too. Leaders address individual emotional needs. Encouraging people to believe in themselves builds confidence, persistence and performance. Leaders who give individuals feedback on their work provide a yardstick by which progress can be measured and confidence can be built.

Reinforcement for the performances of team members can be positive or negative. Positive reinforcements are rewards that can be symbolic (trophies), material (money) or psychological (praise, satisfaction, sense of belonging). Negative reinforcements are punishments such as the loss of privileges (even the ride!) or dismissal from the team.

In most cases positive reinforcement is preferable, but negative feedback can work more effectively on some people some times. Over the long-term, however, the power of rewards can fade. The ante must be boosted to make an impression. In a team setting individual rewards sometimes can backfire by becoming a source of disruptive rivalry or by being viewed as symbols of favoritism.

Long-lasting motivation comes from within -- pride. People who have experienced success and self-satisfaction want more. The functional team allows all members to share equally in the joys of success and responsibility for coming up short. If a team is to stay loose and take the risks required to achieve new heights, the desire for success must be stronger than the fear of failure.

A supportive leader strives to maintain unity and to make sure each member understands his or her importance to the effort. Helping people understand the roles of others encourages cohesion and support. Research has found that cohesion can be a better predictor of team success than ability.

Realistic goal-setting helps good leaders keep team members striving toward progress. If teammates consider themselves successful more often than not (viewing a top-five or top-ten finish as an achievement rather than a loss, for example) they will persist through adversity. Goals should be flexible -- raised after success and possibly lowered after a string of failures.

It is important to remember that most racing teams run on the hearts and muscles of volunteers who devote countless hours to the cause for the love of the sport. They require far more encouragement and coddling than professionals who work for a paycheck as well as personal satisfaction.

Keeping It In Perspective

Racing should be fun. Period. Most participants are amateurs who spend mountains of hard-earned time and money on their passion. Those who have achieved professional status should never forget how fortunate they are. If racing becomes unceasingly stressful, frustrating or dissatisfying, maybe that indicates the need for a time out. There are less expensive ways to have fun and safer ways to make a living. If it isn't fun, it isn't worth doing.

Racing can provide immense rewards, win or lose, because it allows us to test ourselves and tread where few others dare go. As Dr. Denis Waitley explains, "True Winning is no more than one's own personal pursuit of individual excellence."

Adventurer and President Theodore Roosevelt once said:

"The credit in life does not go to the critic who stands on the sideline and points out where the strong stumble, but rather, the real credit in life goes to the man who is actually in the arena, whose face may get marred by sweat and dust, who knows great enthusiasm and great devotion and learns to spend himself in a worthy cause, who, at best if he wins, knows the thrill of high achievement and if he fails, at least fails while daring greatly, so that in life his place will never be with those very cold and timid souls who know neither victory nor defeat."

Many racing engines create noise far beyond the exposure levels that the U.S. Occupational Safety and Health Administration (OSHA) applies to work places. Whether you drive, crew or watch race cars, hearing protection should be part of your track kit.

Chapter 11

HEARING:
YOUR LOSS IS NOBODY'S GAIN

"What?! What'd you say? Somebody say something?"
-- Motorsports journalist and
former power boat racer, age 63

The lusty, awesomely-powerful sound of racing engines is certainly one of the appeals of motorsports. This awesome sound also may be one of the most overlooked hazards of racing.

Unmuffled racing engines can produce noise as a powerful as jackhammers cracking concrete or the blast of a .22-caliber rifle shot -- but continuously. Two-cycle racing engines can churn out noise energy that is several times the threshold of human pain.

According to exposure limits imposed by the U.S. Occupational Safety and Health Administration (OSHA) on industrial noise sources, people should not be exposed to sound levels produced by typical racing engines for more than a few minutes to a couple of hours unless hearing protection is worn. While crew members and spectators sitting some distance from cars are not subjected to the same volume of engine noise found at the edge of the track, the exposure experienced over a long day, night or weekend of racing is sufficient to cause at least temporary hearing loss.

And hearing loss is a sneaky creature. By the time one realizes there may be a problem it is too late to do anything about it. A long career as a racer or fan can prompt a slow, almost imperceptible loss of hearing that is <u>permanent</u>. Hearing aids may offer some benefit but cannot fully replace the hearing qualities that have been lost.

The Ear

Hearing -- after vision -- is our second most important sensory ability. It is very fragile. The outer ear, the part which hangs on the side of our head, is only a small part of our hearing equipment. The invisible parts are complex and extend deep into the skull.

Sound follows the auditory canal -- that hole in the ear -- into the middle ear, where it reaches the eardrum. The eardrum vibrates and transmits energy to three tiny bones that in turn vibrate the fluid-filled cochlea in the inner ear. Inside the cochlea, shaped like a tiny snail shell, these vibrations cause movement in 24,000 tiny hairs that are connected to nerve cells. These nerve cells pass information on sound to the brain.

Noise

Sound is energy that causes the air to vibrate. Noise is sound that is annoying or loud enough to cause discomfort or hearing damage.

Sound is measured in a unit of energy called the decibel (dB). Hearing injury can occur at a wide range of decibel levels because the effects of noise vary with the pitch of sound, the duration of exposure to it, distance from the source and weather conditions. In addition, some individuals are more prone to hearing damage than others.

People with normal hearing begin to perceive sound beginning at zero decibels. A normal conversation is conducted at about 60 decibels; noise begins to interfere with conversation at 65dB. An automobile horn hits about 90dB.

Sound intensity increases sharply as decibel readings climb because the decibel is a logarithmic, not linear, measurement. That means that the total energy of sound doubles with each 3dB-increase: 93dB is twice as severe as 90dB and 96dB is four times as loud as 90dB.

Noise and the Ear

When the ears are exposed to excessively loud noise they can protect themselves to a limited extent. A muscle in the ear can lower the energy of sound transmitted into the ear by as much as 30dB. This muscle tires very quickly, however, and cannot protect the ear from the steady noise levels generated by racing.

Short-term exposure to moderately high noise may cause a temporary hearing loss that will be recovered in hours, days or weeks. On the other hand, lengthy exposure to high sound levels, or short-term exposure to an exceedingly loud noise such as an explosion, causes permanent hearing loss by destroying the receptive hairs and their connective cells. When the damage is mild the hair cells can replace themselves. Following serious injury the hair cells may be destroyed and replaced with scar tissue. Nerve fibers may be damaged, too.

Hearing loss first becomes evident by difficulties in understanding speaking voices, especially in crowded places. The first hearing losses tend to affect higher-pitched sounds, such as music and the voices of women and children. Hearing loss spreads into lower pitches as deterioration and damage continue.

Another symptom is tinnitus -- hearing loss accompanied by ringing in the ears. Tinnitus often is temporary but can be extraordinarily maddening if it becomes permanent.

Susceptibility to hearing injury is an individual matter, with some people suffering far more damage than others in similar circumstances. Young people may be at a higher risk of injury. Research conducted by the U.S. Institute on Aging found that men over 30 lose their hearing about twice as fast as women. Eventually the difference reaches the equivalent of 20 years, with 60-year-old men hearing as well as 80-year-old women.

How Loud Are Racing Machines?

The Sports Car Club of America (SCCA) has studied noise exposure at auto races since 1980. Its statistics, based on more than 200,000 readings, show that large-displacement racing engines without mufflers average 107.9dB. Some exceed 110dB, the volume of a .22 rifle shot and the loudest rock concerts.

Large engines running with mufflers average 102.1dB. Smaller engines, as found in Formula Ford and Sports 2000 racers, average 99dB to 99.8dB. Showroom stock cars were measured at 80.1dB. Studies of snowmobiles and hearing have found that two-cycle racing engines produce energy ranging up to 136dB. Similar engines are used in two-wheeled and four-wheeled racing.

How much can these noise levels affect hearing? According to the OSHA regulations, people should not be exposed to 115dB (the level of the noisiest big-block engines) longer than 15 minutes a day unless they wear ear protection. Exposure at 110dB should be limited to 30 minutes; at 100dB to two hours; and at 90dB (the smaller racing engines) to eight hours.

How about the two-cycle snowmobile engines? According to some experts, hearing is at risk after 11 minutes unless ear plugs or muffs are being worn.

HEARING

Protecting the Ears

Significant degrees of hearing protection are offered by readily-available and affordable hearing protection products. Both ear plugs and ear muffs can work well if properly fitted -- and worn! Additional hearing protection can be provided if plugs and muffs are worn together. Hearing protectors do not eliminate all sound reaching the inner ears but rather diminish its energy.

Racing helmets diminish the sound pressure reaching drivers' ears, too, but wearing plugs underneath still is advisable.

Ear plugs are available in molded soft plastic or a flexible polyurethane that expands after being compressed and inserted in the ear canal. The polyurethane plugs are so cheap that they can be considered disposable. They are highly preferable to wads of cotton, which do not offer hearing protection. Ear plugs must fit tightly in order to provide noise suppression -- a pair that fits effectively may be slightly uncomfortable when first worn.

Sound is conducted to the inner ear by the skull bones around the ear as well as by the middle ear. Ear plugs do not bar bone conduction transmissions of sound. Ear muffs, if properly fitted, are effective at limiting noise exposure through bone conduction. Muffs consist of a solid cup filled with sound-absorbing material and held over the ear by a flexible band. The material which seals the muff to the side of the head -- typically a rubber gasket filled with liquid or rubber foam -- is critical. Any object that can interrupt the snug seal between the muffs and the head (glass frames, long hair) negates the protection being offered.

Ear plugs and muffs carry an NRR (noise reduction rating) that indicates their sound-muffling abilities. Ear plugs can lower the energy of sound reaching the inner ear by 20dB to 35dB. Disposable plugs should cost less than a dollar a set and can actually do a better job than reusable plugs which cost a couple of dollars per pair. Ear muffs can provide 20dB to 30dB of protection and cost $10 to $40.

If ear plugs are worn under ear muffs, add 5dB to 7dB of additional muffling to the rating of the muffs.

Ear protection should be part of every motorsports buff's track kit.

Chapter 12

SUNBURN:
AN OCCUPATIONAL HAZARD OF RACING

A dark tan used to be one of the special extras enjoyed by people who basked in the sunshine at race tracks. Then our sun-worshiping society was struck by a plague of potentially fatal skin disease that made the great outdoors seem less friendly.

The sun can cause problems far more serious than a painful burn. Skin cancer is the most common form of cancer. About one in six Americans eventually will encounter it -- more than 600,000 cases are reported in the U.S. annually. Many victims require surgery; some lose skin, muscles or pieces of noses and ears. And 8,500 people DIE from skin cancer each year.

To make matters worse, the earth's thinning ozone layer allows more of the sun's most harmful ultraviolet rays to reach those of us attending races. These rays can damage skin cells, making them reproduce erratically to form tumors rather than new skin. If not treated in time, tumor cells can migrate to produce cancerous tumors in the brain, lungs, liver, heart or other tissues.

Doctors now try to convince people that a deep tan signfies injury, not beauty. In minor cases, long-term exposure to sunlight will cause the skin to wrinkle, thicken and discolor. Spending just 15 minutes to an hour under bright sunlight can cause harm. Even when one is sitting in shade nearby reflective surfaces, such as pavement, can reflect more than half the ultraviolet rays in sunlight.

People who do not tan well or have fair, milky-white skin; blue eyes; or blond or red hair are at the highest risk of injury. People who have had serious sunburns or spend a lot of time outdoors face elevated risks. Even dark-skinned people considered immune to sunburn can get skin cancer.

Young people face still higher risks. Infants should never sit in the sun uncovered. Children should not be outdoors without suitable clothing and sunscreen.

Folks who race during the day should make long pants and shirts part of their uniforms even during the hottest months. Light colors will reflect sunlight and minimize heat gain. Hats and high-quality, ultraviolet-screening sunglasses should be worn, as should a sunscreen with a sun protection factor (SPF) of at least 15.

When you go racing, burn up the track -- not your skin.

Drivers racing in close quarters are responsible for the safety not only of themselves but of fellow competitors, crew members and fans. Many drugs and medications, illegal or legal, carry potentially harmful side effects which must be understood.

Chapter 13

DRUGS AND RACING

Drugs and medications can have many side effects, some of which may affect performance and safety in racing. The most common hazardous medication side effect is impaired mental alertness; dizziness is a side effect of more than 1,000 prescription drugs. Some of the classes of such drugs are briefly reviewed below to make one aware of potential hazards.

It is strongly suggested that labels be read carefully and/or a physician be consulted before taking any medication within days of operating a racing machine or working in environments, such as machine shops or pit areas, where injury risks exist.

Medications

Prescription and over-the-counter medications may cause a wide range of side effects. These may not be caused by all drugs within each category or affect all people. Again, it is important to carefully read labels and/or consult with a physician before taking any medications and participating in motorsports.

ALLERGY, COLD AND COUGH medications often contain ANTIHISTAMINES that counteract runny noses, watery eyes, itches and rashes. Antihistamines also may cause blurred vision, anxiety, decreased performance and drowsiness, an effect that can be worsened if these products are taken in conjunction with alcohol, sleeping pills or some other medications.

BETA BLOCKERS, prescribed for heart ailments and migraine headaches, also can cause fatigue, lethargy and impaired concentration.

CONTRACEPTIVES (ORAL) can cause headaches and mood changes that may affect performance.

COUGH SUPPRESSANTS diminish activity in the part of the brain that stimulates the cough reflex. These drugs can contain codeine or other narcotics that can cause drowsiness or dizziness.

DIARRHEA medications may cause some people to become dizzy or drowsy and experience blurred vision.

DIURETICS, which may be prescribed for a number of physical conditions, may prompt dehydration and fatigue.

DRUGS AND RACING

HIGH BLOOD PRESSURE medications may be diuretics that cause the body to eliminate water and minerals. Exposure to heat and sweating therefore can lead to excessive loss of body fluids and minerals.

LAXATIVES may cause dehydration.

MUSCLE RELAXANTS may cause drowsiness and dizziness.

NAUSEA medications sometimes cause drowsiness, blurred vision and accelerated heart beat.

PAIN MEDICATIONS may contain narcotics that can make people drowsy or dizzy and impair mental performance. Using over-the-counter pain products in large amounts, such as to dull the pain of an injury in order to continue driving, can lead to anemia and gastrointestinal blood loss.

SLEEPING MEDICATIONS can induce drowsiness that lasts into the day after they are taken. These medications can contain strong drugs that depress the central nervous system.

ULCER medications may cause drowsiness or dizziness.

WEIGHT-LOSS medications usually contain the same ingredients as decongestants and can have the same effects. They also may carry high doses of caffeine.

Recreational or "Performance Enhancing" Drugs

ALCOHOL is a depressant and society's most popular drug. It has been estimated that 30 gallons of beer, 3 gallons of wine and 2.1 gallons of liquor are consumed for each person in the U.S. each year -- and one-third of its people don't drink!

The influence of alcohol diminishes coordination, reaction times and balance. It can impair the body's ability to regulate heat and can lead to dehydration that lasts after intoxication has ended. The body uses eight ounces of water to metabolize one ounce of alcohol. For health and safety a driver or crew member should not drink alcohol in the 24 hours preceding a race, particularly during hot weather.

A study of alcohol's effects on the skills of airline pilots found that coordination and visual-motor skills were impaired up to 14 hours after three to four drinks were consumed. A U.S. Navy study determined that the body may need 36 hours to fully recover from drunkenness.

Alcohol leaves the body much more slowly than it enters. Regardless of how much is consumed, the body can process only about 0.5 ounce of alcohol per hour. That's about the same amount found in 3/4 of a standard serving of beer, wine or hard liquor.

It should not be necessary to point out that it is unwise to drive a race car on the track or the tow vehicle on the highway while under the influence of alcohol. Intoxication impairs judgment, coordination and vision. Even at blood alcohol levels below the legal limits of intoxication peripheral vision is reduced by 30 percent.

Experts suggest athletes probably would be better off by consuming no alcohol, but they acknowledge that daily consumption of one or two drinks is unlikely to cause harm unless taken prior to competition. We have observed drivers consuming a beer or two on the way to the track to take the edge off their nerves. Doing so probably has taken the edge off their performance and margin of safety, too.

It also is dangerous to consume alcohol to quench the thirst immediately after competition. When a beer or other alcoholic drink is poured into a dehydrated body that has an empty stomach, the intoxicating effects are magnified. At least a quart of water should be consumed before a celebration begins.

AMPHETAMINES are stimulants that have been used for years to give athletes energy boosts or keep weary people awake. These drugs stimulate the nervous system to make one feel stronger, more alert and less fatigued. There are side effects, too, including addiction, nervousness, fever, insomnia, anxiety, hallucinations, agitation, paranoia and -- a very important factor in racing -- inability to regulate heat loss in hot environments. The stresses that amphetamines place on the heart and blood vessels, particularly in the brain, can be dangerous, too. Amphetamines have caused death through hyperthermia, brain hemorrhages and cardiac failure.

ANABOLIC STEROIDS are synthetic derivatives of testosterone taken to build muscle strength and mass. They also can build liver disease, high blood pressure, violent mental instability, severe acne, baldness, sexual impotence, decreased sperm production and atrophy of the testicles. The increased muscle strength and size produced by steroids do not improve aerobic performance, so they are of no benefit to endurance athletes such as racing drivers.

BARBITURATES (DOWNERS) cause fatigue, drowsiness, disorientation and impaired task performance. Alertness, attention span, judgment and reaction times can be affected for hours after a barbiturate is taken. Sleep disturbances may follow use.

DRUGS AND RACING

CAFFEINE, found in coffee, tea, soft drinks or tablets, is a drug. Many athletes use it in efforts to enhance their endurance because it potentially may boost the metabolic rate 8 to 16 percent. Some studies dispute the endurance benefits of caffeine, but others have shown it can increase oxygen consumption and diminish sensations of fatigue by stimulating the brain. Caffeine is listed as a banned substance by the International Olympic Committee.

Caffeine also is a mild diuretic that can increase urination as much as 30 percent up to three hours after consumption. Therefore it increases the risks of dehydration. Because of its potential to relax the muscles of the large intestine, caffeine may prompt diarrhea. None of these experiences would be pleasant during a long race.

As with other stimulants, caffeine also can impair coordination and cause nervousness and irritability, additional concerns for people involved in racing. Caffeine may cause some people to have higher blood pressure during intense exercise by increasing the resistance of the blood vessels. Moderate caffeine consumption can be tolerated by most people. People who may have severe reactions to it or find themselves competing in hot weather might want to consider avoidance.

COCAINE is a powerful stimulant that affects chemical reactions within the brain. It produces feelings of decreased fatigue, euphoria and speeded-up reflexes -- but in an uncoordinated way. Athletes may think they are stronger, faster and more capable while using cocaine, but actually these feelings result from impaired perceptions of reality. Cocaine increases the pulse, blood pressure, body temperature and respiratory rate. Its use generally leads to nasal and sinus disease, psychological instability, agitation, restlessness, insomnia, anxiety, paranoia, seizures and potentially fatal cardiovascular disease. Crack is a pure form of cocaine.

HALLUCINOGENS, known by names such as mescaline, LSD, PCP and acid, produce irrational behavior with visual and auditory hallucinations, possibly with panic attacks, suicide or accidental death resulting. The effects may last for eight hours. Hallucinogens also may cause chromosome damage that is passed on to children.

MARIJUANA is a recreational drug with dangerous side effects. Marijuana releases inhibitions, impairs judgment and can affect the cardiovascular system, prompting episodes of sharply decreased blood pressure. Marijuana inhibits sweating and, therefore, the body's ability to maintain a safe temperature. Marijuana also impairs mental functions and muscular coordination for up to 24 hours after usage. Among the impaired functions are motor control, depth perception, sense of timing and communications. Personality alterations -- lack of motivation, loss of ambition, impaired memory and concentration -- can result from long-term use.

NICOTINE is a highly addictive substance in tobacco products. It affects the nervous system in ways similar to those of caffeine. In regular smokers nicotine improves concentration and memory. On the other hand, smoking decreases muscle tone and, despite folk tales, does not improve cardiovascular endurance.

Nicotine speeds the heart rate, increases blood pressure and carries the additional risks of lung, lip and mouth cancer, regardless of whether tobacco is smoked or chewed. Tobacco use is the leading cause of preventable illness and death in the U.S.

OXYGEN, inhaled through a mask placed over the nose and mouth, often is used by athletes to speed recovery from shortness of breath. This practice may speed the recovery of a resting athlete by a few seconds, but the benefit ends when competition is resumed. When the athlete returns to competition, the blood oxygen level quickly returns to its unassisted state.

PHENYLPROPANOLAMINE is a stimulant found in many non-prescription drugs such as appetite suppressants, nasal decongestants and cold remedies. Its side effects may include life-threatening hypertension, paranoia, hallucinations or seizures. The side effects can be worsened when this compound is taken in excessive doses or in conjunction with caffeine.

Sleep is the maintenance break your body needs to stay in peak form.

Chapter 14

SLEEP:
SLOWING DOWN TO STAY FAST

Racing forces people to work long hours and do a lot of traveling -- things that conflict with regularly getting a good night's sleep. But let us not forget that sleep is one of life's necessities.

Sleep is the daily pit stop our bodies need for basic maintenance and recharging. Many critical chemical substances are created and neurologic changes occur during sleep. These are necessary to keep the brain, muscles and organs humming. If you're not getting enough sleep, your racing performance and enjoyment of life will suffer.

Most adults need seven to eight hours of sleep each night; some normal people get by quite well with an hour more or less than that. Many people with fast-paced lifestyles fall far short of those hours and may be so chronically sleep-deprived they don't remember what it's like to feel fully rested and alert. Some physicians believe sleepiness may be one of the most overlooked physical disabilities in our society, causing chronic fatigue, poor work performance, irritability and accidental injuries.

Racing, more than any sport, requires quick-thinking, vigilant concentration and responsible judgment, whether one toils on the track or in the pits. People who don't get enough sleep may not be as mentally alert as they need to be. In laboratory tests, people deprived of sleep have trouble performing simple mathematics or other routine manual tasks.

Sleep deprivation also can make people cranky and irritable, conditions that are not conducive to a relaxed state of mind behind the wheel or a productive relationship with crew members. A lack of sleep can cause another physical change harmful to racers -- depression of the body's heat regulation and sweating systems.

Most of the body's physiologic functions are tied to sleeping and waking cycles. Strength, alertness, stress and energy levels ebb and flow around the clock with individual body rhythms.

SLEEP

Naps are of limited help in providing catch-up sleep or a mid-day boost, but naps that are too long or taken too late in the day disturb the quality of the coming night's sleep. Occasionally sleeping late does not make up for hours that have been lost -- they're lost for good.

People should get just as much sleep as they need to feel refreshed. Sleeping too much reduces the quality of sleep and throws off the body clock. Getting up at the same time each morning makes it easier to fall asleep at night. Daily exercise encourages sound sleep, too.

Travel and changing time zones or daily schedules can interrupt sleep patterns and affect performance. A three-hour time change is enough to throw the body seriously out of whack. Compensating in advance for a schedule change, by altering bed and wake-up times and turning on bright lights to simulate the coming morning time, can help. The body's internal clock is highly responsive to light.

People over the age of 45 should pay particular attention to sleep needs because they are beginning to experience diminished soundness and quality of sleep.

While making sure you get a good night's sleep, don't work right up until bedtime or fall onto the pillow and start analyzing daily problems and events. Before hitting the sack allow a sufficient winding-down period to get relaxed; different individuals may require 10 minutes to an hour to get ready for restful sleep.

Hot baths or showers before bed can help bring solid sleep. Caffeine, alcohol and tobacco do not. Caffeine can affect people for eight to 14 hours after it is consumed. Alcohol can make people think they are falling asleep more quickly, but in reality it disturbs the important high-quality sleep later in the night. Nicotine can affect people in the same way as caffeine. When consumed in large quantities it is arousing rather than relaxing. An occasional sleeping pill may be helpful but should not be relied upon often or expected to cure sleep difficulties.

Up to one-third of all people may not be getting enough rest due to sleep disorders such as breathing obstructions, nighttime muscle twitches, psychological stress or poor sleep habits. Most sleep disorders are treated through medication or behavioral education. In rare cases sleep disorders may require surgical correction. Anyone who encounters ongoing sleep difficulties should consult a doctor.

144

Chapter 15

THE OBLIGATORY SEX SCENE

"Remember when sex was safe and racing was dangerous?"
-- 1990's T-shirt slogan

Many people have said that every successful creative modern work must contain sex. So here is a brief review of current knowledge on sex, athletic performance and the age-old question: Should sex be avoided the night before a big race?

A search of the medical literature reveals little scientific research on this issue that is <u>so</u> important to the racer.

The traditional belief has been that sexual abstinence on the eve of the big game builds energy and psychological tension that will improve athletic aggressiveness and performance. Sex actually requires very little energy so athletic strength and endurance are not affected at all. (Unless one stays awake all night to participate.)

Most of today's sports medicine experts, however, believe sex can be effective in relieving pre-game stress and anxiety. Sexual activity can help many people get a good night's sleep before a major event. Other people may have difficulty falling asleep after sex, however, so they should consider abstaining or starting earlier in the evening.

And whatever one does during race weekends or between them, keep safety in mind -- on or off the track, have and use protective equipment when that would be wise.

Chapter 16

UNDERSTANDING RACING INJURIES

"Motor racing worldwide, whatever the formula -- it doesn't have to be Indy or Formula One -- is dangerous. You go more than 30 miles an hour, you can hurt yourself."
> -- Nigel Mansell,
> ESPN's Speedweek, June 13, 1992

How Dangerous Is Racing?

Despite the sport's daredevil image, a non-scientific comparison of sporting fatality rates indicates that racing may be about as dangerous as activities that millions of people -- young and old -- take for granted. Viewed statistically, race driving may be as death-defying as swimming or boating and safer than mountain hiking, scuba diving, parachuting and hang gliding.

Other data suggest that a driver's odds of being injured in an Indy-car crash are about the same as the chances of being hurt in a highway collision.

When compared to Indy-car accidents on speedways with average speeds under 145 m.p.h., highway crashes are almost six times MORE likely to cause injuries. During the 1984 CART season and Indianapolis 500, one Indy-car driver was injured for every 7.2 accidents. By comparison, one person is injured in every 8.2 accidents on U.S. highways, according to a paper, "Championship Car Racing Accidents and Injuries," published in The Physician and Sportsmedicine, May 1986, by Terry R. Trammell, M.D., Stephen E. Olvey, M.D., and Diane B. Reed, M.S.N.

No fatalities were found in a study of crashes reported in the Southeast Division of the Sports Car Club of America in 1984 and 1985 by M. Rick Timms, M.D., chairman of the International Council of Motorsports Sciences.

Timms concluded, "From the data presented, 325 drivers involved in 175 accidents with only eight moderate or severe injuries, it is clear that while racing accidents occur with relative frequency, injuries are infrequent and usually minor."

Overall data on auto racing, however, are sketchy. The authors could find no source of comprehensive figures or even estimates on racing risks. The most reliable estimate believed possible, therefore, was derived by comparing data from two motorsports publications.

Performance Racing Industry magazine, in November 1990, estimated that approximately 350,000 people drive a race car at least once each year in the U.S.

For the most reliable estimate on fatalities, National Speed Sport News, the respected weekly, was reviewed for 1989, 1990 and 1991. The newspaper reported 7 driver fatalities in 1989, 14 in 1990 and 8 in 1991. These results would produce fatality rates (per 100,000 participants) of 2.00 for 1989, 4.00 for 1990 and 2.29 for 1991. While the newspaper may have missed an occasional incident, it should be safe to assume the annual incidence of driver fatalities falls between 7 and 14.

According to participation and fatality data from the National Safety Council, those rates would put driving race cars in the same hazard range as swimming, alpine ski racing and boating. Race driving would be slightly less risky than scuba diving and mountain hiking and far less dangerous than parachuting and hang gliding.

The National Safety Council cautions that its numbers reflect only estimates and should not be used to make comparisons. Nonetheless, for the sake of discussion the accompanying chart compares our best estimates of racing events of 1989-1991 to estimates for other sports.

Fatality statistics alone, of course, do not reflect the incidence of non-fatal and potentially serious injuries that racing participants can suffer. The remaining pages of the book are devoted to educating drivers, mechanics, spectators and track operators to accident factors and possible solutions that can prevent the large numbers of preventable injuries that occur at race tracks.

The North American Racing Insurance Database

In attempting to find broad-based statistics on motorsports injuries for informed discussion of preventive and treatment measures, the authors contacted many sources and repeatedly were told data were not available or were considered proprietary. The authors were, however, given access to the files of North American Racing Insurance in Independence, Mo., one of the major motorsport insurers in the U.S.

Relative Risk Factors of Sporting Activities

Activity	Estimated Annual Participation	Estimated Annual Fatalities	Fatality Rate Per 100,000
Softball+	20,900,000	1	0.004
Tennis+	18,000,000	1	0.006
Downhill skiing+	14,400,000	1	0.007
Baseball+	13,900,000	2	0.01
Soccer+	8,200,000	1	0.01
Basketball+	21,200,000	7	0.03
Water skiing++	NA	NA	0.30
Boxing+	500,000	4	0.80
Football+	12,000,000	12	0.10
Auto Racing/1989	350,000**	7***	2.00
Auto Racing/1991	350,000**	8***	2.29
Swimming*	70,500,000	1,700	2.41
Alpine Ski Racing++	NA	NA	2.50
Boating*	32,500,000	865	2.66
Auto Racing/1990	350,000**	14***	4.00
Scuba Diving*	2,500,000	114	4.56
Mountain Hiking++	NA	NA	6.40
Parachuting*	115,000	23	20.00
Hang Gliding*	30,000	8	26.66

SOURCES:

*   Accident Facts, 1990-1991 editions, National Safety Council
**   Performance Racing Industry
*** National Speed Sport News, 1989-91
+   Accident Facts, 1987, National Safety Council
++ U.S. News & World Report, Jan. 15, 1990

NA = Not Available

Several thousand preliminary injury reports, filed with the company for the 1987 through 1990 racing seasons and part of the 1991 season, were surveyed. While NARI's business is limited largely to short tracks, these tracks do host a large portion of the races conducted in the country. In addition, the statistics provide some insight into injuries and causal factors experienced in other forms of racing.

The statistics offered on the following pages were derived from preliminary incident reports filed with NARI by rescue workers or track managers. The reports listed such information as the age of the driver, crew member or spectator injured; type of vehicle involved, if any; type of injury; body part injured; track size and surface; and factors causing or contributing to the incident, such as collision, mechanical failure or rollover. Many reports were incomplete or offered only preliminary diagnosis of injuries. In some cases NARI's detailed case files were consulted to provide further information on specific incidents.

Since some of NARI's data was not computerized at the time of review, detailed analyses of all incidents were not possible. The data also could not be analyzed to provide insight into the rate of injuries per participant because NARI does not receive data on the number of participants at each event.

The data gathered from NARI were entered into a computer database software package which permitted analysis by specific type of race car and by driver, crew member and spectator populations.

For ease of comparison, some closely-related classes of cars were combined to provide results of more statistical significance.

For example, classes described by such names as bombers, "beer stox" and "thundercars" were considered street stocks. Pony cars and four-cylinder stock cars were grouped as ministocks. Limited late models and other titles suggesting cars falling somewhere between street stocks and late models were classified as sportsman cars. The numbers for minisprints, midgets, enduro and demolition derbies may not be representative because the surveyed populations of these cars in NARI's coverage were particularly small.

How Often Do Injuries Occur?

Very good question. It is difficult enough to determine the number of racing fatalities that occur during a year. Establishing precise numbers for injuries sustained by hundreds of thousands participants is not possible given the lack of cooperation found today in the sport.

While North American Racing Insurance does not have estimates on participation levels at the tracks it covers, it does track the number of claims (and therefore injuries) that arise per event. During 1990, NARI received .21 claims per racing meet. The incidence of injuries has dropped steadily since 1986, when the rate was .37 per event. The rate fell to .30 per meet in 1987, .28 in 1988 and .23 in 1989.

Published data from Indy-car racing (the Trammell-Olvey-Reed paper) suggest that injuries at that level of the sport are more likely on high-speed courses. One injury occurred in every 2.4 Indy-car crashes with average speeds over 145 m.p.h. Injuries resulted from one in 47 crashes on courses at which cars averaged less than 145 m.p.h. But the incidence of crashes was approximately the same, 6.5 per race at high-speed tracks and 5.2 per race at slower tracks.

NARI President George England has no statistics on the subject, but his observations over years in the industry lead him to believe that low-speed racing can be as dangerous as faster forms.

"In the early- to mid-80s, if a promoter indicated his racing program primarily consisted of slower, entry-level cars we gave him a discount. We thought of the late models and sprints as faster cars that deserved a premium surcharge," England said.

"What I've determined over the years is that it's a matter of six of one and half dozen of the other. In the entry-level cars you have inexperienced drivers and the equipment may not be as good. There may be only a simple roll bar with no fire suits. There are a lot of cars on the track at the same time with a lot of contact between the race cars. This results in a higher frequency of claims.

"With the faster cars, we see more severity in accidents but less frequency. They have better equipment, more experienced drivers and longer tracks. Once you get past the starts, we don't see as much contact as in the lower divisions. So we would just as soon insure the high-speed cars because the factors wash out," England said. "At the end of the year, our numbers are going to come out the same. There is no justification for giving cheaper rates for street stocks and hobby cars."

England said his claim experience is higher for open wheel cars. "We need to get all the premium dollars we can get from open-wheel tracks. A 30-percent increase would not be out of line for an open-wheel track. We are doing no better than breaking even with our loss ratio on them. The sprint cars are pretty safe race cars considering the violent accidents that you see. I think the wings have helped that. But still, there are a lot of claims presented from sprint cars and those claims usually cost some money."

England believes midgets may be riskier than sprint cars. "I dislike them more than sprints from an underwriting viewpoint. We are very selective of the midget business we choose to insure."

The claim ratios resulting from demolition derbies and enduros (slightly controlled racing of junk cars) are vastly higher than those of other racing classes. NARI receives about two claims for each demo derby, about 10 times the average for all races, and 3.5 to 4 claims per enduro, nearly 20 times the average.

The NARI data suggest that drivers suffer about 7 in 10 (71.3 percent) of all injuries that occur at race tracks. Injuries in the pits, involving crew members, officials, the media and drivers not competing at the time of injury, represent about 2 of 10 (18.3 percent) of injuries. Spectators experience 1 in 10 motorsports injuries (10.4 percent).

A listing of the data is printed at the end of this chapter.

What Causes Injuries?

Trauma -- direct blows or sudden, twisting, deceleration forces applied to the body -- appears to cause 93 percent of all driver injuries reported to NARI. Burns, either from fire or contact with hot materials, are responsible for 4.3 percent of driver injuries. Illnesses -- from heat, seizures, nausea and fainting -- account for less than 1 percent.

Collisions were cited in nearly three-quarters (72.4 percent) of all driver injuries in racing. Crashes involving walls were listed as factors in 28.1 percent of the accident reports filed from 1987 through 1991. Crashes involving other race cars were listed on 23.2 percent of reports; collisions with berms and dirt embankments on 1.4 percent of reports; and collisions with tire barriers on 0.7 percent of accidents. Another 19 percent of the reports listed collisions, crashes or accidents but did not specify the objects contacted. (Because multiple factors may be listed in one accident report, the percentages do not round to 100 percent when totalled.)

Collisions with fixed barriers were involved in 66 percent of 175 accidents studied in the SCCA Southeast Division by Dr. Timms. These accidents accounted for 80 percent of 41 injuries sustained during races held in 1984 and 1985.

A review of the 29 driver fatalities reported in National Speed Sport News from 1989-1991 show that these incidents involved 11 collisions with walls; 8 collisions with other cars; 4 unspecified collisions; three accidents involving roll-overs; one accident in which debris was thrown into a car; 1 collision with a deer; and one unspecified crash.

Vehicle rollovers were cited in 20.5 percent of driver injuries in the NARI files. The files do not reflect roll-overs that occurred without injury. Spins were mentioned in 5.6 percent of injury reports filed with NARI.

In Dr. Timms' study, roll-overs occurred in 49 of 175 accidents but were implicated in only 14 injuries, none considered serious.

Driver contact with objects or surfaces within the car were specifically cited on 2.8 percent of the NARI reports, but this number is probably far lower than the actual occurrence.

Cars leaving the track, sometimes over walls but more often over unguarded embankments, were offered as accident factors on 2.0 percent of the reports. Debris hurled into a car -- often rocks and mud clods -- caused 2.4 percent of driver injuries.

Mechanical failures contributed to 10.1 percent of the accidents in the NARI files. Cars stalling (16.2 percent), engine failures (15.7 percent) and steering malfunctions (12.4 percent) were at the top of the list. Radiator, radiator cap and radiator hose failures, which caused the majority of burns suffered by drivers, were listed on 9.6 percent of the reports. Throttle problems were fifth in frequency at 9.0 percent. A number of other items caused cars to stall or lose control. Some mechanical failures caused components to leave cars and strike drivers. The remaining sources of mechanical failures were, in order of occurrence, body parts, axles/rear ends, wheels, tires, drive shafts, brakes, transmissions, suspensions and exhaust components.

A number of the injury reports suggest that some race cars should not have been permitted on the track. The tales include floor pans falling out of cars, roll bar welds breaking in collisions, a roll cage that completely collapsed and one car that was constructed so the driver's leg was able to touch an exhaust pipe during a spin.

George England of North American Racing Insurance believes many race tracks and sanctioning bodies could do more to promote the safety of race cars. "Every track should have good tech inspectors. And the sport is taking steps, such as through workshops, to produce better tech inspectors," he said. "I would like to see the tech inspections emphasizing safety as well as looking for illegal items."

Loss of car control was cited on 4.0 percent of the reports filed with NARI. Driver error probably contributes to far more crashes than indicated in these statistics, however.

Driver error is believed to contribute to about 70 percent of road and highway accidents. A research report prepared two decades ago by the Jim Clark Foundation, "Grand Prix Accident Survey: 1966-1972," examined 224 Formula 1 accidents during seven racing seasons. Even at the highest level of the sport driver error was believed the cause of 48.6 percent of accidents.

Dr. Michael Henderson, author of <u>Motor Racing in Safety: The Human Factors</u>, studied 277 crashes in 200 race meets during 1967 in Great Britain. He found that drivers, through their own errors, are responsible for 52 percent of accidents in which they are involved. Another 25 percent of the drivers involved in accidents could blame the errors of other drivers.

Eternal safety vigilance is required from all of those who drive or prepare race cars. At the upper levels of the sport vehicle speeds range from 200 m.p.h. to 300 m.p.h. on any given Sunday. In amateur classes even the crudest racing machines reach 60 to 100 m.p.h. Meanwhile, decades of research into passenger automobile safety has proven that impacts at speeds as slow as 35 m.p.h. can be fatal.

What Gets Hurt?

The NECK is clearly the body part most often injured, being listed on 31.5 percent of incident reports. Centrifugal forces and whiplash strains encountered in collisions and rollovers probably are responsible for the large incidence of neck injuries. Neck injuries are slightly more common in enduro and street stock classes than the overall average. This may be due to the lack of high-backed racing seats and neck collars, both of which minimize neck movements during impacts.

In the analysis of SCCA races performed by Dr. Timms, neck injuries accounted for seven of 41 injuries (17 percent) sustained.

A new type of safety device that can help prevent neck and head injuries, called HANS for "Head and Neck Support," has been developed by Biomechanical Design Inc. of East Lansing, Mich. Robert P. Hubbard, Ph.D., is vice president of engineering for the firm and professor of biomechanics at Michigan State University. According to data provided to Hubbard by K&K Insurance Group Inc., neck injuries accounted in 1990 for 10 to 13 percent of all stock car injuries reported; 2 to 3 percent of road course injuries; 8 to 12 percent of demolition derby injuries; and 2 to 4 percent of drag racing injuries.

The BACK is the second most-injured part of the body, representing 19.5 percent of all NARI reports. Centrifugal forces pulling at the head and arms probably are responsible. Impact forces transmitted into the driver compartment also may be at fault, as three small classes of cars experience the highest percentages of back injuries. According to the data, 28.6 percent of all minisprint incidents, 21.6 percent of all modified incidents and 19.2 percent of all midget incidents result in complaints of back pain or injury. These types of cars are likely to have small, tight driver compartments which do not have a lot of "crush" room between drivers and the cruel outside world. Back injuries accounted for 12 percent of the injuries found by Dr. Timms in his SCCA analysis.

HEAD injuries, making up 15.8 percent of all diagnoses, are third on the list. Head injuries may be caused by impact of the head against roll bars, steering wheels, debris thrown into cars or other objects within or outside of the car. Head and brain injuries also can result from severe centrifugal forces which exert shearing movements upon the brain or cause the brain to impact the interior surface of the skull even in the absence of contact to the head.

Minisprints (23.8 percent of all injuries for the class) and enduro cars (23.5 percent of injuries) are at the top of the head injury frequency list. This may again be due to the lack of proper racing seats and other safety equipment which minimize head movement during accidents. Sprint cars also created a higher-than-average percentage of head injuries -- 22.9 percent. In this case, the high power-to-weight ratio of the cars and the particular violence of tumbles may be the cause.

The SHOULDER, cited on 14.2 percent of reports, came in fourth on the injury frequency list. Centrifugal forces and side impacts probably are the cause. The shoulder injury average for all classes was surpassed by modifieds (16.1 percent of all class injuries) and ministocks (16.0 percent), possibly due to close quarters within the driver compartment and proximity to the left outside of the car. Figure 8 cars produced a 15.4-percent shoulder injury rate, in this case probably due both to left side impacts and inadequate seats, safety equipment and side protection.

Even when the torso is belted securely into an adequately anchored seat, momentum forces can cause the extremities and head to be flung about and strike objects within -- or outside -- the car. For these reasons, the extremities also rank highly in the NARI sample: Leg (10.1 percent); knee (9.1 percent); foot (3.4 percent); ankle (3.1 percent); arm (8.0 percent); hand (7.5 percent); and wrist (6.6 percent).

The driver's compartment of every car should be as free of potentially hazardous objects and surfaces as possible. High-quality, energy-absorbent padding must be placed on any surfaces which the head or extremities may contact.

A variety of factors contribute to injuries affecting the ribs (9.3 percent of injuries) and chest (4.9 percent). These include impacts in the driver's door; centrifugal forces hurling the body against the seat or belts; and impact with objects within the car.

Types of Injuries

What types of injuries are incurred? Due to the preliminary nature of many of the reports studied, descriptions such as "pain" and "soreness" were most often mentioned. When specific or suspected diagnoses were given, the most common injuries were fractures (20.4 percent) and bruises (12.8 percent). Both represent impact causes.

Third in frequency (at 7.2 percent) was an injury the authors categorized as "wheelwhip" -- strain exerted on the arms, hands or wrists when steering wheels spin violently during collisions. These injuries, which can be severely painful and disabling, could be largely prevented by the use of spoke-less, dish-type steering wheels or by a using a hand position which keeps the thumbs on top of, rather than inside, the steering wheel.

Rounding out the list of most common injuries were lacerations (7.0 percent); concussions (5.4 percent); sprains (5.4 percent); and burns (4.3 percent). Loss of consciousness was cited in 3.7 percent of driver injuries.

Fatalities resulted from 0.5 percent of the driver incidents reported to NARI during the period examined. About one-third of these involved heart attacks which may have caused, rather than followed, accidents on the track. Heart attacks accounted for 0.1 percent of all incidents in which drivers required medical attention.

Three of the 29 driver fatalities reported in <u>National Speed Sport News</u> from 1989-1991 involved heart attacks; in another the driver died of a stroke the day after a crash which left him apparently uninjured.

Where Do Injuries Occur?

Not surprisingly, most injury-producing accidents (for which an on-track location was cited) occurred in the turns -- 66.7 percent. The straights on oval tracks hosted 30.9 percent of injury-producing accidents. Another 0.4 percent of driver injuries occurred in the pits after race cars lost control or were driven at excessive speeds in them. The remaining two percent of accidents in the total sample occurred at the center intersection of figure-8 tracks.

Driver Injuries by Type of Race Car

The statistics offer insights, some predictable and others surprising, into the accidents experienced in different classes of racing.

As might be expected, open wheel cars are more likely to get airborne and flip than full-bodied cars. While 20.5 percent of all incidents involved flips, 61.8 percent of midget, 52.4 percent of minisprint, 46.5 percent of sprint car and 25.3 percent of supermodified accidents included a rollover. The higher-level late models and stock cars, likely to be the most mechanically reliable cars driven by more experienced chauffeurs, rolled over in 13.8 percent of their accidents.

Open wheel formula cars were involved in 50 percent of the 30 injury-producing accidents in 12 amateur road races held at the Mid-Ohio and Waterford Hills, Mich., tracks during a nine-year period, according to research by M.A. Boitano, M.D. ("Driver Injuries in Auto Road Racing," <u>The Physician and Sportsmedicine</u>, August 1985). While the article did not provide data on the numbers of full-bodied vs. formula cars that participated, the statistics suggest that fendered cars may be able to tolerate a little more rubbing and banging than open wheel cars.

Another foreseeable finding was that the less-sophisticated, or "entry-level," classes of cars encounter more mechanical failures, which were cited in 10.1 percent of all reports. Demo derby (22.2 percent), enduro (14.2 percent) and street stocks (10.8 percent) exceeded the over-all average for mechanical causes of injuries. On the other hand, so did supermodifieds (13.8 percent), sprint cars

(13.6 percent) and modifieds (11.4 percent).

There could be debate over the relative safety and danger of different classes of race cars. Which cause the more serious injuries, the faster, better-prepared cars or the slower, less well-constructed cars? The answer appears to be "both." Both the high-tech and low-tech cars exceed overall averages for the more serious injuries (fractures, concussions, whiplash and dislocations).

In the total sample, fractures averaged 20.4 percent of all injuries. Fractures made up 42.3 percent of all demolition derby injuries, 29.4 percent of all figure-eight injuries, 25.0 percent of all ministock injuries and 21.5 percent of all street stock injuries. But sprint cars (27.4 percent) and stock cars (21.6 percent) also had higher-than-average proportions of fractures, probably due to the greater speeds being traveled when accidents occur.

About 5.4 percent of all injuries involved concussions. This average was surpassed by the lightning-fast sprint cars (16.5 percent) and supermodifieds (7.8 percent) as well as the humble street stocks (5.5 percent).

The survey average for whiplash was 1.9 percent. This average was topped by supermodifieds (3.1 percent) as well as enduro (5.1 percent), ministocks (3.9 percent), street stocks (3.1 percent) and sportsman stocks (2.2 percent).

The 1.6-percent average for dislocations was exceeded by sprint cars (2.4 percent), stock cars and supermodifieds (both at 1.6 percent) as well as the entry-level classes of figure 8 (5.9 percent), sportsman (2.2 percent) and street stocks (1.7 percent).

Because of the small size of some groups of cars in the sample and the lack of numbers on cars that participated in each class, a valid comparison of fatality rates is not judged possible. The percentages are listed for review, however.

The 29 driver fatalities reported in National Speed Sport News from 1989-1991 involved stock cars, 8; supermodifieds, 4; midgets, 3; modifieds, 3; sports cars (road racing), 2; street stocks, 2; sprint cars, 2; off-road truck, 1; hill climb, 1; and not specified, 3.

Injuries in the Pits

The typical pit/paddock injury is a cut, burn or fracture of the arm or hand suffered while working on a car. Falls over or off of things also are common as are, unfortunately, people getting struck by cars and trucks.

Lacerations (36.8 percent), burns (23.8 percent) and fractures

(14.3 percent) led the list of injuries suffered in the pits or on the track by non-drivers. Those were followed by sprains (7.2 percent), bruises (6.4 percent) and abrasions (1.4 percent).

Fingers and thumbs accounted for 14.0 percent of wounds, followed by arms (12.8 percent), hands (12.2 percent), legs (11.1 percent) and the face (10.6 percent).

About one in five pit injuries (21.6 percent) occur while the victim is working on a car. Many are burns resulting from the regrettable and inexcusable act of removing a radiator cap while an engine is overheated. Falls (15.7 percent), being struck by vehicles (15.5 percent) and mechanical failures (15.2 percent) each comprised about one in six pit incidents. Often the people struck by vehicles are on the race track itself, either officials who should be more careful on the track or pit crew people who have no business being on the track.

Debris thrown into the pits from the track causes 10.2 percent of injuries while crashes are linked to 3.2 percent of infield injuries. These point to the need for better protection or isolation of pit areas.

Fights lead to 2.1 percent of pit injuries. People running through the pits, especially onto the race track to gawk at accidents, are cited in 1.9 percent of pit incidents.

Many pit medical incidents result from illness rather than accidents. The reports included heart attacks and heat illness (both 1.0 percent of all pit medical calls), fainting and seizures (both 0.2 percent of all reports). One of two pit fatalities found in the NARI data involved a heart attack. The other fatality was suffered by a track official who was struck by a race car while standing on the track during a caution period.

Spectator Injuries

Is it hazardous to be seated in bleachers near a speedway with those fast-moving race cars so close at hand? Somewhat, but actually it is more dangerous to walk up and down those bleachers.

Slips and falls were listed in nearly 6 of 10 spectator injuries (58.1 percent) reported to NARI. About one in four audience injuries (24.2 percent) are linked to debris thrown from the track or by other people in the stands. Rocks and mud clods are mentioned most often. About 6.5 percent of injured spectators are struck by moving vehicles, either racing machines striking walls and fences in front of them or cars and trucks moving in parking lots.

Grandstands or other viewing areas were the location of 89.3 percent of spectator incidents. These numbers point out the need to do everything possible to make grandstands safer (especially to prevent bleachers from becoming slick when wet or covered with dew) and to keep spectators at safe distances back from track fences and retaining walls.

Smaller numbers of spectator injuries were incurred in parking lots (6.1 percent), concession areas (2.7 percent) and rest rooms (1.9 percent).

Two-thirds of spectator fatalities resulted from people standing next to guard rail fences when the walls were struck by race cars. The other one-third of spectator fatalities occurred in parking lots. In one instance, a spectator died after falling from the back of a pickup truck he was riding across the parking lot to his car. All the spectator fatalities could have been avoided.

Most spectator injuries are minor. Lacerations (38.0 percent) and bruises (17.9 percent) are most common. Those are followed by fractures (16.6 percent), sprains (8.5 percent) and abrasions (5.8 percent). The injuries most often involve the head and face (both at 17.8 percent), legs (14.6 percent), ankles (12.9 percent), arms (8.0 percent) and back (7.7 percent).

Many of spectator medical calls result from illnesses. Heart attacks, fainting, seizures, dizziness and asthma each accounted for about 0.9 percent of spectator cases. Heat illness and nausea each made up about 0.4 percent of the sample.

About 2.3 percent of incidents which injured spectators involved fights.

MOTORSPORTS INJURY DATA, 1987-1991
NORTH AMERICAN RACING INSURANCE
PRELIMINARY INCIDENT REPORTS
Due to multiple injuries and causes in individual incidents, totals can exceed 100%.

DRIVER INJURY DIAGNOSIS:

Pain	29.4%
Fractures	20.4%
Bruises	12.8%
"Wheelwhip"	7.2%
Lacerations	7.0%
Concussion	5.4%
Sprains	5.4%
Burns	4.3%
Lost consciousness	3.7%
"Shaken"	2.8%
Abrasions	2.2%
Whiplash	1.9%
Dizziness	1.8%
Dislocations	1.6%
Swelling	1.1%
Fatality	0.5%
Heat illness	0.3%
Heart Attack	0.1%
Seizure	0.1%
Nausea	0.1%
Lost memory	0.1%
Fainting	0.1%

ACCIDENT FACTORS AND CAUSES CITED

Crashes, all	72.4%
Crash with wall	28.1%
Crash with car/cars	23.2%
Crash, not explained	19.0%
Crash with dirt berm	1.4%
Crash w/ tire barriers	0.7%
Flip/Rollover	20.5%
Mechanical failure	10.1%
Spin	5.6%
Loss of control	4.0%
Driver contact with object(s) within car	2.8%
Driver struck by debris	2.4%
Car left track	2.0%

DRIVER INJURIES:
PARTS OF BODY INJURED

Neck	31.5%
Back	19.5%
Head	15.8%
Shoulder	14.2%
Leg	10.1%
Ribs	9.3%
Knee	9.1%
Arm	8.0%
Hand	7.5%
Wrist	6.6%
Chest	.9%
Foot	3.4%
Ankle	3.1%
Thumb	2.9%
Finger	2.7%
Eye	2.7%
Face	2.6%
Elbow	2.3%
Hip	1.9%
Nose	0.7%
Collarbone	0.7%
Groin	0.6%
Teeth	0.5%
Toes	0.3%
Lung	0.3%
Heart	0.3%
Tongue	0.2%
Jaw	0.2%
Ear	0.2%
Abdomen	0.1%

LOCATION OF ACCIDENTS
CAUSING DRIVER INJURIES

Turns	66.7%
Straights	30.9%
Pit	0.4%
X (Crossing of Figure 8)	2.0%

UNDERSTANDING RACING INJURIES

MECHANICAL FACTORS CITED IN RACING INJURIES:

"Stall" unspecified	16.2%	Wheel	6.2%
Engine	15.7%	Tire	3.8%
Steering	12.4%	Driveshaft	2.9%
Radiator	9.6%	Brakes	1.9%
Throttle	9.0%	Transmission	1.9%
Body	7.1%	Suspension	0.5%
Axle/Rearend	6.7%	Exhaust	0.5%

PIT INJURY DIAGNOSIS

Lacerations	36.8%
Burns	23.8%
Fractures	14.3%
Sprains	7.2%
Bruises	6.4%
Pain	3.1%
Abrasions	1.4%
Heart attacks	1.0%
Concussions	1.0%
Heat illness	1.0%
Heart injury	1.0%
Dislocations	0.6%
Swelling	0.6%
Fatalities	0.3%
Head injury	0.3%
Internal injury	0.3%
Loss of memory	0.2%
Fainting	0.2%
Seizure	0.2%
Hospitalized	0.2%
Shaken	0.2%
Dizziness	0.2%

PIT INJURY CAUSES CITED

Working on car	21.6%
Falls	15.7%
Struck by vehicle	15.5%
Mechanical failure	15.2%
Cuts	12.0%
Thrown debris	10.2%
Crashes	3.2%
Fights	2.1%
Running	1.9%
Heat illness	1.1%
Heart attacks	0.9%

PIT INJURIES: PARTS OF BODY INJURED

Finger/Thumb	14.0%
Arm	12.8%
Hand	12.2%
Leg	11.1%
Face	10.6%
Head	6.7%
Knee	6.4%
Ankle	6.0%
Eye	6.0%
Wrist	5.5%
Back	5.3%
Chest	4.7%
Neck	3.8%
Shoulder	3.6%
Foot	3.1%
Ribs	2.2%
Elbow	1.8%
Abdomen	1.8%
Hip	1.5%
Lung	0.9%
Heart	0.9%
Nose	0.7%
Collarbone	0.7%
Toe	0.7%
Groin	0.4%
Tongue	0.2%
Tooth	0.2%
Jaw	0.2%
Ear	0.2%

DIAGNOSIS OF SPECTATOR INJURIES

Lacerations	38.0%
Bruises	17.9%
Fractures	16.6%
Sprains	8.5%
Pain	7.6%
Abrasions	5.8%
Dislocations	1.3%
Burns	1.3%
Loss consciousness	1.3%
Concussion	1.3%
Fatality	1.3%
Hospitalized	1.3%
Shaken	1.3%
Heart attack	0.9%
Swelling	0.9%
Fainting	0.9%
Seizures	0.9%
Heart injury	0.9%
Dizziness	0.9%
Asthma attack	0.9%
Trauma	0.9%
Loss memory	0.4%
Heat illness	0.4%
Nausea	0.4%
Miscellaneous illness	0.4%

SPECTATOR INJURIES: PARTS OF BODY INJURED

Head	17.8%
Face	17.8%
Leg	14.6%
Ankle	12.9%
Arm	8.0%
Back	7.7%
Hand	4.5%
Hip	4.5%
Shoulder	4.2%
Knee	3.8%
Nose	3.8%
Ribs	3.1%
Wrist	2.4%
Eye	2.4%
Neck	2.4%
Foot	2.1%
Finger/Thumb	2.1%
Chest	1.7%
Elbow	1.4%
Abdomen	1.0%
Mouth	0.7%
Heart	0.7%
Tongue	0.7%
Teeth	0.7%
Jaw	0.3%
Collarbone	0.3%
Groin	0.3%

FACTORS CITED IN SPECTATOR INJURIES

Falls or slips	58.1%
Struck by debris	24.2%
Struck by vehicles	6.5%
Mechanical failures (race cars)	3.2%
Fights	2.3%
Crashes on track	1.9%
Accidents while running	1.6%
Heat illness	0.6%
Heart attack	0.6%
Miscellaneous bumps	0.6%

LOCATION OF ACCIDENTS CAUSING SPECTATOR INJURIES

Grandstands, bleachers or viewing areas	89.3%
Parking lots	6.1%
Concession areas	2.7%
Restrooms	1.9%

UNDERSTANDING RACING INJURIES

AGE DISTRIBUTION
OF INJURED DRIVERS

Under 20	7.6%
20-24	19.0%
25-29	25.9%
30-34	20.2%
35-39	14.4%
40-44	6.2%
45-49	3.5%
50-54	2.1%
55-59	0.8%
60-64	0.2%
65 and over	0.2%

AGE DISTRIBUTION
OF INJURED IN PIT AREAS

Under 15	0.9%
15-19	10.7%
20-24	18.8%
25-29	24.9%
30-34	14.5%
35-39	7.6%
40-44	9.3%
45-49	4.0%
50-54	5.0%
55-59	2.8%
60-64	0.7%
65 and over	0.7%

AGE DISTRIBUTION OF INJURED SPECTATORS

Under 5	11.3%	40-44	7.0%
5-9	14.8%	45-49	3.1%
10-14	9.0%	50-54	3.1%
15-19	9.0%	55-59	2.3%
20-24	7.4%	60-64	3.1%
25-29	12.1%	65-69	2.7%
30-34	4.7%	70 and over	4.3%
35-39	5.9%		

OCCURENCE OF RACING ACCIDENT FACTORS BY CAR TYPE
(Percentage of Each Class' Reports Listing Each Factor)

CRASHES INVOLVING WALLS
(Percentage of class reports)

Sportsman	34.5%
Ministock	32.3%
Modified	32.2%
Supermodified	32.2%
Stock car	30.4%
Sprint	29.8%
Midget	29.4%
TOTAL SAMPLE	28.1%
Street stock	26.4%
Minisprint	9.6%
Enduro	8.9%
Figure 8	7.4%
Demo	0.0%

CRASHES WITH OTHER CARS
(Percentage of class reports)

Figure 8	85.2%
Demo	55.0%
Enduro	46.1%
Ministock	37.4%
Modified	32.3%
Midget	23.5%
TOTAL SAMPLE	23.2%
Street stock	22.7%
Supermodified	19.5%
Minisprint	19.1%
Stock cars	17.1%
Sportsman	12.0%
Sprint	10.6%

CRASHES NOT DESCRIBED
(Percentage of class reports)

Enduro	28.3%
Stock cars	21.3%
Sportsman	20.7%
Ministock	20.2%
TOTAL SAMPLE	19.0%
Modified	17.3%
Supermodified	17.2%
Street stock	16.6%
Minisprint	14.4%
Sprint	14.1%
Midget	5.9%
Figure 8	3.7%
Demo	0.0%

FLIPS AND ROLLOVERS
(Percentage of class reports)

Midget	61.8%
Minisprint	52.4%
Sprint	46.5%
Supermodified	25.3%
TOTAL SAMPLE	20.5%
Street stock	19.9%
Sportsman	19.8%
Modified	18.6%
Ministock	16.1%
Enduro	14.1%
Stock cars	13.9%
Figure 8	0.0%
Demo	0.0%

CRASHES INVOLVING BERMS
(Percentage of class reports)

Minisprint	4.8%
Street stock	4.3%
Enduro	3.5%
Midget	2.9%
Stock cars	2.7%
TOTAL SAMPLE	1.4%
Modified	1.4%
Supermodified	1.1%
Ministock	0.0%
Sprint	0.0%
Sportsman	0.0%
Figure 8	0.0%
Demo	0.0%

CRASHES: TIRE BARRIERS
(Percentage of class reports)

Street stock	1.3%
Ministock	1.0%
Sprint	1.0%
Sportsman	0.9%
Modified	0.9%
TOTAL SAMPLE	0.7%
Stock cars	0.4%
Enduro	0.0%
Supermodified	0.0%
Midget	0.0%
Minisprint	0.0%
Figure 8	0.0%
Demo	0.0%

SPINS
(Percentage of class reports)

Sportsman	13.8%
Modified	12.6%
Ministock	11.1%
Supermodified	6.8%
Street stock	6.3%
TOTAL SAMPLE	5.6%
Minisprint	4.8%
Stock cars	4.4%
Enduro	4.4%
Sprint	4.0%
Midget	2.9%
Figure 8	0.0%
Demo	0.0%

MECHANICAL FAILURES
(Percentage of class reports)

Demo	22.2%
Enduro	14.2%
Supermodified	13.8%
Sprint	13.6%
Modified	11.4%
Street stock	10.8%
TOTAL SAMPLE	10.1%
Minisprint	9.6%
Stock cars	8.6%
Sportsman	8.6%
Ministock	7.1%
Midget	2.9%
Figure 8	0.0%

LOSS OF CAR CONTROL
(Percentage of class reports)

Minisprint	9.6%
Sprint	6.1%
Street stock	6.0%
Ministock	5.0%
Supermodified	4.6%
Modified	4.5%
TOTAL SAMPLE	4.0%
Stock cars	3.1%
Midget	2.9%
Enduro	0.9%
Sportsman	0.9%
Figure 8	0.0%
Demo	0.0%

DRIVER STRUCK BY DEBRIS
(Percentage of class reports)

Demo	11.0%
Supermodified	9.2%
Stock cars	5.2%
Figure 8	3.7%
Midget	2.9%
Modified	2.7%
Enduro	2.6%
TOTAL SAMPLE	2.4%
Sprint	2.0%
Sportsman	1.7%
Street stock	0.5%
Ministock	0.0%
Minisprint	0.0%

DRIVER CONTACT WITH OBJECT IN CAR
(Percentage of class reports)

Enduro	7.1%
Ministock	5.0%
Modified	5.0%
Supermodified	3.4%
Sportsman	3.4%
TOTAL SAMPLE	2.8%
Stock cars	2.3%
Sprint	2.0%
Street stock	0.5%
Midget	0.0%
Minisprint	0.0%
Figure 8	0.0%
Demo	0.0%

CAR LEFT TRACK
(Percentage of class reports)

Minisprint	4.8%
Street stock	3.3%
Midget	2.9%
Stock cars	2.2%
TOTAL SAMPLE	2.0%
Sportsman	1.8%
Enduro	1.7%
Modified	1.4%
Supermodified	1.1%
Sprint	1.0%
Ministock	0.0%
Figure 8	0.0%
Demo	0.0%

DRIVER INJURY DIAGNOSES BY RACE CAR TYPE

FRACTURES
(Percentage of class reports)

Demo	42.3%
Figure 8	29.4%
Sprint	27.4%
Ministock	25.0%
Stock cars	21.6%
Street stock	21.5%
TOTAL SAMPLE	20.4%
Sportsman	20.0%
Midget	19.2%
Supermodified	17.2%
Modified	15.2%
Enduro	8.2%
Minisprint	6.7%

LACERATIONS
(Percentage of class reports)

Minisprint	20.0%
Stock cars	9.9%
Ministock	7.9%
Modified	7.6%
Sprint	7.3%
TOTAL SAMPLE	7.0%
Supermodified	6.2%
Figure 8	5.9%
Sportsman	5.6%
Midget	3.8%
Street stock	3.5%
Enduro	0.0%
Demo	0.0%

BRUISES
(Percentage of class reports)

Figure 8	35.3%
Midget	19.2%
Sprint	18.3%
Stock cars	13.7%
Modified	12.9%
TOTAL SAMPLE	12.8%
Supermodified	12.5%
Street stock	10.8%
Enduro	9.3%
Ministock	9.2%
Sportsman	7.8%
Minisprint	6.7%
Demo	0.0%

CONCUSSIONS
(Percentage of class reports)

Sprint	16.5%
Supermodified	7.8%
Street stock	5.5%
TOTAL SAMPLE	5.4%
Stock cars	4.8%
Ministock	3.9%
Midget	3.8%
Modified	2.9%
Sportsman	1.1%
Enduro	1.0%
Minisprint	0.0%
Figure 8	0.0%
Demo	0.0%

WHEELWHIP
(Percentage of class reports)

Stock cars	13.7%
Street stock	10.4%
TOTAL SAMPLE	7.2%
Enduro	6.2%
Sportsman	4.4%
Modified	1.8%
Ministock	1.3%
Sprint	0.6%
Supermodified	0.0%
Midget	0.0%
Minisprint	0.0%
Figure 8	0.0%
Demo	0.0%

SPRAINS
(Percentage of class reports)

Ministock	7.9%
Stock cars	7.2%
Minisprint	6.7%
Figure 8	5.9%
TOTAL SAMPLE	5.4%
Modified	5.3%
Street stock	5.2%
Sportsman	4.4%
Midget	3.8%
Sprint	3.7%
Supermodified	1.6%
Enduro	1.0%
Demo	0.0%

UNDERSTANDING RACING INJURIES

BURNS
(Percentage of class reports)

Demo	28.6%
Supermodified	14.1%
Sprint	7.9%
Sportsman	7.8%
Midget	7.7%
TOTAL SAMPLE	4.3%
Modified	4.1%
Enduro	3.1%
Ministock	2.6%
Stock cars	2.4%
Street stock	2.4%
Minisprint	0.0%
Figure 8	0.0%

WHIPLASH
(Percentage of class reports)

Enduro	5.1%
Ministock	3.9%
Supermodified	3.1%
Street stock	3.1%
Sportsman	2.2%
TOTAL SAMPLE	1.9%
Modified	1.8%
Stock cars	1.0%
Sprint	0.0%
Midget	0.0%
Minisprint	0.0%
Figure 8	0.0%
Demo	0.0%

LOSS OF CONSCIOUSNESS
(Percentage of class reports)

Minisprint	26.7%
Figure 8	5.9%
Street stock	4.2%
Midget	3.8%
Sprint	3.7%
TOTAL SAMPLE	3.7%
Modified	3.5%
Stock cars	3.4%
Sportsman	3.3%
Enduro	3.1%
Supermodified	1.6%
Ministock	1.3%
Demo	0.0%

DISLOCATIONS
(Percentage of class reports)

Figure 8	5.9%
Sprint	2.4%
Sportsman	2.2%
Street stock	1.7%
Stock cars	1.6%
Supermodified	1.6%
TOTAL SAMPLE	1.6%
Enduro	1.0%
Modified	0.6%
Ministock	0.0%
Midget	0.0%
Minisprint	0.0%
Demo	0.0%

ABRASIONS
(Percentage of class reports)

Figure 8	11.8%
Sportsman	5.6%
Ministock	3.9%
Midget	3.8%
Sprint	3.0%
TOTAL SAMPLE	2.2%
Enduro	2.1%
Stock cars	1.6%
Supermodified	1.6%
Modified	1.2%
Street stock	1.0%
Minisprint	0.0%
Demo	0.0%

FATALITIES
(Percentage of class reports)

Midget	5.40%
Sportsman	1.10%
Sprint	0.90%
TOTAL SAMPLE	0.50%
Modified	0.40%
Stock cars	0.25%
Ministock	0.00%
Enduro	0.00%
Supermodified	0.00%
Street stock	0.00%
Minisprint	0.00%
Figure 8	0.00%
Demo	0.00%

MOST COMMONLY INJURED PARTS OF BODY BY RACE CAR TYPE

NECK
(Percentage of class reports)
Enduro	33.9%
Street stock	32.6%
TOTAL SAMPLE	31.5%
Minisprint	28.6%
Modified	26.7%
Stock cars	26.2%
Ministock	25.0%
Supermodified	23.6%
Figure 8	23.1%
Sportsman	21.8%
Sprint	16.0%
Midget	11.5%
Demo	0.0%

SHOULDER
(Percentage of class reports)
Modified	16.1%
Ministock	16.0%
Figure 8	15.4%
TOTAL SAMPLE	14.2%
Sprint	13.3%
Street stock	12.8%
Stock cars	11.6%
Midget	11.5%
Sportsman	11.3%
Demo	9.0%
Supermodified	5.9%
Minisprint	4.8%
Enduro	3.5%

BACK
(Percentage of class reports)
Minisprint	28.6%
Modified	21.6%
TOTAL SAMPLE	19.5%
Midget	19.2%
Street stock	17.0%
Stock cars	16.0%
Ministock	16.0%
Sportsman	14.5%
Sprint	13.8%
Supermodified	13.0%
Enduro	12.2%
Figure 8	11.6%
Demo	9.0%

LEG
(Percentage of class reports)
Midget	15.4%
Figure 8	15.4%
Supermodified	15.3%
Sportsman	11.3%
Modified	10.2%
TOTAL SAMPLE	10.1%
Ministock	10.0%
Minisprint	9.6%
Sprint	8.5%
Stock cars	8.2%
Enduro	6.1%
Street stock	5.8%
Demo	0.0%

HEAD
(Percentage of class reports)
Minisprint	23.8%
Enduro	23.5%
Sprint	22.9%
TOTAL SAMPLE	15.8%
Supermodified	15.3%
Street stock	13.0%
Modified	12.7%
Midget	11.5%
Stock cars	11.1%
Ministock	10.0%
Sportsman	9.7%
Figure 8	7.7%
Demo	0.0%

RIBS
(Percentage of class reports)
Demo	18.1%
Ministock	14.0%
Sportsman	9.7%
TOTAL SAMPLE	9.3%
Modified	8.9%
Street stock	8.8%
Enduro	8.7%
Figure 8	7.7%
Stock cars	6.8%
Sprint	4.8%
Supermodified	4.7%
Midget	3.8%
Minisprint	0.0%

KNEE
(Percentage of class reports)

Minisprint	33.3%
Sportsman	17.7%
Figure 8	15.4%
Sprint	13.3%
Modified	10.6%
TOTAL SAMPLE	9.1%
Street stock	6.3%
Enduro	6.1%
Ministock	5.0%
Stock cars	4.6%
Midget	3.8%
Supermodified	3.5%
Demo	0.0%

WRIST
(Percentage of class reports)

Minisprint	9.6%
Stock cars	7.9%
TOTAL SAMPLE	6.6%
Street stock	6.5%
Sportsman	4.8%
Sprint	4.3%
Modified	3.4%
Ministock	2.0%
Enduro	1.7%
Supermodified	0.0%
Midget	0.0%
Figure 8	0.0%
Demo	0.0%

ARM
(Percentage of class reports)

Demo	27.2%
Midget	11.5%
Modified	8.1%
Ministock	8.0%
TOTAL SAMPLE	8.0%
Stock cars	7.7%
Supermodified	7.1%
Sprint	6.9%
Sportsman	4.8%
Street stock	4.5%
Enduro	3.5%
Minisprint	0.0%
Figure 8	0.0%

How much abuse can the human body tolerate? Understanding the mechanisms of trauma can help racers recognize and minimize the injury risks faced during their participation.

Chapter 17

UNDERSTANDING TRAUMA

"In relation to trauma it is important to recognize that, as the Harvard crash investigator, A.L. Moseley, once remarked, 'It's not speed which kills, it's the sudden stop.'"

-- Dr. Murray Mackay, Accident Research Unit, University of Birmingham, England

By medical definition, trauma is injury inflicted upon the body by external force or violence. More than nine of 10 injury-causing racing accidents involve collisions, flips and spins, all of which create impacts and sudden acceleration or deceleration forces that lead to trauma. Trauma can occur in three forms:

-- Penetrating trauma results when an object strikes and enters the body (or the body strikes the object and is entered).

-- Blunt trauma occurs when the body strikes or is struck by an object which causes compression and rupture of body tissues.

-- Acceleration/deceleration trauma occurs in the absence of external impact when the body experiences an abrupt change of motion which causes body tissues to stretch, separate or even strike internal bodily structures such as the ribs and skull lining. Whiplash is a common term applied to some of these injuries.

When a moving vehicle strikes something and comes to a stop, its occupants continue moving at the vehicle's pre-impact speed until they, too, come into contact with something -- preferably the safety harness.

Collisions are cited in nearly three-quarters (72.4 percent) of all driver injuries in racing, according to the North American Racing Insurance reports. Crashes involving walls were listed as factors in 28.1 percent of the accident reports filed from 1987 through 1991.

Crashes involving other cars were listed on 23.2 percent of reports; collisions with berms or dirt embankments on 1.4 percent of reports; and collisions with tire barriers on 0.7 percent of accidents. Another 19 percent of the reports listed collisions or crashes but did not specify objects contacted.

Vehicle rollovers were cited in 20.5 percent of driver injuries. Spins were mentioned 5.6 percent of the time. Even in the absence of severe impacts, these phenomena can precipitate whiplash-type injuries that can be serious.

Driver contact with objects or surfaces within the car were specifically cited on 2.8 percent of the reports but this number is probably far lower than the actual occurrence. Cars leaving the track, sometimes over walls or embankments, were offered as factors on 2.0 percent of the reports. Debris hurled into a car -- often rocks and mud clods -- caused 2.4 percent of driver injuries.

Gauging Impact Forces

The severity of trauma injury hinges upon the number of gravitational (or "G") forces the body experiences during impacts or sudden accelerations/decelerations. During violent flips, spins or collisions, the body can experience forces equal to many times the force of gravity and therefore many times its own weight.

When a crash causes a driver's head (about 10 pounds without helmet) to snap forward at 10 Gs, for example, the head briefly weighs 100 pounds and passes that strain on to the neck. The brain weighs about three pounds itself, so its delicate tissues may bang into the inside of the skull with a force of 30 pounds.

According to crash dummy tests undertaken by the developers of the HANS (Head and Neck Support) device, the head briefly experiences 25 Gs and a weight of about 250 pounds in a 35-mile-per-hour impact into a solid barrier. At that force, the delicate brain may strike the inside of the skull at a force equalling 75 pounds.

One G is equal to the force with which the earth pulls objects downward. Mathematically, one G equals the force which causes an object to accelerate at the rate of 32 feet per second per second. When a car corners at one G, for example, it is creating a sideways force equal to the gravitational force pulling it to the pavement.

Gravitational forces encountered in collisions are highly dependent, of course, on the speed at which a vehicle -- and, therefore, its driver -- are traveling at the moment of impact. A doubling of speed quadruples G forces.

The severity of deceleration also depends upon how suddenly the crashing car slows. If a race car crumples during a collision, strikes an object that "gives" or strikes at a glancing blow rather than head-on, the body experiences fewer Gs because deceleration stretches over many milliseconds, and hopefully seconds, rather than occurring instantly.

Sudden acceleration also can create multiple G loadings. This occurs, for example, when a stationary or nearly-stationary race car is hit by a faster-moving car, causing the occupant's body to be snapped in the direction of the hit.

To determine the number of G forces which result from a head-on collision, one multiplies the square of the vehicle's speed (in miles per hour) times .0333 and divides it by the stopping distance (in feet). The formula is:

$$Gs = .0333 \text{ X (M.P.H. X M.P.H.)} \div \text{(Distance)}.$$

The computation is slightly more complex when a moving race machine strikes something at an angle. Because the car is likely to encounter a glancing blow and continue moving, the kinetic energy present before impact is expended over a longer period of time and creates a lower peak G force. To portray the potential energy present at high -- or low -- racing speeds, the accompanying chart offers potential, worst-case G forces for head-on collisions.

Race cars that largely crush or disintegrate during crashes are less likely to transmit high G forces to the driver. This may explain the fatality reports found in National Speed Sports News from 1989 through 1991. Indy cars, which can currently reach 240 m.p.h. but disintegrate in collisions, were involved in no deaths.

"The primary reason why today's drivers are able to walk away from so many serious accidents is the car's deformable structure construction," wrote Rick Amabile in his book, Inside Indy Car Racing: 1990. "This type of aircraft construction dates back to the mid 1960s. Before then, race cars were constructed of tubular frames. Frame construction would lead to a much stronger car. When a car would crash, about 80% of the impact was felt by the driver. Today that number is just about the opposite at 20% on the driver, 80% on the car."

Full-bodied stock cars, by far the most numerous racing machines found in the U.S., accounted for 8 deaths from 1989 through 1991. Supermodifieds and modifieds were probably far less common but accounted for 7 deaths. Could their rigid chassis and relative lack of crushable body structures be contributing factors?

THEORETICAL POTENTIAL COLLISION "G" FORCES

In the real world many complex factors determine the actual deceleration forces experienced during a crash. For the sake of comparison, however, the following chart assumes theoretical, worst-case, head-on collisions, at a variety of speeds and deceleration distances resulting from vehicle crush and/or barrier displacement.

SPEED	STOPPING DISTANCE									
	1'	2'	3'	4'	5'	6'	7'	8'	9'	10'
50 mph	83G	42G	28G	21G	17G	14G	12G	11G	9G	8G
75 mph	187G	93G	62G	47G	37G	31G	27G	23G	21G	19G
100 mph	333G	166G	111G	83G	67G	55G	48G	42G	37G	33G

SPEED	STOPPING DISTANCE										
	1'	5'	10'	15'	20'	25'	30'	35'	40'	45'	50'
125 mph	520G	104G	52G	35G	26G	21G	17G	15G	13G	12G	10G
150 mph	749G	150G	75G	50G	37G	30G	25G	21G	19G	17G	15G
175 mph	1,020G	204G	102G	68G	51G	41G	34G	29G	25.5	23G	20G
200 mph	1,332G	266G	133G	89G	67G	53G	44G	38G	33G	30G	27G
225 mph	1,686G	337G	169G	112G	84G	67G	56G	48G	42G	37G	34G

SPEED	STOPPING DISTANCE										
	1'	10'	20'	30'	40'	50'	60'	70'	80'	90'	100'
250 mph	2,081G	208G	104G	69G	52G	42G	35G	30G	26G	23G	21G
275 mph	2,518G	252G	126G	84G	63G	50G	42G	36G	31G	28G	25G
300 mph	2,997G	300G	150G	100G	75G	60G	50G	43G	37G	33G	30G

Another factor in trauma is the integrity and spaciousness of the car's cockpit. If the car is constructed so that direct blows to the driver are avoided or minimized, serious injury is less likely to result.

The driver is also a factor in the risks of trauma injury. People who are more physically fit may be able to withstand more severe forces because their muscles and even their bones are stronger. The direction of impact also determines the chances of fracture. Because bones are shaped triangularly or elliptically rather than being perfectly round, either thicker or thinner cross-sections may receive the forces of blows.

Age can be a factor, too. Bones begin to decrease in density after about age 40, making fractures somewhat more likely. A study of shoulder belt loads applied to the chest found that people under 30 could withstand loads up to 1,650 pounds while the ribs of people over age 50 would start to fracture at 950 pounds of force. When compared to their tolerance against fracture during the ages of 20 to 39 years, the arm and leg bones fracture at 9.8 percent lighter bending forces during the 40s; 13.5 percent lighter forces during the 50s; and 16.7 percent lighter forces during the 60s. (See chart at end of chapter.) The bones of women, due generally to smaller size, fracture at lighter loads than the bones of men.

The occurrence of bone breaks also is dependent upon the length of exposure to force -- studies have found that the bones can withstand about 1.5 times as much energy in impacts lasting milliseconds than when loads are applied statically, as when a heavy object lands and remains on the bone.

The Biomechanics of Collision

Automotive safety engineers base their efforts on the theory that three distinct collisions occur during a crash. The first collision involves the vehicle and whatever it strikes. The second collision is between the human body and anything with which it makes contact -- roll bars, dash boards, pedals or seat belts.

The third collision occurs within the body as soft tissues (brain, muscle, organs) slam into skeletal tissue. During severe deceleration, brain injuries can result without impact to the head or driver's helmet because the skull comes to a stop briefly before the brain. The brain then strikes the interior of the skull in the direction of impact. Brain tissues and blood vessels can shear as they move and twist. While the skull itself can withstand hundreds of Gs, the brain may not.

Other internal organs can be injured during high-G impacts or decelerations. Organs can strike the ribs; ribs can compress onto organs; organ tissues and blood vessels can stretch and shear. And bones, of course, can be broken with or without impact.

How much force can the body withstand during a crash? That is a difficult question because so many variables are involved. Research has been shown that a 35-m.p.h. passenger-car crash will kill one in four occupants who are not restrained by seat belts. That should be sobering information to anyone who races. All race cars demand the best safety equipment available and that equipment needs to be installed and maintained properly.

Doug Gore explored trauma in the August 1990 issue of <u>Stock Car Racing</u> magazine:

> The National Highway Traffic Safety Administration crash tests new model passenger vehicles each year by propelling them at 35 m.p.h. into an immovable concrete barrier. These tests . . . typically show dummy deceleration forces in the range of 20 to 40 Gs spread over a time period of around 50 to 100 milliseconds, or 1/20th to 1/10th of a second.
>
> A 35-m.p.h. head-on crash may not sound bad to you but in reality it is. These relatively low speed (by racing standards) crashes typically result in the front ends of the crashed cars being deformed between 1-1/2' and 2-1/2' feet . . . At a deceleration of 40 Gs, a 160-pound driver is propelled forward against his seat belts with a force of 6400 pounds! . . . even at 35-m.p.h. impacts, good tight seat belts are required . . .
>
> At a deceleration rate of 40 Gs most adult skeletons can resist these forces without breaking. But at this same rate of deceleration, the human heart is at risk of suffering severe damage . . . the heart is not particularly well supported within the chest cavity. Since the walls of the heart must constantly move as they pump blood, they cannot be tightly connected to anything within the chest. The human heart basically hangs from the large blood vessels connected to it. Furthermore, when the heart is full of blood it is relatively heavy.
>
> Sudden high decelerations can result in forces which can literally tear open the heart's aorta, the large blood vessel

leading from the heart. The aorta is the heart's main support and once it's severed, the heart's owner perishes . . . Deceleration forces in the range of 40 to 50 Gs are often considered to be the limiting horizontal deceleration that a seated and well restrained human's heart can reliably survive without life-threatening damage. (Reprinted by permission)

To keep deceleration forces under 40 Gs, deceleration from 50 m.p.h. theoretically must occur over at least two feet; at 100 m.p.h. over at least eight feet; and at 200 m.p.h. over at least 33 feet.

40-G Stopping Distances, Head-On Collisions

50 mph	2'
75 mph	5'
100 mph	8'
125 mph	13'
150 mph	19'
175 mph	25'
200 mph	33'
225 mph	42'
250 mph	52'
275 mph	63'
300 mph	75'

In Gore's analysis of a fatal modified stock car crash, he estimated that the driver's body was subjected to 200 Gs.

A 1992 Indy-car crash into the concrete wall at a one-mile oval produced a 10.8-G deceleration as the car backed in and bounced off the wall at an estimated 170 m.p.h. At that force, the driver's head briefly weighed about 108 pounds and his heart about 7.5 pounds. According to telemetry on the car, the rebound off the wall subjected the driver to an instantaneous reverse force of 7.4 Gs. Nelson Piquet's 1992 Indianapolis Motor Speedway practice crash, which resulted in severe leg and foot injuries, reportedly produced 11 Gs.

While most cars have significant crush space at the front and rear, the sides of many race cars generally offer little or no structure that can absorb energy and lengthen deceleration. This lack of structure often causes side impacts to cause serious injuries and fatalities that would not have resulted from front or rear impacts imparting similar G forces. About one in five passenger-car collisions involves side impacts. Due to the lack of side crush material on many racing cars and the presence of rock-solid roll cages, the driver's body can receive a G-loading equal to nearly the total impact speed of the striking car.

Despite their spectacular appearance, roll-over accidents can be less dangerous than crashes during which a car remains upright. During a flip a car's momentum can be scrubbed off in small doses over a large distance, therefore limiting G forces. In violent "snap rolls" or flips accompanied by hard impacts against the ground, walls or other cars, of course, the car's inertia may not be burned off so gently.

The North American Racing Insurance reports analyzed for this book do not contain numbers on the roll-overs that occurred without injury. In a study of accidents occurring in the Southeast Division of the SCCA in 1984 and 1985, Dr. M. Rick Timms determined that injuries were associated with 14 of 49 reported roll-overs. None of those injuries were fatal or serious and only six were considered moderately serious. "This study indicates that roll-over is much less hazardous than barrier contact," he wrote in a paper presented to the International Council of Motorsports Sciences.

Head Injuries

Snell Foundation and SFI Foundation helmet certification tests are based on the theory that the head can briefly withstand 300-G forces. The head, due to neck movement and impacts during accidents, can encounter higher G forces than other parts of the body. The seriousness of head injuries depends upon head movements during impacts or decelerations, the duration of an incident and the total G forces experienced.

When the head is contacted directly, shock waves can be passed to the brain directly through the skull, which may or may not fracture. Shock waves may travel through the brain tissue and even rebound off the skull and pass through the brain several times. Distortion of the skull can cause fractures at locations other than the point of contact. Skull fractures may or may not be accompanied by brain injuries. Helmets are designed to distribute impact loads over a wide surface area of the skull to minimize the possibility of fracture and the forces transmitted to the brain.

Inertial forces can cause head injuries -- brain damage or skull fracture -- even without impact to the head. Brain tissues and blood vessels can be torn by inertia, especially if the head rotates while the G forces are experienced. In severe collisions, the weight of the head pulling at the neck can be sufficient to fracture the skull. These injuries, known as basilar skull fractures, can be quickly fatal.

The most common head injury is termed a "concussion" and is common in many sports. It results from a blow to the head or head-snapping deceleration that at least briefly disrupts brain function. The brain, a delicate organ that runs on billions of tiny electrochemical impulses, may only be momentarily stunned by a mild concussion. Moderate to severe concussions follow damage of brain tissues. The Committee of the Congress of Neurological Surgeons officials defines brain concussion as "a clinical syndrome characterized by immediate transient impairment of neural function such as alteration of consciousness, disturbances of vision, equilibrium, etc., due to mechanical forces."

-- A mild concussion causes no loss of consciousness or only a fleeting loss, making such an injury difficult to diagnose. The victim may have momentary difficulties in thinking, seeing, standing and/or moving with a sense of coordination. There may be a brief loss of memory. Sports medicine doctors practicing in other sports suggest that anyone who encounters a mild concussion should be kept out of competition and observed for 20 to 30 minutes. If the athlete remains alert and coherent and can recall events that happened before the injury, it may be safe to resume play. If the victim exhibits confusion, headache, disorientation or dizziness, a medical examination is required. The effects of concussions may be additive -- if a second concussion is experienced within a sports season, at least two weeks out of action are suggested. Statistically, it is believed that an athlete's odds of incurring a concussion increase four times after a first concussion is suffered. About half of all concussions are of the mild nature.

-- A moderate concussion is accompanied by a loss of consciousness lasting less than five minutes as well as amnesia that may arise 5 to 20 minutes after injury. Examination by a doctor is required; if the victim remains unconscious or disoriented for a longer period a neurological evaluation is needed. After a moderate concussion, if there are no signs of continuing symptoms, two weeks of layoff are suggested. If a second moderate concussion occurs during the same season the athlete should be held from competition for a month and then undergo neurological examination before returning to action. A doctor should determine the wisdom of finishing the season.

-- A severe concussion also involves a loss of consciousness and amnesia that may develop after the injury and last 12 hours or more. The length of amnesia may indicate the severity of the injury. Hospitalization and neurological examination are needed. Because of the possibility of other severe injuries, the spine and airway should be stabilized before transport. A severe concussion should keep athletes off the field, court or track for at least one month, and that is only if there are no signs of continuing symptoms. A second severe concussion should end the athlete's season and possibly career in the sport.

Neck Injuries

Injuries of the neck are a significant risk of motorsports -- the data from the North American Racing Insurance files indicate that the neck is the most-injured part of a driver's body.

In passenger-car collisions, whiplash injuries to the neck most often follow rear-end impacts which create backwards acceleration of the head. Cadaver tests have found that the neck can tolerate up to about 42-foot-pounds of backward whiplash force before injuries begin to occur.

In motorsports the neck may be more subject to decelerations which snap the head forward during impacts. Fortunately, the neck is better able to handle these forces. The muscles to the rear of the neck are much larger than those supporting the front, enabling the body to deal a bit better with sudden forward head movements. Forward neck extensions of 140 foot-pounds of force are believed to be tolerable before injuries begin to occur.

Neck injuries are somewhat more likely if the head is turned sideways when an acceleration/deceleration is felt because the muscles and ligaments already will be under some strain and less able to move.

The neck is less tolerant of forces exerted in sideways collisions. If a T-bone crash snaps the head sideways at a 90-degree angle, the neck can tolerate an average of 33 foot-pounds of force before injury commences. Sometimes blows to the top of the head, such as in a roll-over where the roof collapses or the ground makes contact with the driver, can transmit energy through the neck to the body. Studies have found that impacts to the top of the head averaging 1,620 pounds of force produce neck injuries.

Blows directly to the front of the neck are very dangerous. The thyroid and cricoid cartilages, which help keep the airway open, are capable of withstanding only 40 to 100 pounds of impact force before they can collapse, allowing the victim's airway and breathing ability to collapse, too.

Neck and spinal injuries, like those to the head, pose significant risks which may warrant a driver's abstinence from competition for many months or, in some cases, retirement. Any neck injury requiring surgery could require a year out of action; fractures that do not require surgery typically demand strength therapy and three months out of the cockpit. Any driver who previously has had neck problems should take special precautions, such as wearing a supportive collar between the shoulders and helmet.

Internal Injuries

When the body is suddenly decelerated the internal organs slam about inside of the chest. The chest, meanwhile, can be compressed by the bending of the ribs. During a particularly violent deceleration the organs can actually be squeezed between the ribs and the spine. As the speed of impact increases so do the impact and shearing forces experienced by the organs.

As explained previously, the heart can withstand about 40 Gs of deceleration, depending upon the duration of the G-loading. United States Federal Motor Vehicles Safety Standards require that automobile designs limit chest decelerations to 60 Gs, "except for intervals whose cumulative duration is not more than 3 milliseconds." Injury is more likely if the heart, which weighs about 11 ounces, is full of blood at the moment of impact. Each heart beat contains about 60 cubic centimeters of blood, so the heart is both larger and heavier when full.

Human tests conducted years ago on rocket sleds found that decelerations of 26 to 38.5 Gs were sufficient to produce a drastic drop in blood pressure immediately following deceleration.

Fractures

Considerable research (using cadavers) has been devoted to the tolerance of bones, particularly the skull, neck and legs, to impact and bending forces. These tolerances may be expressed in pounds of force. In motorsports environments it usually is the human body which strikes objects within or outside of the vehicle, so the pounds of force experienced in accidents vary according to the G forces with which the body strikes them.

Force also varies with the surface area of the impact. A 200-pound force applied over four square inches of flat surface equals 50 pounds per square inch. The same force applied over a .2-square-inch sharp-edged surface creates 1,000 pounds of force per square inch.

The skull's tolerance of impact varies by the location of a blow on the skull, the size of the object that strikes it and the density of an individual victim's bone tissue. The frontal bone (forehead and front of skull) can withstand an average blow of 1,000 to 1,600 pounds of force. The tempero-parietal bones (the sides of the head) tolerate blows averaging 700 to 1,900 pounds of force. The occiput bone (the back of the head) can bear impacts averaging 1,440 pounds of force.

The facial bones are significantly more delicate. The cheekbones can handle impacts of 280 to 520 pounds of force before breaking, the upper jaw about 260 pounds of force. The lower jaw's impact tolerance averages 700 pounds of force in frontal blows and 430 pounds in side blows.

The skull can be fractured without impact when severe G forces cause the skull to break near its union with the neck. This phenomena, according to reports, caused a 1991 NASCAR Winston Cup fatality at Watkins Glen.

Cadaver tests have shown that the chest can tolerate compression of up to 20 percent without causing rib injury. This amounts to about 3.5 inches of bending in the average male body. By 40-percent compression, however, rib fractures have certainly occurred. Breaking ribs can penetrate internal organs and cause severe injury. Rib fractures begin as shoulder belt forces pass 1,300 to 1,500 pounds.

Potential injury to the long bones (arms, legs, collarbone) is assessed in terms of lateral forces (pressure applied to the side of the bone) and compression (pressure applied to the end of a bone, as a nail would be struck).

Considerable research has been devoted to the strength of the leg bones since crash standards for passenger cars concentrate heavily upon them. Fractures of the femur (thigh bone) can be life-threatening. This bone is so large that bad breaks can prompt considerable blood loss and other serious complications.

Research has found that the femur, when the leg is struck on the knee, will break at 2,300 to 2900 pounds of force. The kneecap will break at impacts of 1,000 to 1,300 pounds. The knee ligaments are damaged by blows averaging 1,140 pounds of force. When rearward pressure is applied to the lower leg, the knee joint fails at an average force of 560 pounds.

The thigh is the strongest bone in resisting bending forces, tolerating an average of 882 pounds of lateral force in males. The tibia, the larger calf bone, follows in strength at 756 pounds. The fibula, the small bone in the calf, is one of the body's weakest bones, fracturing at an average force of 90 pounds. The humerus (upper arm) bone is quite sturdy, tolerating average bending forces of 610 pounds before fracture. In the forearm, the ulna tolerates an average of 277 pounds and the radius an average of 270 pounds.

The bones can withstand considerably higher compression forces. When average tolerances before fracture are compared, the femur is the strongest bone, tolerating 2,867 pounds of force. It is followed by the humerus, 1,874 pounds; tibia, 1,323 pounds; ulna, 1,213 pounds; radius, 1,159 pounds; and fibula, 664 pounds.

The following charts indicate the relative strengths of bones.

Long Bone Fracture: Bending & Compression, Static Loads in Pounds

	Bending Male	Bending Female	Comp. Male	Comp. Female
Clavicle (Collarbone)	220	135		
Humerus (Upper Arm)	610	385	1,874	1,323
Radius (Outer forearm)	270	151	1,159	862
Ulna (Large forearm bone)	277	182	1,213	684
Femur (Thigh)	882	581	2,867	2,426
Tibia (Large calf bone)	756	504	1,323	1,433*
Fibula (Small calf bone)	90	68	664	684*

* Larger tolerances may represent anomalies in bones studied.

Fracture Tolerance and Age:
Average Bending Load at Fracture in Pounds

(Percentages Indicate Decline from 20-39 Age Group)

	20-39	40-49	50-59	60-69
Femur	612	556	529	525
		-9.2%	-13.6%	-14.3%
Tibia	653	567	547	534
		-13.1%	-16.2%	-17.6%
Fibula	99	90	88	83
		-9.1%	-11.4%	-15.9%
Humerus	333	313	288	277
		-6.1%	-13.5%	-16.9%
Radius	133	119	117	108
		-10.2%	-11.9%	-18.6%
Ulna	160 lb.	142	137	133
		-11.3%	-14.1%	-16.9%
Average Loss By Age Group, All Bones		-9.8%	-13.5%	-16.7%

An example of the deceleration forces which can occur during a crash: In a test of the HANS (Head and Neck Restraint System), a dummy wearing a racing helmet was subjected to a 40-m.p.h. head-on crash which (above) stretched the neck with a load of nearly 1,000 pounds. Recreating the impact with the dummy wearing a HANS, (below) the neck received a loading of less than 130 pounds, well below the thresholds of neck or head injury, according to Hubbard/Downing Inc. (Photos courtesy Hubbard/Downing Inc.)

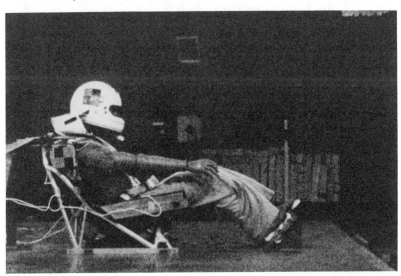

Safety innovations have drastically reduced the incidence of racing fires over recent decades, but danger continues to lurk in any class of racing -- wherever high heat and fuel are present.

Chapter 18

UNDERSTANDING BURNS

"It took just three seconds to destroy the skin on my hands -- my own fault for taking my gloves off. If I had been wearing an open-face helmet, who knows what my face might look like today."
> -- Tony Siscone, <u>Stock Car Racing</u>, November 1987

Many racing drivers wear insufficient fire-protective clothing, both in quantity and quality, when competing. There are many sources of intense heat, all beyond the skin's tolerance, that can injure racing drivers as well as mechanics.

Siscone was wise enough to use good equipment, but he made the mistake of removing his sweat-soaked gloves during a caution flag to dry them. As <u>Stock Car Racing</u> explained, "When the green flag came out before he could get the gloves back on, Siscone tossed them beside the seat, planning to put them back on during the next caution period. Little did he realize at the time that he would be the cause of the next caution!"

In the North American Racing Insurance data, burns represented 4.3 percent of injuries incurred by racing drivers. In pit and paddock areas, burns were second only to lacerations in frequency, accounting for 23.8 percent of injury reports.

People tend to assume that terrible accidents will not happen to them, especially if they drive at relatively slow speeds in lower classes of racing. At some tracks, drivers are not required to wear fire-resistant clothing or equip their cars with fuel cells. Many drivers who do wear driving suits have models that provide little protection; some wear open-face helmets and no protective gloves, socks or shoes, exposing large parts of the body to fire and heat dangers. The nose, ears, hands and fingers are especially prone to destruction. Their size and shape allow heat to attack from several sides and quickly penetrate throughout the tissues.

UNDERSTANDING BURNS

In addition, many people underestimate the risks of burns lurking in their motorsports environment. Unfortunately for many people, a fuel fire or radiator hose explosion does not care where it occurs: Flames and heat can be as fierce during the trophy dash at Jimmy-Bob's Speedbowl as during the Grand Prix of Monaco.

The mechanisms of the burn process begin when the skin reaches approximately 108 degrees Fahrenheit; exposure to this temperature for six hours can destroy the skin. Blistering begins at 118 degrees. By 122 degrees, the rate of damage has increased 100 times -- this temperature kills the outer layer of skin in three minutes of exposure.

When the skin reaches 149 degrees all layers are destroyed, leaving it incapable of healing and regeneration. Heat transmitted deeper into the body can cause serious injury at lower temperatures. The vital organs can be killed at about 108 degrees; osteoblasts (the cells which form bone tissue) at 111 degrees; leukocytes (white blood cells) at 115 degrees; and erythrocytes (red blood cells) at 122 degrees.

The body's absorption of heat is dependent upon the temperature and duration of exposure. For example, an air temperature of 212 degrees (the boiling point of water and roughly the operating temperature of automotive lubricants) causes skin redness in 4 to 5 seconds and blisters in 7 to 10 seconds.

Air temperature of 414 degrees (less than the boiling point of brake fluid) causes redness in 1.5 seconds and blistering in 2 to 3 seconds.

Air temperature of 616 degrees causes redness in 0.6 second and blistering in 0.7 second.

Air temperature of 818 degrees causes redness in 0.2 second and blistering in 0.25 second.

Air temperature of 1,060 degrees causes redness with 0.1 second and blistering in 0.2 second.

Brake rotors and exhaust headers generally operate at still higher temperatures. Fuel fires may attain 2,200 degrees. Skin exposed to those temperatures begins burning instantaneously and the heat quickly sinks deep into the body, where it may consume muscles, tendons and bone.

Racing poses many hazards which far exceed the skin's tolerance against burns. If these hot objects or fluids remain in contact with the skin long enough, burns are inevitable.

Here are some potential temperatures encountered in racing:

Radiator coolant	200 °-230 °
Rear end gear oil	200 °
Power steering fluid	200 °
Transmission oil, 90W	220 °
Tires (on pavement)	200 °-300 °
Engine oil	195 °-225 °
Brake fluid, boiling	550 °-600 °
Brake rotors	1,100 °-1,500 °
Exhaust headers	1,450 °
Brake rotors (glowing yellow/white)	2,000 °
Petroleum fuel fire	1,300 °-2,000 °
Methanol fire	2,200 °
Acetylene flame	2,325 °
Oxy-acetylene torch	5,710 °

It takes quite a while for the skin and muscle to dissipate heat so burning continues after the body is removed from a heat or fire source, as long as tissues remain above a dangerous temperature. Skin exposed to a gasoline explosion lasting a fraction of a second remains overheated for one to two minutes. A 20-second exposure to steam keeps body tissues overheated for three minutes.

That is why the treatment of burns involves the rapid application of cool, moist towels to quickly lower the temperature of the injury. Exposure to steam for three minutes keeps the body overheated for more than 18 minutes. Applying water cooled to 45 degrees can shorten the cooling process to five minutes and reduce tissue damage.

Burns are classified into three groups:

-- First-degree burns are red, hot, swollen and tender because nerve endings are irritated. These burns usually heal in about seven days and are accompanied by peeling skin.

UNDERSTANDING BURNS

-- Second-degree burns usually result in blisters. The outer layer of skin, the epidermis, is destroyed but can heal in about 14 days. Infection, however, can elevate second-degree burns to third-degree burns.

-- Third-degree burns destroy both the epidermis and dermis, the second layer of the skin that binds the outer layer to the body. These burns are not painful because nerve endings are destroyed. Skin grafts are required because the skin is unable to regenerate itself.

Burns over a significant portion of the body can result in the permanent impairment or loss of limbs and appendages. The skin performs two functions, keeping body fluids in and germs out. If the skin cannot do these jobs survival is jeopardized.

Thanks largely to the availability of impact-resistant fuel cells, the incidence of burns caused by racing fires has been reduced dramatically in recent decades. In the NARI sample, fires accounted for 15.5 percent of the reported burns. But that is not to downplay the severity of the risk of fire. Burns resulting from fire can be devastating.

Burns classified in medical terms as "thermal," or resulting from heat without fire, made up 70.1 percent of burn injuries. Of these, about 75 percent resulted from exposure to hot engine coolant. At least ten percent of the burns were suffered by people who made the mistake of removing a radiator cap while an engine was very, very hot. This percentage may have been higher since many burns indicated the involvement of hot coolant but not the mechanism of its release.

The following charts list burn factors found in the NARI files.

Burn Reports, 1988-1991:
North American Racing Insurance Files

Thermal	70.1%
Fire	15.5%
Acid (battery)	2.7%
Fireworks	1.1%
Concession accidents	0.5%
Not specified	10.2%

Thermal Burn Factors

Radiator/hose/cap failure or removal	60.3%
Radiator cap removal specified	14.5%
Contact with hot object on race car	10.7%
Engine block oil or coolant leak	8.4%
Power steering fluid	3.1%
Hot grease	1.5%
Transmission fluid	0.7%
Tire grooving iron	0.7%

Detail of Skin and Underlying Tissue

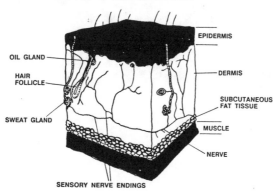

Classification of Burns by Degree of Injury

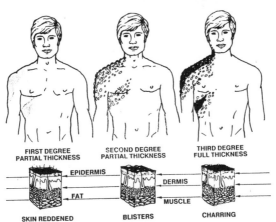

Off-the-shelf safety equipment can reduce -- if not eliminate -- many of the injury risks facing racers. Do you know all you should about selecting and using it?

Chapter 19

UNDERSTANDING SAFETY EQUIPMENT

Just about every driver uses some motorsports safety equipment, but some people don't use enough of it or don't use it correctly. Others don't know what they're getting when they buy it. This seems especially true when it comes to driving suits, gloves, underwear and socks, despite the educational efforts of many in the motorsports press. Let's take a look at the differences and standards applied to these indispensable racing components.

Helmets

The helmet may be the oldest form of racing safety equipment. Even in the early days of the sport, when drivers still wore short-sleeve shirts in competition, most wore some crude form of head protection. The old leather aviator-style helmets used decades ago offered little or no protection. The sturdy shells of today's helmets are fiberglass or, in the expensive, light-weight models, Kevlar or carbon fiber. The lining is made of a material similar to styrofoam.

The shell's first job is to distribute impact force over a wide area of the liner. The shell may disintegrate in the process, but in doing so can manage substantial impact energies that might otherwise injure or kill an unprotected wearer. Helmet maker Bill Simpson told Dick Berggren for the January 1990 issue of Stock Car Racing magazine. "This year at Indy we had 13 major impacts but in every case the driver was OK but 13 helmets were trashed."

Today the Snell Memorial Foundation and SFI Foundation, both non-profit corporations, define the standards for racing helmets.

The Snell Foundation was founded in 1957 after the death of William "Pete" Snell of massive head injuries sustained in a racing accident. The foundation maintains testing laboratories in St. James, New York; North Highlands, California; and Farnham, United Kingdom. Snell publishes standards for helmets used in motorcycling, bicycling, harness (horse) racing and automobile racing. The foundation subjects helmet types to a series of tests before deciding whether to certify them. It then randomly procures copies of helmets available to the public to make sure production models continue to meet the standards. Companies that maintain compliance with Snell standards may contract with the foundation to use the Snell name and logo on products, packaging and advertising.

Helmets are tested to determine their ability to withstand fire and penetration by blunt objects and to limit the G forces transmitted to the head. Helmets must pass these tests under a variety of conditions including exposure to heat, cold, water, solvents, fuels and other chemicals common to racing and motorcycling.

Snell subjects motorcycle helmets to stronger impacts than do other U.S. standards for motorcycle headgear. These are DOT FMVSS 218 (U.S. Department of Transportation Federal Motor Vehicle Safety Standard) and ANSI Z90.1 (American National Standards Institute). While Snell-certified motorcycle helmets are tested with generally the same impact energy levels and must meet the same G-load standards as auto racing helmets, motorcycle helmets should never be worn in racing. Auto racing helmets are subjected to additional tests, such as to simulate repeated blows against a roll cage.

The basic Snell standard calls for helmets to be smooth and free of fixed protrusions so friction against external objects does not catch or twist the head during an accident. There also must be no internal projections which could injure the wearer. Full-faced helmets must permit peripheral vision of 90 degrees to both the left and right of the helmet's center and a vertical field of vision of at least 45 degrees.

In initial certification tests, Snell requires manufacturers to submit six copies of each helmet type. Five are destroyed by testing. The sixth is retained for reference. One helmet is tested at room temperature, one is chilled to 14 degrees Fahrenheit, one is heated to 122 degrees Fahrenheit and another sprayed or soaked in water. The fifth helmet is used in tests simulating roll cage impacts and measuring flame resistance. To simulate the effects of exposure to chemicals, the helmets may be swabbed with a solvent mix consisting of equal parts of toluene and isooctane.

The ability of the first four helmets to absorb shock is gauged by exposing them to nine precise, repeatable impacts at five specific locations. The fifth helmet, to simulate roll cage impacts, is struck three times at each of two sites -- one at the rear of the helmet and the second on either the left or right side. The helmets are strapped to an instrumented "headform" and supporting assembly that weigh no more than 14.3 pounds. The helmets are dropped from about 10 feet onto anvils that are flat, hemispherical, flat edge (2.4 inches wide) and "steel bar" (two inches in diameter) in shape. During these impacts the helmet must remain "structurally intact" and must not transmit a "peak acceleration" of more than 300 Gs to the headform.

The chin strap is tested by being stressed by a 50.6-pound weight while receiving a jolt from an 83.6-pound weight dropped 4.72 inches.

The chin bar of full-face helmets is tested by having an 11-pound weight dropped onto the bar at a specified speed.

To test the ability of the helmets to withstand penetration, a 6.6-pound, cone-shaped weight is dropped onto the helmet, again from about 10 feet. According to the Snell standards, "The test striker must not penetrate to achieve even momentary contact with the test headform."

The face shields of full-face helmets also are tested for resistance to penetration. A soft lead pellet, .2 inches in diameter and weighing one gram (.03527 ounces), is shot against three locations on the shield at a speed of about 300 miles per hour. The pellet must not penetrate the shield or create a dent deeper than about a tenth of an inch.

A propane flame of about 1,450 degrees Fahrenheit is used to test the helmet for flame resistance. After the flame is applied to the helmet shell for 30 seconds and removed, the shell must stop burning within 10 seconds. The helmet lining, where it would touch a wearer's head, must not exceed 158 degrees Fahrenheit during the flame test.

The chin strap is exposed to the flame for 15 seconds. It must not melt or continue burning longer than five seconds after the flame is removed. The face shield is exposed to flame for 45 seconds and must not melt or continue to burn longer than 20 seconds.

The SFI helmet standard is in many ways similar to the Snell standard. Like Snell, SFI prohibits any headform impact exceeding 300 Gs. SFI also limits any acceleration beyond 200 Gs to 2.5 milliseconds and any acceleration beyond 150 Gs to 4 milliseconds. The SFI standard evaluates the optical properties of face shields and tests shields for penetration resistance by dropping a 1.56-ounce steel cone onto them from a height of 14 feet.

No helmet should be worn in racing unless it carries a Snell or SFI racing certification. Snell recommends that helmets be replaced after five years of service or less if the manufacturer suggests it.

The Snell standard requires that helmets be labelled to address fit issues. The label explains that "for maximum protection, the helmet must be of good fit and all retention straps must be securely fastened to retain the helmet.

Modifications should not be made to a helmet. Some adhesives, paints and cleaning solvents may damage helmets.

Safety experts say helmets should be very tight -- so tight, in fact, that they will move wearers' eyebrows up and down if jiggled. Properly-fitting helmets, like shoes, may be almost too tight upon first wearing but can be expected to loosen and, with time, become comfortable.

A simple test will determine if a helmet is not sufficiently snug: strap it on and try to roll it forward. If it can be rolled off the head, a smaller size or different design is needed.

Snell recommends that any helmet involved in an accident should be discarded or returned to the manufacturer for complete inspection before it is worn again. (Other experts recommend the same for any helmet that is thrown against anything solid. An empty helmet probably can withstand considerable abuse without losing protective capacity, but why take chances?)

As the Snell standards explain, "A helmet's protective capability may be exhausted protecting the wearer in an accident. Helmets are constructed so that the energy of a blow is managed by the helmet, causing its partial destruction. The damage may not be readily apparent . . . . "

Maintaining helmets also is important to their integrity. Helmets should be cleaned and dried after each use. Rivets and chin straps should be examined often to make sure there are no signs of rusting, fraying or other deterioration.

The latest Snell helmet standard is designated "Snell SA-90" ("SA" means "Special Application"). The SFI standard for open face helmets is designated "Specification 31.1." For full-face helmets the standard is "Specification 31.2."

The Snell standards are upgraded every five years to account for improving technological capabilities and expanding knowledge of head injury mechanisms, which still are not fully understood. Nonetheless, Snell explains, even the best helmets cannot prevent injuries under all conditions that racing may create:

"Although helmet use has been shown to reduce the risk of head injuries significantly, there are limits to a helmet's protective capability. No helmet can protect the wearer against all foreseeable accidents. Therefore injury may occur in accidents which exceed the protective capability of any helmet including even those helmets meeting the requirements of this Standard."

Driving Suits

Analysis of the accident/injury data in the North American Racing Insurance files suggests that fires are rare in motorsports these days, no doubt thanks to the development of impact-resistant fuel cells. But the fires that do occur can have devastating results. It seems that many motorsports participants do not realize that driving suits must do more than merely provide clothing that does not burn. Driver suits almost must serve as insulators that provide sufficient thermal protection to keep the heat of fires and other heat sources from being transmitted to the body. Driving suits are, in effect, snow suits in reverse -- designed to keep heat out rather than in.

Nonetheless, many race tracks and sanctioning organizations allow drivers to compete without wearing fire-protective clothing at all -- or to wear cheap, single-layer suits than can provide only a few seconds of protection from flame and heat. In addition, many drivers wear two-piece suits (separate pants and jacket) that could leave that tender belly and those internal organs exposed during a dive out of a burning car or a fall onto a flaming puddle of fuel.

Slow race cars can burn, too -- the North American Racing Insurance data analyzed for this book showed that demolition derby cars experience the highest rate of burn injuries (as a percentage of all injuries reported) for all classes of racing covered. Demo drivers suffered burns in 28.6 percent of all injury-producing accidents, nearly seven times the average burn experience for all racing classes combined.

Here are some thoughts on driving suits:

"They talk about a single layer doing the job. That's bullshit," says Bill Simpson of Simpson Safety. "All the single layers are going to give you (is) 4-6 seconds. The heat goes right through."

"With a single layer," says Jim Deist of Deist Safety, "they have nothing more than a flame-retardant uniform. Instead of a fire hazard like a tee shirt, all they have is a uniform that won't flame up. You haven't gotten any protection. You just haven't made the problem worse."

A single layer firesuit isn't sufficiently insulating to prevent heat from a fire from burning the driver. The suit doesn't burn but given several seconds of exposure to flame, the driver inside it does!

Six seconds isn't enough time to stop a burning car and get out of it without being burned.

Jim Deist has . . . a slogan . . . "Guys who can't afford a good firesuit can't afford to race."

> -- Dick Berggren," Firesuit Fabric Test,"
> Stock Car Racing, April 1986 (Reprinted
> with permission)

Berggren's article tested a number of driver suit materials and layers to determine their ability to keep a 1,700-degree propane flame from passing through 180 degrees of heat -- the theoretical blistering point of skin. While a single layer of Nomex (used in many suits) would have begun to burn a driver in only four seconds, four layers of fabric delivered 20 to 35 seconds of protection. In fact, by the time the inside layer of one fabric sample reached 180 degrees, the outside layer was glowing.

Driver suits are certified by the SFI Foundation through SFI Specification 3.2A. SFI applies a TPP (Thermal Protection Performance) rating that indicates a material's resistance to heat transfer. SFI tests are based on Stoll's Curve, a model which estimates the initiation of skin blistering by measuring temperature and the duration of exposure to it.

SFI fabric testing uses a heat source, consisting of two laboratory burners and nine electric quartz tubes, that creates 2,100 degrees Fahrenheit -- the range of a fuel fire. Racing fires, however, can differ in temperature, depending upon type of fuel, wind conditions and other ignited materials. The SFI procedures evaluate the fabric's resistance to flame, glow propagation and charring. The testing is repeated on each product every 24 months.

SFI Driver Suit Specifications

SFI Spec	TPP Rating	Estimated Protection in Fuel Fire
3.2A-1	6	3 seconds
3.2A-5	19	9.5 seconds
3.2A-10	38	19 seconds
3.2A-15	60	30 seconds
3.2A-20	80	40 seconds
3.2A-25	100	50 seconds
3.2A-30	120	60 seconds

For many racing uses, two-layer driving suits are considered acceptable when fire-proof underwear are worn to provide additional insulation. Some two-layer suits provide more seconds of protection than some three-layer suits, so it is important to base selections on SFI ratings rather than on numbers of layers.

While neither machine-washing nor dry-cleaning can damage most of the materials used in today's suits, manufacturer's recommendations for cleaning and care must be followed to the letter. Drivers also should avoid wearing their suits while they work on their cars. Grease or oil soaked into the fabric may briefly support flame if exposed to fire in an accident.

A driving suit is not all that is needed to provide the best protection possible -- the feet, hands and head must be protected, too, to prevent disabling injuries or deaths. A significant loss of skin, no matter where on the body it occurs, can prompt life-threatening complications.

Many drivers compete in athletic shoes which offer no protection against flame or heat. To make matters worse, these shoes are likely to contain cotton, vinyl and rubber which can melt and stick to the driver while they burn.

Restraint Systems

The SFI Foundation evaluates driver restraint assemblies and issues certification to those that meet SFI Specification 16.1. Buyers should demand that restraint systems bear a certification label. Users should follow careful installation, maintenance and replacement practices.

SFI issues four certifications for seat/shoulder/anti-submarine belt assemblies. Three of them require the lap belt to withstand a load of 5,000 pounds, theoretically enough to restrain a 200-pound driver in a 25-G deceleration. The fourth standard demands tolerance of a 3,000-pound load -- 15 Gs for that 200-pound driver.

Two of the certifications require that shoulder harnesses handle 2,500 pounds -- a 12.5-G load if a 200-pound driver's entire weight is forced against them. The other two certifications call for 1,500-pound loads -- approximately 7.5 Gs. Anti-submarine (crotch) straps also are tested at 1,500 pounds of pull.

Belts must survive these loads without failures or deformations of metal parts that would affect the functioning of the assembly. During the test, total slippage in the belt system must not exceed one inch.

The certifications differ in the required widths of belts. Shoulder and lap belts may be either three or two inches wide. All anti-submarine belts must be 1.72 inches wide. Three-inch belts are about 50-percent stronger than two-inch belts. The wider belts also distribute G forces over a wider surface area of the body and reduce the risks of injury.

Specification 16.1, of course, also addresses the strength and functionality of belt buckle release mechanisms. These components must "be designed to minimize the possibility of accidental release," according to the standard. They also must "be capable of being easily released" whether the car is upright, upside-down or on its side. Buckles shall consist of "a quick release connector with no more than two separate motions required to release the entire restraint assembly" and "shall be capable of being easily released in any of the release directions by an individual wearing driving gloves and not able to see the mechanism."

SFI requires that test results for restraint assemblies be resubmitted at least once every 24 months following initial certification. SFI also specifies that "the useful life of the webbing in the straps shall not exceed two years and they must be replaced at or before that time."

The nylon material of which belt straps are made are deteriorated by exposure to sunlight, chemicals, friction and other types of wear. The straps lose an estimated 30 percent of original strength in two years of typical use. In test conditions belts have lost 80 percent of their strength over six months of exposure to severe elemental conditions.

SFI Specification 16.1: Restraint Systems

SYSTEM TYPE	1	1A	2	3
Lap Belt Width	3"	3"	3"	2"
Lap Belt Test Load (lb.)	5,000	5,000	5,000	3,000
Shoulder Belt Width	3"	3"	2"	2"
Shoulder Belt Test Load (lb.)	2,500	2,500	1,500	1,500
Crotch Strap Width	1.72"	1.72"	1.72"	1.72"
Crotch Strap Test Load (lb.)	1,500	1,500	1,500	1,500

The installation of restraint assemblies is critical to their maximum performance and longevity. Manufacturer guidelines and recommendations should be followed precisely. For example, belts should not be exposed to abrasion from moving components within the car. The belts should be mounted to prevent them from slipping off of a driver (particularly from the shoulders) and so as to be as short as possible to minimize the amount of stretch that could occur during an impact. Seat padding should not be so thick as to permit excessive looseness in belts that are apparently tight.

Belts and hardware should be cleaned often, particularly if used on dirt tracks. Grit can speed wear and deterioration. Simple soaps, not solvents, should be used for cleaning. Hardware should be inspected often to make sure no bends or cracks have developed. After a serious crash, restraint assemblies (like helmets) should be discarded or used only after examination by the manufacturer.

No race car, even the most simple, should roll onto a race course without a restraint system designed for competition. Some accidents reported to North American Racing Insurance noted that injured drivers were wearing only three-point harnesses intended for passenger-car use.

Neck Protection

Muscle-strengthening and flexibility exercises are one way to prevent collision forces from causing neck injuries. Wearing protective equipment is another. The standard "horse collar" neck support should be a part of every driver's wardrobe. It provides some protection against excessive neck extension during impacts, violent spins or tumbles.

A new device which could become more common in racing cockpits is the HANS (Head and Neck Support) offered by Hubbard/Downing Inc., 5096 Peachtree Road, Atlanta, Ga. 30341.

HANS consists of a yoke that slips over the driver's shoulders and is held in place by the shoulder belts. A network of tethers connects the driver's helmet to the yoke. The tethers allow the head to be turned but resist cornering forces to minimize driver fatigue during the race and limit extreme head motions and neck loads during crashes to minimize risks of injuries.

In crash-dummy tests, a 40-m.p.h. impact was determined to place a load of nearly 1,000 pounds on the neck. When the impact was repeated with the dummy wearing HANS, the neck load remained under 130 pounds, within the neck's safe limits, and the movement of the head was significantly reduced, according to the manufacturers of the device.

HANS was developed by Dr. Robert H. Hubbard, professor in the department of biomechanics at Michigan State University and founder of Biomechanical Design Inc. It has been worn in competition since 1988 by, among others, five-time IMSA champion Jim Downing.

A HANS unit was exposed to a real-world motorsports test in 1991, when a boat racer was involved in an accident that otherwise could have caused severe or fatal injuries, Hubbard reported. A boat became airborne at about 70 m.p.h., rotated and struck the water on its left side, front and top. The driver experienced a 50-m.p.h. deceleration in about five feet for an estimated 26-G deceleration. While he sustained a concussion, broken nose, neck strain and bruised lung, he was released from medical care the following day and recovered within a few weeks.

Similar accidents, said Hubbard, had caused skull fractures and five fatalities in powerboat racing since 1985. Neck loadings and head motions of the same nature also have been known to cause fatal skull fractures in auto racing.

"Among these is the recent death of (NASCAR Winston Cup driver) J.D. McDuffie. According to the Schuyler County Sheriff's Department and Coroner in Watkin's Glen, N.Y., McDuffie died due to a basilar skull fracture with bruising and abrasions from the chin strap and without any significant damage to the helmet from direct impact," Hubbard wrote in a paper he delivered to the International

Council of Motorsport Sciences in 1991. "His skull fracture was probably caused by excessive loading of the base of the skull through the neck during the side impact of the car with a barrier."

Seat Liner

The rapid hospital transport of a critically injured person can be crucial to survival. Critical minutes, however, often are consumed in the careful removal of racing drivers from their cars to prevent the aggravation of suspected head, neck and back injuries. Before these drivers are removed, their bodies and heads are carefully secured to a backboard that must be squeezed between their backs and their driving seats.

Another recent innovation in racing is the "Safety Quest" seat liner which is custom-fitted to a driving seat. The liner is an aluminum backboard which slips into the seat. It contains several fire-resistant straps that can be used to secure the driver's body. The driver's helmet can be affixed to the upper portion of the board with duct tape. Handle straps in the seat portion of the liner then can be used to quickly lift the driver from the car.

The device is sold by Safety Quest Inc., c/o P/SL Healthcare System, 4896 Chambers Road, Denver, Colorado, 80239.

Advance planning and training prepare track safety workers for the special situations and conditions that may arise during motorsports competition.

Chapter 20

UNDERSTANDING TRACK SAFETY

Motorsports safety often hinges upon conditions at race tracks and the ability of track personnel to handle emergencies. Many fatalities can be prevented and many injuries avoided or made less severe by eliminating or minimizing hazardous conditions and better preparing track personnel to respond to accidents.

Track Conditions

Injury reports in the North American Racing Insurance files suggest that many accidents result from hazardous conditions on or near racing surfaces and in pit, paddock, spectator and parking areas.

The NARI data indicate that 58.1 percent of all spectator injuries at race tracks are caused by slips and falls. People step in holes, trip over debris and slip on slick pavement or bleachers. Another 6.5 percent of injured spectators are struck by vehicles in parking lots or race cars -- meaning either spectators or race cars were allowed to go where they should not have been. Spectators, on rare occasions, are struck by race cars because guard rails and cable barriers are insufficient or people are allowed to hang on to catch fencing at the very edge of the track. Secondary spectator fences should be positioned several feet behind all race track catch fencing to increase the margin of safety between fans and cars.

"We want a secondary fence behind the crash wall or barrier and/or wheel fence in both the participant pits and spectator areas to provide a buffer zone for safety," said George England of North American Racing Insurance, who conducts track inspections at the beginning of each racing season.

Inadequate fencing and security allow crew members as well as fans to venture where they have no business being during races. The NARI data suggest that 15.5 percent of those who are hurt in pits and paddocks are struck by moving vehicles. People are struck by cars because insufficient barriers allow racing cars to strike people or permit people to run on the track to gawk at crashes.

UNDERSTANDING TRACK SAFETY

Drivers are unnecessarily injured by track conditions, too. Race cars can be launched into the air by steep dirt berms or flipped or spun out of control by barriers erected simply to keep drivers from cutting turns too tightly.

Berms and embankments were cited as contributing factors in 1.4 percent of the driver injury reports filed with NARI. On another 2.0 percent of the driver injury reports cars were reported to have left the track. While it is safer to have run-off areas rather than guard rails where possible, these numbers suggest that changes of slope at race tracks can be too severe and contribute to vehicle launches that create high centrifugal forces or rollovers.

England said he would rather not see barriers unless they guard something that would be worse for a car to hit. "I don't want walls or barriers if there is nothing behind them to protect."

In his study of accidents in the Southeast Division of the SCCA in 1984 and 1985, Dr. M. Rick Timms determined that injuries were associated with 14 of 49 reported roll-overs, none of the injuries fatal or serious. "This study . . . suggests that efforts to limit barrier contact through the use of gravel pits in runoff areas are indeed justified, even if the likelihood of inducing roll-over is increased," he wrote in a paper presented to the International Council of Motorsports Sciences. "This is obviously an area that needs much additional study."

Timms said "Contact with barriers or another vehicle is associated with most injuries noted, and points out the importance of course design and the proper use of energy absorbing barriers. It is clear that improvements in barrier design, specific for the types of race cars utilizing the circuit, could reduce injury in cases of high speed barrier contact. It should be possible to identify the design elements best suited for each type of race car and incorporate them into an affordable, versatile barrier suitable for use at multipurpose race tracks."

Similar advice was offered by members of the Indy-car-racing medical team. "Less rigid, more energy-absorbing barrier material should be developed to line the retaining walls, especially on the turns. Topographical changes should be made to decrease or eliminate the chance of cars becoming airborne and cartwheeling," wrote Terry R. Trammell, M.D., Stephen E. Olvey, M.D., and Diane B. Reed, M.S.N. ("Championship Car Racing Accidents and Injuries," The Physician and Sportsmedicine, May 1986.)

Medical Planning

The treatment of injured participants at motorsports facilities can be aided by the immediate availability of medical information. Track administrators and sanctioning organizations can assist emergency medical personnel and emergency room physicians by providing medical background data on injured participants.

Major racing organizations and facilities require all drivers, crew members and officials -- anyone who may be exposed to moving race cars or pit/paddock accidents -- to complete medical information cards. (Anyone permitted to enter pit areas, even a spouse or girlfriend, is at risk of injury from collisions, fuel fires, exploding radiator hoses, etc.)

Medical information cards should include such crucial facts as:

Blood type
Allergies
Medications being taken
Date of last tetanus immunization
Other significant medical history or conditions
        (diabetes, heart disease, seizure disorders, major illnesses or injuries, particularly fractures)

Treatment also may be expedited by the inclusion of a signed informed consent release through which the participant gives doctors permission to provide blood transfusions.

The medical information cards and consent forms should be stored in a sturdy container or briefcase that is placed on the primary emergency response vehicle at the beginning of each competitive meet or practice session.

The medical crew and track director also should be equipped with lists of all specialized medical facilities in the track's region so the emergency crew can immediately select, notify and depart for the appropriate center.

These sheets must list hospitals qualified in trauma, burns, orthopedics, oral surgery, neurosurgery, thoracic surgery, vascular surgery, cardiology, spinal cord injuries, ob/gyn, ophthalmology, urology, ear/nose/throat surgery, gastroenterology, nephrology, plastic surgery, pediatrics, etc. Travel times, telephone numbers, emergency radio frequencies, licensed bed and emergency room bed totals and maps should be included, too. (Sample forms are printed at the end of this chapter.)

The medical crew's copies will speed the selection of the appropriate facility. The race director's copies of the forms can assist crew and family members of injured people in going to the treatment facility.

The emergency destination list obviously must provide for the treatment of non-participants who may be injured or become ill. It has been estimated that one spectator emergency occurs each hour for every 40,000 spectators attending sporting events. The emergencies can arise from trauma or medical problems such as heart attacks or seizures. Spectators range from pediatric to geriatric. About 0.7 percent of people injured in pit areas are older than 65 years, according to the NARI data. Children under five years of age make up 11.3 percent of the injured spectator population while 10.1 percent of injured fans are over the age of 60.

Fire Planning

Motorsports fire injuries have become rare. While burns were involved in 4.3 percent of driver injuries and 23.8 percent of pit area injuries found in the North American Racing Insurance files, fires accounted for just one in six -- 15.5 percent -- of these burns. Even the briefest fire, however, can cause fatal or crippling injuries so firefighting remains an essential requirement of motorsports safety.

G. Terry Smith of Swea City, Iowa, has developed an automobile race track fire protection course and has provided services at short tracks in Iowa, Minnesota and South Dakota since 1976. He holds a bachelor's degree with a fire science emphasis from Western Illinois University and has been certified as a fire instructor by Iowa State University.

Smith believes the most-overlooked area of motorsports fire safety is the protection and training of the firefighting crew. He believes these people should wear the same types of protective clothing that drivers wear. He also stresses motorsports-specific knowledge in flash points, fire points, ignition temperatures, vapor densities, specific gravities, flammability and explosive limits, melting points, vaporization, pyrolysis and the effects of weather and wind on fires.

Next on Smith's preparation list is the fire extinguisher supply.

"The size of fire extinguishers should be in the 10- to 20-pound range. An extinguisher smaller than a 10-pound unit does not contain enough extinguishing agent and does not discharge at a sufficient rate to cope with the many possible situations that could develop at a race track," he said. "A unit larger than a 20-pounder is too difficult to carry around and maneuver."

He recommends "Purple K" as the extinguishing agent of choice for motorsports environments. "Our primary concern is flammable liquid motor fuels and combustible liquid lubricating and hydraulic oils. Purple K -- potassium bicarbonate -- is an economical, non-toxic, readily-available dry chemical extinguishing agent which has been shown to be very effective on flammable liquid fires. Purple K will do a better job on a flammable liquid fire than a multipurpose (ABC) or sodium bicarbonate (regular BC) extinguishing agent. Carbon dioxide and halogenated agent extinguishers do not work well in open areas, especially with any degree of wind that will disperse the agent."

Smith believes halogen extinguishers may be suitable for use inside race cars. "Halogenated agents are excellent fire extinguishers in closed areas such as the interior of a race car but there are other associated problems. When halogenated agents, also known as halons, are exposed to flame the decomposition products have varying degrees of toxicity to the human. Plus, they environmentally attack the earth's ozone layer."

Smith says water is not to be used as a firefighting agent except in special situations. Other experts advise, however, keeping buckets of water handy in pit environments when methanol fuel is being used. This practice is followed by many major sanctioning bodies.

Smith believes tracks should have firefighting foam available for major incidents. Foam would need to be based on a truck, which also could carry larger Purple K extinguishers. He recommends the use of oil-dry absorbent material on spills, even at dirt tracks.

"Oil dry is a fire prevention agent. Remember, the best way to fight a fire is to prevent it. Use plenty of oil dry to cover flammable and combustible liquids when they are spilled to prevent their vaporization and thus prevent their ignition. Another advantage of oil dry is that it gives the rescuers better footing during extrication procedures," Smith said.

When high-tech machines race another firefighting agent may be needed, Smith said. MET-L-X is designed for magnesium fires, which cannot be fought with water. Water can intensify magnesium flames because the metal burns at a high temperature that may disassociate, or separate, water's hydrogen and oxygen molecules, creating gases that then burn.

UNDERSTANDING TRACK SAFETY

Jack Gilmore, director of safety at Indianapolis Motor Speedway, believes short tracks should have at least 10 20-pound dry powder extinguishers, five 2.5-gallon water extinguishers and one 150-pound dry powder extinguisher stationed in the pits.

The small dry powder units, he said, should be distributed at the entrance and exit to each turn, along the straights and in the pits. The water extinguishers should be spread about the pits for use in methanol fires on people. He said the numbers of extinguishers should be increased for larger tracks.

To prevent program delays or having inadequate equipment to complete a race program, tracks should have sufficient fire extinguisher capability to handle repeated accidents -- either extra extinguishers or facilities to recharge them.

Firefighters and their equipment need to be placed at locations that protect them from racing vehicles (usually on the inside of the track) and that provide quick access to all parts of the track. Since even the best drivers' suits available can be expected to give no more than 30 seconds of protection against burns (and only if the driver also wears protective underwear), fires need to be extinguished well within that time window. Small tracks should consider having at least one vehicle carrying heavy-duty supplies to supplement hand-held extinguishers.

Smith trains racing rescuers to position their vehicles during on-track responses so that they can work behind the vehicles and be protected from race cars circling the track. At shorter facilities with little room on the track, Smith advises that the red flag be thrown whenever emergency personnel or vehicles need to enter the racing surface. Drivers should be directed to bring their vehicles to an immediate safe stop and should not be allowed to drive past the incident.

"When driving an emergency response vehicle to the scene of an incident, extra precautions must be taken," Smith said. "If possible, make your direction of travel the same as the racers' direction of travel. Also keep in mind the speed difference of your vehicle as compared to the racing machine.

"Always be aware of the type and condition of the surface being driven upon. Each racing facility will be different so one must survey the facility and determine the safest and best positions for personnel and equipment. And maybe you should tatoo this in mirror image on your forehead so you'll be reminded each morning: "Never turn your back to the racing machine."

Incident Control

The track's competition director should meet with safety and security personnel to make sure they understand track procedures and are positioned for the most effective response and crowd control for all anticipated needs. As this book was being written, the authors witnessed many examples of poor emergency training and discipline at several tracks.

-- At one track two ambulances were on hand. Rather than being positioned separately for maximum coverage of the half-mile track and its outside pit area, they parked side by side in the inner pits. To make matters worse, the crews sometimes stood along the front-straight pit wall to watch races. When a car rolled over in a turn, the crews had to run 50 feet just to get to their vehicles.

-- On another occasion, firefighters began leaving their stations at trackside and stowing equipment at the start of the final feature.

-- During hot laps a firefighter left his turn to get a soda and was standing at the pit concession stand when a sprint car flipped over the wall. The firefighter then had to run -- wearing heavy boots, coat and hat and carrying his extinguisher -- back to his post a quarter-mile away. If the car had caught fire and the driver been unable to flee from it, the protective limits of even the best driver's fire suit would have been exceeded in the time it took the firefighter to reach the car.

-- A midget took a rough tumble in a turn. Before other cars on the track had stopped moving, a photographer ran onto the track. Was he trained to offer any assistance? Did he have any reason to risk his life by running onto the track?

-- Two firefighters, sitting in a truck in the middle of a track, responded to an accident in a distant turn -- by exiting the truck and running on foot with their fire extinguishers.

-- At a small dirt track, a three-car collision stunned or winded one driver. As the ambulance traveled toward the crash, three men assigned themselves the responsibility of yanking the driver from the car and, for some reason, lugging him 50 or 60 feet into the pits by his armpits and knees. They laid him on the ground where, due to guardrails, parked race cars and a milling crowd, the ambulance could not reach him. These well-meaning but irresponsible actions delayed for many potentially crucial seconds the initiation of treatment by qualified medical personnel. If the driver had sustained a neck or spinal injury or needed to have an airway promptly established to restore breathing, he also could have been killed, paralyzed or subjected to brain damage by his "rescuers."

213

ANY DRIVER, CREW MEMBER OR SPECTATOR WHO HAS BEEN INVOLVED IN AN ACCIDENT SHOULD BE ASSUMED TO BE INJURED UNTIL A TRAINED MEDICAL PROFESSIONAL HAS DETERMINED OTHERWISE. IF A DRIVER IS UNABLE TO EXIT THE CAR HIMSELF OR HERSELF, HE OR SHE MUST BE EXTRICATED WITH THE GREATEST CARE AND ONLY BY EXPERTS. UNLESS THERE IS AN IMMEDIATE THREAT OF FIRE OR OTHER LIFE-THREATENING DANGER, AN INJURED PERSON SHOULD NEVER BE MOVED BY AMATEURS. ANYONE WHO IS NOT TRAINED IN EMERGENCY MEDICINE HAS NO RIGHT TO JEOPARDIZE AN INJURED PERSON'S LIFE OR SAFETY.

Ambulance crews must be poised to roll immediately upon the command of the race director. Prompt response by paramedics or emergency medical technicians may discourage the untrained from "helping." Because track officials such as corner workers may be the first to reach a crash, they should be graduates of an emergency medical technician program, too. This training will enable them to determine quickly whether the ambulance is needed and to initiate any life-saving measures that may be necessary. If an official saves only one life or prevents only one crippling injury during his or her career, the training will be more than justified.

For the best possible protection, firefighting and ambulance coverage should be on hand from the opening of the pit gate to the departure of the last tow rig. Injuries can occur in parking lots and during the loading and unloading of race cars.

Adequate pit security, education and signage also are part of the safety equation. Crew members and spectators must not be permitted to leave the pits to observe or handle accident situations on the track.

Disaster Planning

Advance preparations for extraordinary emergencies will expedite and assist responses by rescue workers. These measures, in turn, will improve the transportation and medical treatment of injured people -- and possibly save lives. The "golden hour of trauma" comes into play after many serious incidents -- it has been proven that treatment within 60 minutes of injury often can mean the difference between a victim's death or total recovery.

There are many disaster risks present at motorsports facilities and some are not related to racing. In addition to multiple car accidents, the remote chance of a race car entering the crowd and explosive fuel fires, there are risks of concession fires, collapsed bleachers and natural disasters such as tornadoes, severe thunderstorms and lightning strikes. Tracks need not only the equipment and personnel to deal with the usual crashes -- they also must have plans in place to rapidly summon other resources to deal with major catastrophes.

A disaster plan should designate a chain of command -- who directs emergency response efforts and the responsibilities which other officials assume. The plan should designate secondary command responsibilities for medical triage, transportation, crowd/traffic control and notification of other needed resources such as additional ambulances, police, highway patrol, fire departments and hospitals to which the injured will be transported. A command succession should be included for the possibility that a major player is among the incapacitated.

Telephone numbers and, if appropriate, radio frequencies for all resources should be immediately accessible to all people who may become responsible for directing the effort. If possible, a cellular telephone should be available in the event that a disaster damages telephones lines or offices.

At least once a year, preferably at the beginning of a season, a meeting should be held for disaster plan review and practice by regional public safety officials, emergency medical personnel, track officials, corner workers, security forces, other employees who could be assigned to the disaster team.

Every race track needs the best emergency-response facilities and personnel it can muster. Some day a life may depend upon it.

DRIVER/CREW MEDICAL INFORMATION CARD   (Front)

Name: _____

Address: _____

City: _____

State & Zip: _____

Home Phone: (_____)_____

Work Phone: (_____)_____

Insurance
Company: _____

Insurance
Plan Number: _____

Social Security
Number: _____

Date of Birth:
(Mo/Day/Yr) _____

DRIVER/CREW MEDICAL INFORMATION CARD   (Back)

Allergies: _____

Medicines That
I Take: _____

_____

Medical Problems (Existing medical history of conditions such as, but not limited to, diabetes, heart disease, seizure disorders, major illnesses or past injuries, particularly fractures):

_____

_____

_____

Contact Lenses?   Yes _____   No _____

Pupils Normally Equal?   Yes _____   No _____

Blood Type: _____

Last Tetanus
Immunization:
(Mo/Day/Yr)   _____

Religion: _____

IN CASE OF EMERGENCY, PLEASE CALL:

Name: _____

Address: _____

Telephone: (___) _____   (___) _____

Doctor: _____

Telephone: _____

CAPABILITIES OF AREA HOSPITALS

	HOSP:	HOSP:	HOSP:
LOCATION			
TRAVEL TIME			
EMERGENCY ROOM LEVEL			
NUMBER OF E.R. BEDS			
HELIPAD?			
TOTAL BEDS			

PHYSICIAN COVERAGE

TRAUMA			
GEN. SURG.			
NEUROSURG.			
THOR. SURG.			
CARD. SURG.			
ORTH. SURG.			
BURNS			
ORAL SURG.			
INT. MED			
PEDIATRICS			
OB/GYN			
OPHTHAL.			
UROLOGY			
NEPHRO.			
E/N/T			
GASTRO			
SPINAL			
VASCULAR			
PLASTIC SUR.			

While significant injuries may occur during only one in five racing meets, track personnel must be prepared to promptly and intelligently respond to any conceivable situation.

Chapter 21

RESPONDING TO INJURIES

Injuries are a fact of life, off the race track as well as on it. More people aged 1 to 34 in the U.S. die each year from trauma than from all diseases combined. After the age of 34 only cancer and hardening of the arteries take more victims than trauma.

Accidents claim about 140,000 lives in the U.S. each year. An estimated 50 million Americans are injured annually, about 10 million of them suffering disabling injuries.

Those of us associated with motorsports spend a lot of time on the highway and working around machinery, so we may face more than our share of risk. Thousands of us hit the road after work on Friday, hurry to a weekend of racing then rush back home Sunday night so we can stumble wearily to work Monday morning. Life is risky enough -- don't drive or use dangerous tools when too tired to handle the responsibility or when under the influence of drugs or alcohol.

The Stages of Trauma

Trauma poses the potential of death at three stages. In the most severe cases injuries are so serious that there is little chance of survival. In the other two levels of severity, survival depends upon the promptness and quality of care.

The first risk of death from trauma occurs within seconds or minutes of injury, usually from lacerations affecting the brain, upper spinal cord, heart, aorta or major blood vessels. Few people with these injuries will live unless they are extraordinarily close to emergency medical transport.

The second chance of death is encountered from minutes to a few hours after injury. These are caused by brain damage, chest and organ injuries or significant blood loss. The third peak of trauma death will be faced within days or weeks, generally from infection or organ failure. The emergency medical care available to a victim within the first hour of injury (known as the "golden hour") will determine the likelihood of overcoming these two periods.

Rapid stabilization (maintaining breathing and oxygenation and immobilizing the spine), controlling external hemorrhages and initiating intravenous lines to compensate for fluid losses are the keys.

Shock from blood loss is a significant cause of death for accident victims. Young people might survive a loss of 20 percent of their blood volume, but a 20- to 40-percent blood loss can cause the classic symptoms of shock -- racing heart beat, lowered blood pressure and impaired mental function. Loss of more than 40 percent of blood volume is life-threatening.

The prevention of shock during blood loss requires the presence of skilled medical personnel to stop bleeding and deliver intravenous fluids -- as much as two to three liters -- as quickly as possible.

First Aid Is Everyone's Responsibility -- Sometimes

Everyone associated with motorsports should have some working knowledge of first aid because injuries often occur in the absence of an ambulance crew while people are working in the shop or traveling along the highway. All of us also need to realize when to simply stay out of the way and permit qualified emergency medical technicians to practice their professions unimpeded.

How many times does a racing incident bring a flood of people running onto a race track like children to "help" or look? These people get in the way and put themselves at risk of tripping, falling, being struck by moving vehicles or burned should a fire or cooling system erupt. At least 1.9 percent of the injuries suffered in pit areas or on race tracks by non-drivers result while people are running to or from something, according to computer analysis of thousands of racing incidents reported to North American Racing Insurance from 1988 through 1991.

First Responders

Anyone at a race track who is considered a "first responder" to accidents should be professionally trained and current in first aid or, preferably, certified in Advanced Trauma Life Support. People without training have no business approaching accident victims unless their assistance is specifically requested by professionals supervising the response.

Nonetheless it is highly recommended that all members of every race team jointly undergo first aid training at least once each year so they can handle injuries that occur away from the track or before or after ambulance crews are present at a track. It is not sufficient to have one or two team members trained -- who will assist them if they are injured?

The First Aid Cookbook

All people who may be required to provide emergency medical care should memorize the basic steps of injury assessment and response and become as comfortable with executing them as they would be with following the directions in a cookbook. Let's summarize an accident response outline that can be used as a refresher following training. (THIS INFORMATION CAN NOT REPLACE PROFESSIONAL TRAINING.)

1. Remain calm. Responders must be able to follow the instructions they have memorized, maintain control of the accident scene and reassure the injured. Panic from aid-givers can frighten victims, boosting their blood pressure and worsening blood loss and other injuries.
2. Approaching the scene: Walk briskly or jog under control. Do not run. You could fall or be struck and make conditions worse.
3. Ask the right questions: First, "Where do you hurt?" Second, "How are you?" Third, "What happened?" These questions require the injured person to take a mental inventory of body systems and provide crucial information about mental and breathing functions. Do not waste an injured person's energy and possibly fading consciousness by asking "Are you OK?" A response to this question provides no useful information. Any person involved in an accident should be presumed hurt until proven otherwise. While talking to the victim, provide reassurance -- this can keep the victim calm and minimize blood pressure increases.
4. Assess the victim's physical signs.
    -- Is the victim breathing? If not, administer mouth-to-mouth resuscitation.
    -- Does the victim have a pulse? If not, administer cardiopulmonary resuscitation.
    -- Is the victim bleeding? If so, use hand pressure or surgical dressings to attempt to stop the bleeding. Use a tourniquet or force on a pressure point only if necessary.
    -- Is the patient in shock? If so, cover with a blanket and elevate the legs.

-- Assess other vital signs: blood pressure, body temperature, skin color, eye pupils, state of consciousness, ability to move, reactions to pain.

5. Assess and Address Injuries.

-- If spinal cord injury is possible, handle patient with extreme care, using a neck brace and spine board.

-- If fractures are possible, apply splints. Do not re-insert protruding bones.

-- If bleeding is present, cover wounds and control bleeding. Do not re-insert protruding intestines. Do not remove foreign objects. Retrieve amputated parts.

6. Transport patient to appropriate medical facility.

Victims of motorsports accidents should be presumed to have suffered head, neck or spinal injuries unless determined otherwise. Therefore it always is necessary to secure them to a backboard before removing them from their vehicle and transporting them to medical treatment. When the victim appears stable, there should be no need to rush removal from the vehicle. When immediately life-threatening injuries are apparent, however, an immediate extraction should be undertaken to insure that transport to the hospital begins within 10 minutes of the accident.

The First Aid Kit

Every race team should keep a well-supplied first aid kit handy in the shop and on the tow vehicle. Fans who travel a lot should keep kits in their cars, too. Basic items that should be included are:

Bandages
Sterile gauze pads, 4" by 4"
Gauze bandage, roll, 3" wide
Butterfly bandages
Adhesive tape, 1" wide
Scissors
Elastic bandage, 3" wide
Cotton-tipped swabs
Absorbent cotton, roll
Aspirin
Acetaminophen
Oral and rectal thermometers

Petroleum jelly
Syrup of ipecac
Tweezers
Safety pins
Hydrogen peroxide, three percent solution
Calamine lotion
Bar of soap
Flashlight
Antihistamine tablets
Snakebite kit

Basic First-Aid Techniques

The following guidelines should serve as a reference and reminder of techniques that can be used in emergencies. This information cannot replace first-aid training, which can be taken from many public organizations, agencies and schools. All members of racing teams and track crews are strongly encouraged to undergo first aid training and refresher courses every year.

MAINTENANCE OF BREATHING is the first step in delivering first aid. One must assure that the victim's airway is clear and open. To do so, lay the victim on the back on a firm, hard surface. Use a finger to clear the mouth and airway of any foreign material. If there does not appear to be a neck injury, open the airway by tilting the head backward, placing the palm of one hand on the victim's forehead and the fingers of the other hand under the bony part of the chin. Using this method lifts the tongue from the back of the throat.

MOUTH-TO-MOUTH RESUSCITATION may be needed if the victim is not breathing. With the victim's head tilted backward, place one hand on the forehead and use the fingers to squeeze the nostrils closed. Take a deep breath, place your mouth snugly over the victim's mouth and deliver two full breaths about a second apart. Stop blowing when the chest is expanded. Wait for air to escape from the victim's chest and repeat, blowing about 12 breaths per minute for an adult; 15 breaths per minute for a child; and 20 breaths per minute for a baby. Continue until the victim begins breathing without assistance or until medical assistance arrives.

STOPPING BLOOD LOSS obviously is another primary requirement of first aid. Applying direct pressure to the wound with a sterile dressing or piece of clean cloth may cause some pain to the victim but will slow the loss of blood. Any blood clots that form as bleeding stops should be left undisturbed. If blood soaks through the dressing, it should be left in place while another is applied over it and held firmly against the injury. (The risk of contracting AIDS from a victim's body fluids -- if the victim has AIDS -- during a first-aid situation are considered extremely low if not non-existent.)

RESPONDING TO INJURIES

If a limb is bleeding, it should be held above the level of the victim's heart while pressure is applied. As the bleeding stops, a bandage can be wrapped around the wound snugly but not tightly.

If a pulse cannot be felt below the bandage after it is affixed, it should be loosened.

Applying firm force to the body's pressure points may be needed to slow blood loss in extreme situations. Pressure points (see diagram) are found where major arteries carry blood through the body: The sides of the head; the sides of the neck; the armpits; the wrists; the creases of the groin; and the backs of the knees.

Tourniquets should be used to stop blood loss only in life-threatening situations, such as a partial or complete amputation, when the risk of death is higher than the threat of losing a limb.

INTERNAL BLEEDING may be evident if the patient vomits or spits up blood, passes black or bright-red stools or exhibits other signs of blood loss such as dizziness, confusion or rapid and weak pulse. If internal bleeding is suspected, the victim must be placed on his or her back and assisted in maintaining a clear airway while medical attention is sought immediately.

BANDAGES and DRESSINGS are essential in most situations requiring first aid. Dressings help control bleeding, prevent germs from contaminating wounds and absorb secretions.

Dressings should be large enough to extend about one inch beyond the edges of a wound. Tape and absorbent materials such as cotton should not be applied directly to the surface of a wound because they can stick and cause further injury. Dressings should be gently lowered directly onto the injury; sliding them can drag contamination from the skin into the wound. Dressings should remain sterile, of course. Torn packages or dressings that are dropped should be discarded.

In medical terminology, a bandage is the wrapping material that holds a dressing in place. Bandages must be applied snugly but not tight enough to slow blood circulation or cause swelling. When applying a bandage to the arm, hand, foot or leg, the fingertips or toes should remain exposed and monitored for indications that the bandage is too tight: swelling, coldness or blue or pale color. Loosen the bandage immediately if these conditions are seen or if the patient complains of numbness or tingling.

Pressure Points for Control of Bleeding

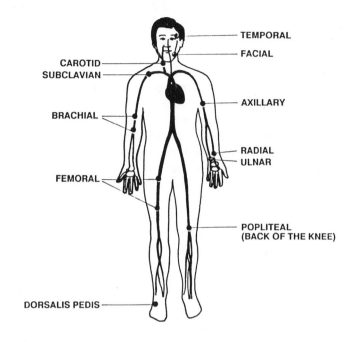

TEMPORAL

FACIAL

CAROTID

SUBCLAVIAN

AXILLARY

BRACHIAL

RADIAL

ULNAR

FEMORAL

POPLITEAL
(BACK OF THE KNEE)

DORSALIS PEDIS

Basic First-Aid Dressings and Bandages

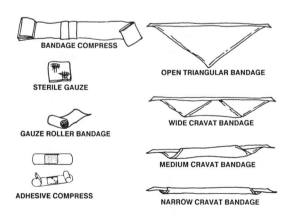

BANDAGE COMPRESS

STERILE GAUZE

GAUZE ROLLER BANDAGE

ADHESIVE COMPRESS

OPEN TRIANGULAR BANDAGE

WIDE CRAVAT BANDAGE

MEDIUM CRAVAT BANDAGE

NARROW CRAVAT BANDAGE

Rectangular bandages, the standard found in stores everywhere, should be kept handy. Some injuries may require larger bandages and knowledge of the techniques for applying them.

Butterfly band-aids and narrow adhesive strips may be needed to hold the edges of a deep cut closed. The wound must be held closed while these are applied.

Roll gauze is useful for bandages that must be larger or wrapped around a finger or limb. To make a circular gauze bandage, hold the end of the gauze at a an angle over the wound and make several wraps (not too tight) around the body part. Make several more circles, slightly overlapping the edges of the gauze until the injury is completely covered. Cut the gauze and secure it in place with tape or a safety pin.

A fingertip wrap is used when the end of the finger is injured. Make a couple of rolls around the base of the finger, turn the bandage sideways and go up, over and down the finger several times to create layers of bandage. Beginning back at the base of the finger, make a series of overlapping rolls up the finger and back down to the base, securing it there with tape.

A figure-eight wrap is useful for the ankle, wrist, foot or hand. To start, make a couple of loops around the injured body part then begin making figure eights around the adjacent body part (ankle, wrist, hand or foot). Continue making overlapping figure-eights until the entire ankle, wrist, foot or hand is covered.

A head bandage is laid across the forehead, just above the eyebrows. The ends are pulled around the back of the head and brought back to the forehead, where the ends are tied. The corner left hanging behind the head is tucked into the fold of the tied ends.

A triangular bandage can be used in an emergency to cover a large injury, such as a head wound, or used as a sling.

NOSEBLEEDS can be stopped by having the victim sit and lean forward. Press together the sides of the nose, below the bone, and hold for 15 minutes. Placing ice against the nose and face can help constrict blood vessels and slow bleeding. Do not allow the victim to touch or blow the nose during bleeding or for several hours after bleeding is halted. If bleeding continues, squeeze the nose for another five minutes. If bleeding still continues or if it is believed the nose is broken, seek medical attention.

Triangular Bandage for the Hand

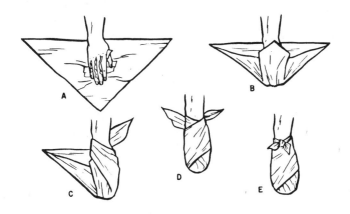

Cravat Bandage for Palm of Hand

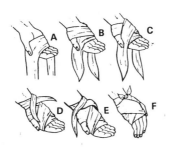

Cravat Bandage for the Leg

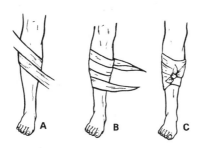

BLISTERS can lead to infections so they should not be taken for granted. Cover a small, unopened blister with a dressing and allow it to heal itself. If a blister is broken by accident, wash it gently with soap and water and cover with a bandage. Blisters caused by burns should not be opened.

Large blisters that are likely to be broken by accident should be seen by a doctor. If medical help is not readily available and it is deemed necessary to open a large blister, it should be done only with a small poke by a needle sterilized over an open flame. After the blister is pressed gently to force out fluid, it should be covered with a sterile dressing. Continually monitor a healing blister for signs of infection.

BROKEN BONES should always be suspected if the victim felt or heard a "snap;" if the injury is painful to the touch or when moved; if it is difficult to move the injured body part (although it also may be easy to move the injured part); if the body part moves unnaturally; if the victim feels a "grating" sensation; or if the body part appears deformed, swollen or blue in color.

Closed fractures are breaks that remain inside the skin and muscle. Open fractures break the skin and are potentially more dangerous due to risk of blood loss or infection.

When giving first aid for a broken bone, make sure the patient is breathing and comfortable. Always suspect a neck or spine injury if the victim is not conscious, feels neck pain or tingling in the extremities or is paralyzed in the arms or legs.

Stop any bleeding by gently applying a sterile dressing and pressure to the wound. Cover the entire injured area with a bandage. Do not attempt to wash a wound or place a broken bone back into the body. Apply a splint to the injury, affixing it well above and below the break. Call immediately for medical assistance.

A fracture can be diagnosed by asking the injured person to do a push test against an immovable force supplied by hand.

For a suspected leg fracture, place a hand on the outside of the foot and ask the person to try to twist the leg outward as far as possible. If there is severe pain or an inability to push, handle the injury as if it is a fracture. If the outward push does not create severe pain, place a hand on the big toe of the injured leg and ask the person to twist the leg inward. Again, if there is severe pain or the person cannot move the leg, there probably is a broken bone.

To diagnose a possible arm fracture, ask the person to grasp

Elbow Bandage

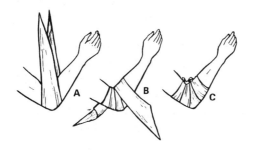

Cravat Bandage for the Knee

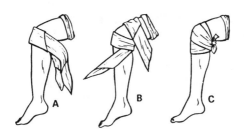

Triangular Bandage for the Foot

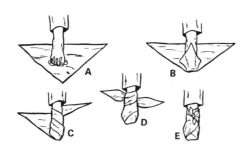

your hand. Ask him to twist his hand toward you then try to rotate the hand to a thumb-down position against the resistance of your hand. If there is no pain in that movement, ask him to attempt to rotate the hand upward against resistance. Severe pain or the inability to move the hand suggests a fracture.

Never move a person with a suspected neck or back injury without trained medical assistance -- unless there is immediate danger of fire, drowning or other fatal threat -- since any further injury may cause paralysis or death.

Do not give the victim anything to eat or drink; treat for shock.

SPRAINS are injuries to joints that include damage to and sometimes tears of ligaments. The ankle is the most likely joint to be sprained.

-- First-degree sprains involve tears of just a few ligament fibers and usually are not painful until the day following injury.

-- Second-degree sprains may be accompanied by a "pop" or "crack" sound when initially sustained. When the ankle is involved, the person may be able to stand but will feel significant pain. Swelling occurs within minutes; within 24 hours the injured joint is black and blue.

-- Third-degree sprains also may occur with popping or cracking sounds and immediate severe pain and swelling. Because ligaments are completely torn, the victim will not be able to stand or walk. Immediate medical attention is needed.

To treat a sprain, remember the words that make up "I.C.E." -- ice, compression and elevation. Apply an ice bag and an elastic bandage to the injury and elevate it about the level of the heart. Leave ice on the injury until the cold becomes painful. Remove the ice until the injury begins to hurt again, then reapply. Continue this procedure until medical attention is sought.

SPLINTS keep injured body parts from moving to ease the pain of injury and prevent further injury during transport. In an emergency, splints may be fashioned from boards, broomsticks, cardboard or even rolled newspapers, towels or blankets. Padding, such as towels, should be placed between the injury and the splint. The splint can be tied in place with string, a belt, bungee cords, handkerchiefs or strips of clothing. As with a bandage, the splint should be affixed snugly but not tightly enough to impair blood flow or cause swelling. Keep a watch on the injured limb and loosen the

Dressing for Injuries to the Scalp, Temple, Ear or Face

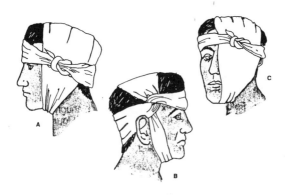

Dressing for Injuries to the Forehead or Back of Head

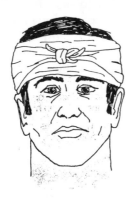

Dressing for Injuries to the Hip

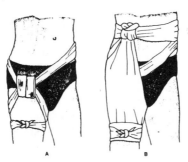

splint if there are signs of tightness.

-- Ankle splints should be made of a pillow or rolled blanket wrapped around the leg from the calf to the end of the foot and tied in place around the foot, ankle and calf.

-- Upper arm splints can be fashioned from a rolled newspaper or magazine. Place a towel or other padding in the armpit and gently lower the arm to the side of the body. Place padding inside the newspaper or magazine and roll it around the arm, then tie it in place above and below the break. Use a sling to hold the forearm across the front of the chest, then use a large blanket or sheet to wrap the arm against the body.

-- Splints for the lower arm or wrist also can be made from a newspaper or magazine. Place padding inside the splint and place it against the arm, making sure it stretches from the elbow to the hand. Tie the splint in place above and below the break and use a sling to hold the forearm across the front of the body.

-- Back splints should never be applied by anyone other than a trained medical professional unless it is ABSOLUTELY necessary to move the victim due to an immediately life-threatening situation. Before moving the victim, immobilize the back with a short, wide board which extends to the buttocks. Place the board behind the body and keep the back, neck and head in a straight line. Tie the board around the forehead, around the chest at the armpits and around the lower abdomen. Move the victim very gently. Do not allow the body to twist or bend. If the victim is not breathing, tilt the head back slightly to maintain an airway.

-- Collarbone splinting is applied with a length of cloth or flexible bandage wrapped in a figure-eight that goes over the shoulders and under the arms and crosses behind the back.

-- Elbow splints should be applied so that the arm remains in its injured position, either straight or bent. Elbow injuries can cause blood circulation problems and should be examined as soon as possible by a physician.

If the elbow is bent, the forearm should be placed in a sling hanging around the neck so that the arm can be wrapped against the body.

If the elbow is straight, padding should be placed under the armpit and splints placed along one or both sides of the entire arm.

-- A hand splint should be applied like a forearm splint. Place a rolled magazine or newspaper lined with padding under the arm so the hand is cradled in the splint. Then place a sling around the

Dressing for Wounds of the Shoulder

A   B   C

Slings

A   B   C
TRIANGLE SLING CRAVAT SLING BASKET SLING

Dressing for Dislocation of the Shoulder

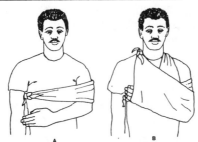

A   B

Bandage/Sling for Fractures of Shoulder, Arm or Collarbone

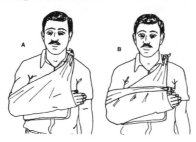

A   B

neck to support the splint in front of the body.

-- A kneecap splint should be applied after the leg is straightened. Place a padded board, four inches or more in width, under the leg. The board should be long enough to stretch from the buttocks to the heel of the foot. Tie the splint in place at the ankle, above and below the knee and at the thigh.

Upper leg splints can be made from two boards, one stretching from the armpit to the heel of the foot on the outside of the leg and the other going from the crotch to the heel on the inside of the leg. Tie the board in place at the ankle, above and below the knee, the thigh, the hip, the lower back and the armpit.

Lower leg splints can be made from two shorter boards long enough to go from above the knee to below the heel. If available, a third board can be placed behind the leg. The splints should be tied in place in three or four places but not directly over the break.

If boards are not available, an injured leg can be splinted to the other leg. Place a rolled blanket between the legs and tie the legs together as recommended in the above guidelines.

-- Pelvis injuries can be supported by tying the legs together. With the victim lying on a large board or door, tie the legs together at the ankles and knees. The legs may be straight or bent, whichever is more comfortable for the victim.

-- Shoulder injuries can be supported with a sling and large cloth wrap. Place the forearm directly across the front of the chest and support it with a sling. Use a large towel or cloth to wrap the upper arm and lower arm against the body.

WHIPLASH is strain to the neck and its muscles resulting from sudden jerking of the head. In severe instances, the head, neck and back should be immobilized and the patient transported to medical care. In minor cases ice should be applied to the injury and the neck should be exercised (see chapter on flexibility). If the neck remains painful more than 24 hours a doctor should be consulted.

BRUISES should be treated by applying an ice pack or cold compress. If the injury is on an arm or leg, the limb should be elevated about the level of the heart to reduce blood flow to the injured area. After 24 hours, the injury should be treated with a moist, wet compress to aid healing. A bruise that is large or extremely painful is cause to seek medical attention due to the possibility of a fracture or other injury.

Splint for Upper Arm, Elbow, Forearm or Wrist

Splint for Elbow Fracture, Arm in Straight Position

Splint for Leg or Ankle

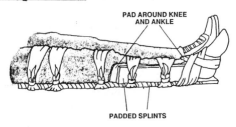

PAD AROUND KNEE
AND ANKLE

PADDED SPLINTS

Splint for Thigh or Knee

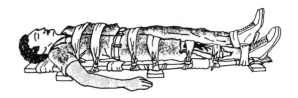

237

RESPONDING TO INJURIES

BUMPS AND LUMPS should be treated by applying an ice pack or cold compress to reduce pain and swelling. Seek medical attention immediately if a bump affects the head injury, especially if there is bleeding from the ears, nose or mouth; the victim is unconscious; has difficulty breathing; experiences severe headaches, vomiting, slurred speech, convulsions or a change in pulse; or exhibits a personality change. Medical attention also should be sought when any bump or lump on any part of the body seems severe.

BURNS are classified according to their degree of injury. The recommended first-aid depends on this severity. The first step always is quickly reducing the temperature of the injury to reduce further damage.

-- First-degree burns affect only the outer layer of skin and cause no blistering. This burn should immediately be placed under cold water until the pain decreases. The injury then should be covered with a clean bandage. Do not apply butter, grease or other home remedies to a burn.

-- Second-degree burns injure tissues beneath the skin and are red, blotchy, blistered, swollen, moist and oozy. The burn should be placed in cold, not icy, water or a clean towel soaked in cold water until the pain subsides. Gently pat the burn dry with a clean towel and cover it with a sterile bandage. Burns on the arms or legs should be elevated above the heart. Do not break blisters or apply any medicine or home remedy. Medical attention should be sought at once.

-- Third-degree burns destroy all layers of skin. These burns appear white or charred. There is little pain because nerve endings are destroyed. Place a cold cloth or cool, not iced, water on the burn. Cover it with a thick, sterile dressing. Do not remove clothing stuck to the burns or apply any medications. Elevate burned hands, feet, arms or legs above the level of the heart if possible. Keep the victim lying down unless the face or neck is burned. Make sure the victim is able to breath. Call an ambulance immediately.

EYE INJURIES are common in racing due to blows to the face and foreign objects, usually dirt, entering the eyes. The common "black eye" is potentially serious and deserves medical attention to rule out internal bleeding. In the meantime, apply cold compresses to the eye and keep the victim lying down with eyes closed.

Splint for Immobilization of Ankle or Foot

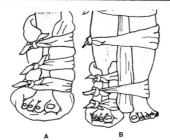

A   B

Splint for Fracture of Foot or Toes

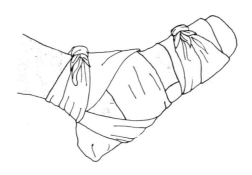

Positioning of Hand in Splint

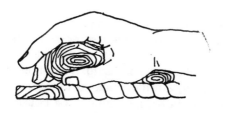

Positioning of Leg in Splint

SUPPORT AND SLIDE WELL-PADDED
SPLINT UNDER LEG

PAD SPACES BETWEEN LEG AND SPLINT
AND BANDAGE SECURELY

Cuts to the eye or eyelid also are dangerous. Cover the injured eye with a sterile bandage but apply no pressure. Cover the uninjured eye to discourage the victim from moving the eyes. Keep the victim lying on the back and seek medical attention immediately.

Foreign objects can be removed from the eyes with caution unless the object is sticking into the eyeball. In either case, do not allow the victim to rub or touch the eyes.

If a foreign object is floating on the surface of the eyeball or under the eyelid, wash your hands with soap and water and gently pull the upper eyelid down over the lower eyelid and hold momentarily. The tears that will flow may flush out the debris. If the object remains, use a medicine dropper or glass to gently flow warm water over the eye. If that fails, use the moistened corner of a clean tissue or handkerchief to remove the particle. Seek medical attention.

If a foreign object is sticking into the eyeball, do not attempt to remove it. Gently cover both eyes, without pressure, with sterile bandages and keep the victim lying on the back. Seek medical attention immediately.

HEAD INJURIES must be assumed in any person who is found unconscious. Most head injuries are caused by sudden deceleration with or without blows directly to the head. Even if the victim remains conscious, head injury may have occurred. Warning signs include cuts, bruises, lumps or depressions to the head; confusion or drowsiness; blood or clear fluid coming from the ears, nose or mouth; an unusual pulse rate; vomiting; convulsions; headache; speech difficulties; or a pale or reddish face. Some symptoms may begin to appear some time after the injury is sustained.

If a head injury is suspected, make sure the victim is able to breathe and splint the neck because a neck injury may accompany a head injury. Control any bleeding that is occurring and keep the victim lying down (face up), quiet and warm. Summon medical attention immediately.

NECK INJURY should always be suspected when a head injury has occurred. Other symptoms of neck injuries include headache, stiff neck, inability to move all or parts of the body or tingling sensations in the feet or hands.

Stabilizing the Head and Neck

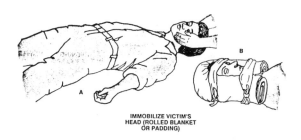

IMMOBILIZE VICTIM'S
HEAD (ROLLED BLANKET
OR PADDING)

Splint for Fractured Pelvis or Hip

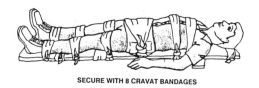

SECURE WITH 8 CRAVAT BANDAGES

Splint for Dislocation of Hip

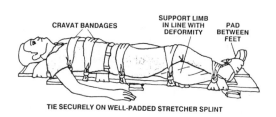

CRAVAT BANDAGES   SUPPORT LIMB   PAD
IN LINE WITH   BETWEEN
DEFORMITY   FEET

TIE SECURELY ON WELL-PADDED STRETCHER SPLINT

241

RESPONDING TO INJURIES

A neck injury victim should be moved only by trained medical personnel unless absolutely necessary due to a life-threatening danger. If it is necessary to move the victim, immobilize the neck by loosely wrapping and securing a rolled towel or newspaper around the neck. Use a short, wide board to stabilize the neck and back; the board should extend from the buttocks to the head and be secured at the forehead and armpits. Move the victim very gently without allowing the body to bend or twist.

Heat Illnesses

MUSCLE CRAMPS are sustained, highly painful contractions of heavily-used muscles, often in the legs and abdominal wall. These cramps result from inadequately replaced water and minerals lost through sweating. The best cramp treatment is the strain/counter-strain maneuver. Passively flex the muscle to maximal relaxation until the muscle relaxes, usually within 90 seconds. For example, if a calf muscle cramps have someone gently push the toes downward as far as possible and hold until the cramp subsides. Rubbing cramps can bruise tight muscles. Applying balm just creates heat in the muscle -- which is what caused the cramp.

HEAT EXHAUSTION is a more serious result of dehydration. The victim may become dizzy, weak and confused and encounter heart palpitations, headaches, intense thirst, nausea, vomiting and diarrhea. The body continues to sweat, so the sufferer may feel cool and clammy despite having a fever.
Prompt treatment is required to prevent heat exhaustion from escalating to heat stroke. The victim needs to drink cold fluids; have wet towels applied to the neck, groin and armpits; and possibly receive intravenous fluids. Place the victim in a shady environment, preferably off the ground. Hot soil or pavement can radiate additional heat into the body.

HEAT STROKE is a life-threatening emergency that can occur suddenly, sometimes without being preceded by heat exhaustion symptoms. A heat stroke victim typically collapses into unconsciousness. Sweating may continue but hot, dry skin indicates sweating has halted and body temperature is rising dangerously. Hyperventilation -- rapid, panting breathing -- can be present.

Once sweating halts, body temperature may soar to or over 106 degrees in as little as 20 minutes. Only minutes of exposure to that temperature can put critical organs at risk. Central nervous system impairment may cause bizarre behavior or coma. Racing drivers approaching heat stroke may exhibit inconsistent lap times or altered driving lines.

The risk of death from heat stroke depends on the elevation and duration of body temperature and the promptness of treatment. Heat stroke symptoms require immediate medical treatment and efforts to lower body temperature. When medical personnel and facilities are available the victim may be immersed in ice water. If immersion is not possible, an excellent alternative is applying ice wrapped in towels to the groin, armpits and back of the neck -- the key pathways of blood flow. If core body temperature has reached 105 degrees intravenous fluids should be started immediately.

SHOCK is a life-threatening reaction to many serious injuries or illnesses. It occurs when an inadequate supply of oxygen is delivered to body tissues such as the lungs, brain and heart. Traumatic injuries may cause shock through the loss of blood and body fluids or lack of sufficient oxygenation. Shock also may arise from an allergic reaction to medications, foods or insect stings. The warning signs of shock may include pale, blue and cool skin; moist or clammy skin; general weakness; a rapid but weak pulse; vomiting; thirst; rapid breathing or shallow, irregular breathing; lack of responsiveness; dilated pupils; or lack of consciousness.

When shock occurs, it is important to make sure the victim is able to breath. (See the section on maintaining an airway.) Then address the cause of the shock, such as bleeding or severe pain. Keep the victim lying down and, if needed, cover with a blanket to prevent loss of body heat. Unless absolutely necessary, do not move the victim if a head, neck or back injury is suspected. Provide reassurance to keep the victim calm. Seek medical attention immediately.

SEVERED LIMBS require immediate medical assistance. Due to the possibility of shock, make sure the victim is able to breath and attempt to slow or stop blood loss, using a tourniquet if necessary. After stabilizing the victim, place the severed limb in a clean container such as a plastic bag. Place ice outside the container to keep the limb cold. Do not allow ice to directly contact the limb.

INDEX

A

Abdomen muscles 46-47, 65
Abrasions 159, 160
Acceleration trauma 173
Accident Facts 149
Accidents in racing 3, 147-170
Accommodation, visual 93, 95, 109-110
Acetylene 191
Acid (battery) burn 192
Acid (drug) 141
Addiction, drug 139
Adenosine triphosphate 21, 35-36
Adrenaline 12, 23
Advanced Trauma Life Support (ATLS) 222
Aerobic fitness 11-12, 22, 24, 36, 38, 140
Age Wave 111
Age and aging 2, 10, 49, 65, 99-117, 133, 165, 177, 186
Agility 49
AIDS 225
Airway 183
Alcohol 68, 87, 138-139, 144
Alcoholism 18
Allergy medications 137
Allison, Bobby 61
Amabile, Rick 175
Amateur racing 121, 154, 158
Ambulances 213-214
American National Standards Institute (ANSI) 196
American Scientist 21
Amnesia 181, 182
Amphetamines 139
Amputation (of limbs) 243
Anaerobic fitness 21
Anemia 138
Ankles 54, 156, 160
Antihistamines 137
Anti-submarine belts 202-203
Anxiety 137, 139, 141, 145
Arousal 122-123
Arms 36, 49, 54, 156, 159, 160, 177, 184-186
Assessment of injuries 223-224
Asthma 160
Athleticism and racing 9, 14-15
Auditory canal 132
Axles 154

B

Back 36, 41-42, 46-47, 49, 53, 123, 155, 160, 183, 205, 221
Balance 94, 138-139
Bandages 226-240
Barbiturates 139
Barriers 153, 208
Baseball 21, 23, 24, 149
Basketball 11, 23, 124, 149
Battery acid 192
Beer 63, 138-139
Belts, seat 173, 177, 178, 201-203
Berggren, Dick 3, 195, 200
Berms 153, 173, 208
Beta blockers (medications) 137
Biceps 43-47
Bicycling 11, 22, 24, 31, 67, 195
Biomechanical Design Inc. 154-155, 204
Biomechanics 177
Birmingham, England, University of 173
Bleachers 159-160
Blinking 94
Blisters 190, 200, 230
Blood 85, 190
Blood loss 222, 225
Blood pressure 25, 26, 106, 119, 140, 141
Blood pressure medications 138
Blood stream (see Cardiovascular system)
Blood vessels 177, 178-179, 180, 221
Blunt trauma 173
Boating 147, 148-149
Boat racing 112, 204
Bodies, car 154
Boitano, Dr. M.A., 157
Bomber race cars (see Street stocks)
Bone 85, 86, 107, 112, 177, 178, 183-186, 190
Boxing 149
Brain 65, 71, 139-140, 143, 155, 174, 177, 180-182, 221
"Brain fade" 21, 61
Brake fluid 190-191
Brakes 154, 190-191
Breathing 142, 225
Bruises 156, 159, 160, 236
Buckles, restraint system 202

Bumps (injuries) 238
Burns 152, 156, 158-159, 189-193, 210, 238

C
Caffeine 18, 68, 82, 140, 142, 144
Calcium 86
Calf muscles 49, 54, 57, 58
Calisthenics 24
Callahan, Tom 5
Calories 27, 31, 64, 75-76, 82, 84
Cancer 135, 141
Carbohydrates 67-68, 76-77, 82, 83
Carbon dioxide 85
Carbon monoxide 28
Cardiopulmonary capacity 9, 11-12
Cardiovascular system 14-15, 19, 21-31, 36, 61, 64, 65, 106, 139-141, 142
CART 101, 147
Cartilage 86
Charlotte Motor Speedway 105
Chest 58, 156, 177, 183, 184, 221
Children 210
Chlorine 86
Cholesterol 80-81, 110
Chromium 86
Clark, Jim 126
Clark Foundation, Jim 154
Clavicle (see Collarbone)
Climbing 31
Cobalt 86
Cocaine 140
Cochlea 132
Cold medications 137, 141
Collarbone 184-186
Collisions 152-153, 156, 173-174, 177, 180-181, 182
Color vision 93, 109
Composure 119
Compression (in bone fracture) 184-186
Concentration 121-122, 125-126, 141, 143
Concession areas 160, 192
Concussion 156, 159, 181-182
Confidence 123-124
Contact lenses 96
Contraceptives (medications) 137
Cool suits 71
Coolant, engine 192-193
Coordination 65, 94, 109, 112, 138-141
Copper 86
Cough medications 137
Crack (drug) 141
Cramps, muscle 65, 242

Cramps, stomach 67
Creatine phosphate 21, 36
Crew members 11, 13, 14, 15, 27-28, 49, 63, 70, 121-122, 152, 160, 207, 214
Crush, structural 155, 180

D
Dairy foods, 79
Dallaire, Dr. Jacques 11, 14
Dancing 24
Dawson, Dr. Glenn A. 9, 12
Debris 153, 154, 159, 174
Deceleration trauma 173
Decibel 132
Decongestants, nasal 142
Dehydration 13, 25, 61-72, 82, 138-139, 140
Deist, Jim 200
Deltoid muscles 40-42, 47
Demolition derbies 150, 152, 155, 157, 158, 199
Depth perception 91, 141
Diabetes 19, 25
Diarrhea 65, 69, 140
Diarrhea medications 137
Dieting 87
Disaster planning 214-215
Disease 95
Diuretic medications 137, 140
Diving, scuba 147, 148, 149
Dizziness 29, 65, 137, 138, 160
Dover Downs International Speedway 105
Downing, Jim 204
Drag racing 155
Dressings 226-240
Drinks, sports 67-68
Drive shafts 154
Driver error 154, 157
Driving suits 63, 151, 189-193, 199-201
Drowsiness 138
Drugs 71, 95, 137-142
Drug abuse 18
Dychtwald, Dr. Ken 111
Dynamic visual acuity 91

E
Ear plugs and muffs 134
Eardrum 132
Earnhardt, Dale 99, 119, 126
Ears 189
Endurance, physical 21-31, 33, 65, 81, 82, 140, 141, 143
Endurance racing 12
Enduro cars 150, 152, 155, 156, 157, 159
Energy consumption 15, 21

INDEX

Engines 153, 191, 193
England, George 151, 152, 154, 207, 208
Enzymes 21
Equilibrium 18
Error, driver (see Driver error)
Erythrocytes 190
ESPN 147
Exercise 12, 14-15, 23, 25, 27, 28-31, 33-47, 69, 83, 144
Exhaust systems 154, 190-191
Expense of racing 4
Experience 111, 123, 158
Eye injuries 238
Eyeglasses 96

F
Face 159, 160, 184
Face shields 94, 197
Fainting 159, 160
Falls 158, 159, 207
Fans (see Spectators)
Fat (food) 76, 79, 81, 82, 85
Fatalities 4-6, 148-149, 153, 156-157, 158, 160, 161, 175, 179-180
Fatigue 25, 36, 65, 76, 140, 143
Federal Aviation Administration 17-19
Federal Motor Vehicle Safety Standards (FMVSS), U.S. 183, 196
Femur 184-186
Fences 160
Fiber 80-81
Fibula (see Leg)
Fights 159, 160
Figure 8 racing 155, 158, 159
Fingers 159, 189
Fire 152, 189-193, 196, 197, 199-201
Fire extinguishers 210-212
Fire suits (see Driving suits)
Firefighting 210-213
Fireworks 192
First aid 221-243
First aid kit 224
Fitness (also see Exercise) 177
Fittipaldi, Emerson 33, 38, 111
Flexibility 13, 49-58, 107
Flips (see Roll-overs)
Fluorine 86
Foot 156, 179, 201
Football 9, 11, 23, 24, 31, 33, 62, 149
Formula 1, 11-12, 13, 147, 154
Formula cars 157
Foyt, A.J. 111
Fractures 156, 157, 158, 160, 177, 183-186, 204-205, 230-232

Fruit 67-68, 77-78, 82
Fuel 190-191, 196, 199

G
G (gravitational) forces 12, 33, 112, 155, 156, 157, 174-180, 196, 197, 202, 208
G-force formula 175
Gant, Harry 99, 111
Garfield, Dr. Charles A. 126
Gastrocnemius muscle 57
Gilmore, Jack 212
Glare 95, 109
Gloves (safety equipment) 189
Glucose 76
Glycogen 22, 76, 82, 85
Goals 124
Goggles 94
"Golden Hour" 221
Golf 21, 24, 31
Gore, Doug 178-179
Grand Prix racing (see Formula 1)
Grandstands 159-160
Grease 193, 201
Great Britain 154
Green, Dr. Robert N. 121
Guard rails 152, 159, 160, 173, 174, 180, 207
Gymnastics 21, 31

H
Hallucinations 139, 141, 142
Hallucinogens 140
Halogen 211
Hamstrings, 49, 56
Hands 36, 156, 159, 189, 201
Hang gliding 147, 148, 149
HANS (Head and Neck Support) 154, 174, 204
Harness (horse) racing 195
Head 155, 160, 174, 177, 180, 184, 201, 205, 240
Headache 65, 123
Hearing 131-134, 141
Heart 9, 11-12, 14, 65, 112, 123, 178, 179, 183, 221
Heart attack 156, 159, 160, 210
Heart disease 25, 110
Heart rate 25, 26, 29, 119
Heart volume 26
Heat 9, 13, 25, 62-72, 109
Heat exhaustion 65, 152, 160, 242
Heat illness 159, 160, 242-243
Heat stress 69
Heat stroke 61, 65, 66, 242

Heat tolerance 109, 138-139
Helmets, driving 177, 180, 189, 195-199
Hemoglobin 28, 86
Henderson, Dr. Michael 1, 89, 119, 154
Highways 147
Hiking, mountain 147, 148, 149
Hill climbing 158
Hips 47, 52
Hockey 11, 23, 111
Hood, Hooker 111
Hormones 23, 27
Howe, Gordie 111
Hubbard, Dr. Robert P. 154-155, 204
Hubbard/Downing Inc. 204
Humerus (see Arm)
Humidity 67
Hydration (see Dehydration)
Hypertension 19, 25, 142
Hypertension medications 138

I
Illness 159, 160
Image of racing 4-6
Imagery, mental 124, 126
Indianapolis Motor Speedway 5, 179,
    195, 212
Indy cars 12, 147, 151, 175, 179, 195,
    208
IndyCar 101
Infection 221
Injuries in racing 33, 34, 147-170
Injury data 3, 6-7, 147-170
Injury prevention 14
Injury rates 147, 148, 149, 151
Injury treatment 221-243
Intelligence 119, 120
Inside Indy Car Racing: 1990 175
Insomnia 139, 141
International Council of Motorsports
    Sciences 6-7, 147, 180, 204-205,
    208
Iodine 86
Iron 86
Isokinetics 39
Isometrics 39
Isotonics 39

J
Jaw 184
Johnsgard, Keith 120
Joints 49
Judgment 140

K
K&K Insurance Group 155

Kidneys 65
Kleiner, Dr. Susan M. 85
Knee 156, 184-185

L
Lacerations 156, 158, 160, 221
Lactic acid 29
Late models 151, 157
Lateral force (in bone fracture) 184-186
Laxatives 138
Leadership 127-128
Legs 49, 53, 55, 65, 156, 159, 160, 177,
    179, 184-186
Leukocytes 190
Ligaments 49
Liguori, Ralph 111
Liquor 138
Liver 65, 140
Loss of control (see Driver error)
Lopez, Carlos 111
Lubricants 190-191
Lumps (injuries) 238
Lungs 22, 107, 119, 123

M
Mackay, Dr. Murray 173
Maclean's 4
Magnesium 86, 211
Manganese 86
Mansell, Nigel 147
Marijuana 140-141
Marisi, Dr. Dan 11, 14
McDuffie, J.D. 204-205
McElreath, Jim 111
McGill University Motor Sport Research
    Group 11, 14
McGriff, Hershel 111
Mechanical failure 153-154, 159
Medical information cards 216-218
Medical planning 209-210
Medications (see Drugs)
Memory 141
Mensa 14
Mental ability 18, 27, 65, 121-122, 126,
    139, 140, 141, 143
Mental illness 18
Mental training 125-126
Mescaline 141
Metabolism 140
Methanol 191, 211, 212
MET-L-X 211
Michigan State University 155, 204
Mid-Ohio race course 157
Midgets 102, 150, 152, 155, 157, 158
Miklasz, Bernie 5

INDEX

Minisprints 150, 154, 155, 157
Minerals 67, 86
Ministocks 150, 156, 159
Modified cars 155, 156, 157, 159, 175
Molybdenum 86
Moseley, A.L. 173
Moss, Stirling 121
Motivation, 127-129
Motor Racing in Safety: The Human
    Factors 1, 19, 154
Motorcycling 195, 196
Motorcycle racing 36
MR (maximum resistance) 37
Muscles 9, 11-13, 26-27, 33-47, 49, 107,
    119, 123, 143, 175, 177, 190
Muscle relaxant medications 138

N
NASCAR 9, 12, 13, 100, 103-105, 113-
    117, 184, 204
National Highway Traffic Safety
    Administration 178
National Safety Council 148-149
National Speed Sport News, 148, 149,
    153, 157, 158, 175
Nausea 62, 65, 71, 152, 160
Nausea medications 138
Neck 12, 34, 36, 49, 52, 154-155, 182-
    183, 184, 203-205, 240-241
New York Times 5, 33
Nervous system 18-19, 66, 108, 112, 119,
    123, 138, 139
Neurological Surgeons, Congress of, 181
Newman, Paul 111
Nicotine 141, 144
Night vision 91
Noise 132-133
Norenephrine 27
North American Racing Insurance 4, 102-
    103, 148, 150-156, 160-170, 173,
    180, 182, 189, 192, 199, 203, 207,
    210
Nose 189
Nosebleeds 228
Nutrition 75-87

O
Occupational Safety and Health
    Administration (OSHA) 131, 133
Off-road racing 158
Officials, racing 11, 13, 14, 15, 28, 152,
    154, 159, 214
Oil 191, 196, 201
Oil dry absorbent 211

Olvey, Dr. Stephen E. 147, 151, 208
Olympic Committee, International 140
Open wheel cars 152, 157
Open Wheel 3
Organs, internal 62, 71, 143, 177, 178,
    183, 190, 221
Ortho-Rehab Bar 39
Osteoblasts 190
Osteoporosis 25, 107-108
Oxygen 11, 21-31, 61, 69, 112, 141, 211

P
Padding, safety 156
Paddock (see Pit areas)
Pain medications 138
Parachuting 147, 148, 149
Paranoia 139
Parking lots 160, 207
Peak Performance: Mental Training
    Techniques of the World's Greatest
    Athletes 125-126
Piquet, Nelson 179
PCP (drug) 141
Pectoralis muscles 45
Penetrating trauma 173
Performance Racing Industry, 103, 148,
    149
Peripheral vision 90, 196
Petroleum fire 191
Petty, Kyle 75
Petty, Richard 99, 111
Phenylpropanolamine 141
Phosphorous 86
Physical examination 17-19
Physician and Sportsmedicine 85, 147,
    157
Pit areas 157, 58-159, 207
Pony cars (see Ministocks)
Potassium 70, 86
Pressure points (and bleeding) 225
Protein 76, 78, 81
Psychology 14, 119-129
Psychology of Winning 121
Purple K 211

Q
Quadriceps 47, 51
Quinn, Hal 4

R
Radiators, hoses, caps 153, 159, 191-193
Radius (see Arm)
Range of motion 38
Reaction times 13, 93-94, 108, 109, 138-
    141

Rear ends, car 154, 191
Reed, Diane B. 147, 151, 208
Relaxation 125
Respiratory system 21-31
Rest rooms 160
Restraint assemblies, driver 201-203
Ribs 156, 178, 184
Riegel, Peter S. 21
Road racing 6-7, 147, 152, 154, 158
Road & Track 9, 14
Roll bars/cage 151, 153, 155, 177, 196
Roll-overs 153, 157, 174, 180, 208
Roosevelt, Theodore 129
Rope jumping 24
Rowing 22, 24, 31
Rudd, Ricky 104
Run-off areas 208
Running 11, 21, 24, 29-30, 31, 62, 63, 122

S
Safety 3-7
Safety crews 28, 49, 70-71
Safety equipment 156, 189, 195-205
Safety Quest seat liner 205
St. Louis Post-Dispatch 5
Salt 69, 82, 86
SCCA 101-102, 133, 147, 153, 155, 180, 208
Screening, medical 17-19
Seats 155, 156, 205
Security, track 207, 213-214
Seebold, Bill 112
Seizures 152, 159, 160, 210
Selenium 86
Severed limbs 243
Sexuality 120, 140, 145
SFI Foundation 180, 195, 197-203
Shock 222, 243
Shoes 201
Shoulders 12, 36, 155, 177
Shoulder harnesses 202-203
Siano, Joseph 5
Silver Crown Series 101
Simpson, Bill 195, 199
Siscone, Tony 189
Skating 22, 31
Skiing, snow 22, 24, 31, 148, 149
Skiing, water 149
Skin 85, 135-136, 189-193, 199-201
Skull 177, 180, 184, 204-205
Sleep 139, 140, 143-44
Sleep medications 138, 144
Smith, G. Terry 210-213
Snell Foundation 180, 195-198

Snell, William "Pete" 195
Snow blindness 95
Sodium 86
Soccer 9, 11, 23, 62, 149
Soft drinks 67-68
Softball 149
Soleus muscle 57
Solvents 196
Sound 132
Space perception 91
Spectators 11, 28, 63, 152, 159-160, 164, 165, 207, 210, 214
Speedweek 147
Spine (see Back)
Spins 153, 174
Sports Injuries: Mechanisms, Prevention and Treatment 121
Sportsman cars 150, 159
Splints 232, 234-242
Sprains 49, 156, 159, 160, 232
Sprint cars, 101, 151, 152, 155, 157, 158
Squash, 31
Stabilization, victim 222
Stamina 10
Static visual acuity 90
Steam 191
Steering 153, 191, 193
Steering wheels 155, 157
Stereoscopic vision 91-92, 110
Steroids, anabolic 139
Strength, muscular 10-12, 33-47, 65, 107, 112, 143
Stress 25, 82, 119, 122-123, 143, 144, 145
Stretching 30, 50-58
Stock cars 155, 157, 158, 175
Stock Car Racing 3, 61, 62, 178, 189, 195, 200
Stoll's Curve 200
Straights (track location) 157
Street stocks 150, 155, 157, 158
Stroke 157
Sucrose 68
Sugar 67-68, 82
Sulfur 86
Sunburn 135
Supermodified cars 157, 159, 175
Suspension components 154
Sweating 63-67, 109, 141, 143, 242-243
Swimming 22, 24, 31, 147, 148, 149

T
Team work 127, 143
Tear-offs 94
Technical inspections 154

INDEX

Teeth 86
Tendons 86, 190
Tennis 149
Testosterone 140
Thermal burns 191-192
Thermal protection 199-201
Thermoregulation 64, 138-139, 141, 143
Thigh bone (see Femur)
Thirst 62, 65
Throttles 153
Thumb 159
Thundercars (see Street stocks)
Tibia (see Leg)
TIME 5
Timms, Dr. M. Rick 6-7, 147, 153, 155, 180, 208
Tire grooving iron 193
Tires 154, 191
Tire barriers 153
Tobacco 18, 28, 141, 144
Track safety 207-220
Transmissions 154, 191, 193
Trauma 152, 173-186, 221-222
Track (sports) 9
Trammell, Dr. Terry 147, 151, 208
Trans Am 63, 70, 101
Travel 144, 221
Tricep muscles 42, 44-47
Truck racing 159
Turns (track location) 157

U
Ulcer medications 138
Ulna (see Arm)
USAC 101-102
U.S. News & World Report 149
Urine 68-69

V
Vegetables 77-78
Velocity judgment 92
Vision 17, 85, 89-96, 109-110, 112, 139, 141
Visualization 124
Vitamins 85-87
Vomiting 65, 69, 83
VO2 max 24, 106

W
Waitley, Dr. Denis 121, 129
Walking 24
Wallace, Rusty 104
Walls (see Guard rails)
Water, as beverage (see Dehydration)
Water, as firefighting agent 211
Waterford Hills race course 157
Watkins Glen race course 184, 204-205
Weight, body 64-65, 70
Weight loss medications 138, 142
Weightlifting 21, 33, 37-43, 122
West, Ted 9
Wheels 154
Wheelwhip 156
Whiplash 154, 158, 173, 182, 236
Windshields 94
Wine 138
Winston Cup Scene 75
Wrestling 31
Wrists 44, 50, 156

Z
Zinc 86